SCOTT'S INTERLEAVED WAVERLEY NOVELS

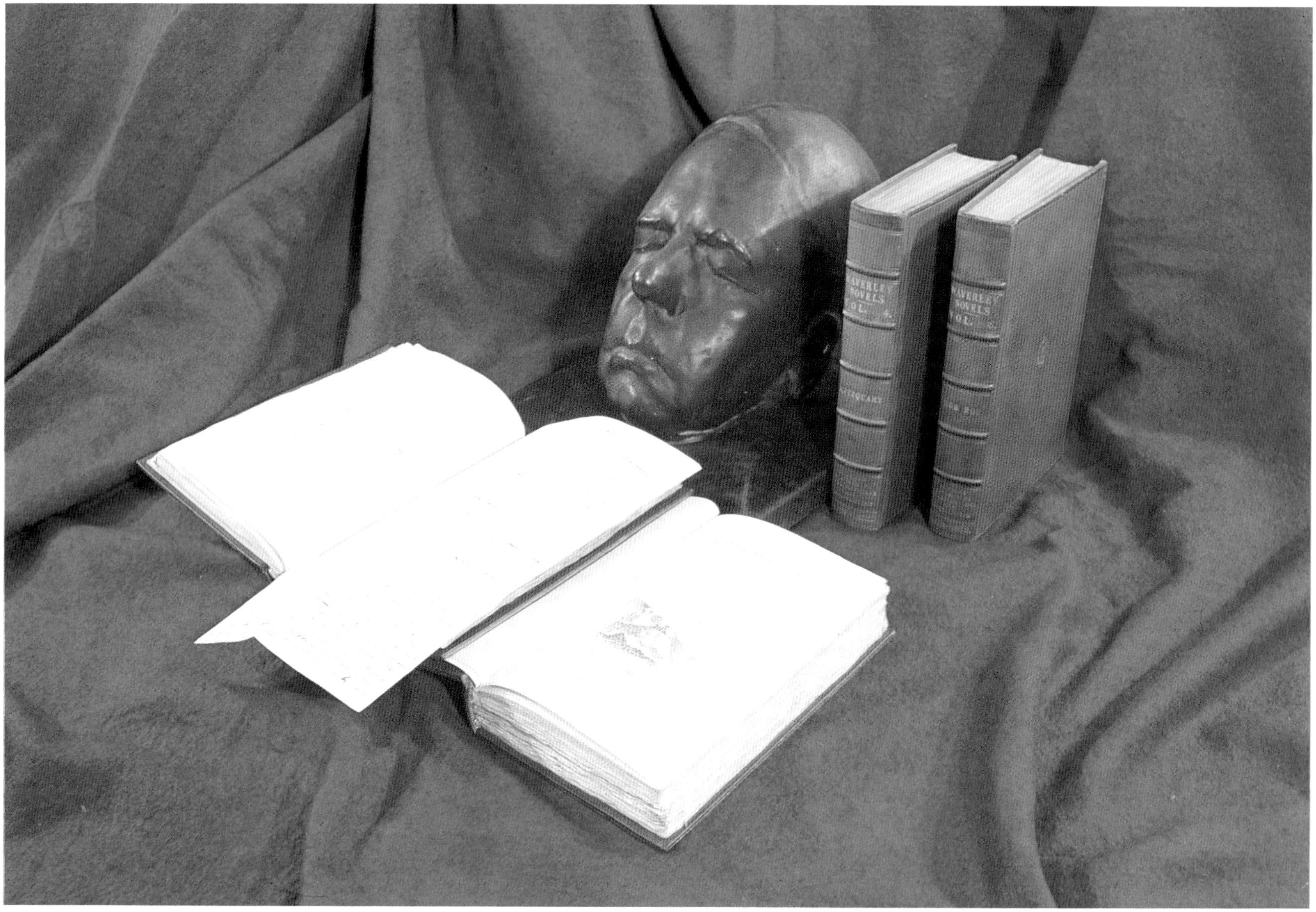

1 A cast of Scott's death-mask with volumes from the Interleaved Set. The two volumes of *The Heart of Mid-Lothian* lie open (one at the description of the prospect of Edinburgh, Scott's 'own romantic town', from Arthur's Seat, and the other at its title-page vignette of the Salisbury Crags); *Rob Roy* and *The Antiquary* stand watch.

SCOTT'S INTERLEAVED WAVERLEY NOVELS

(The 'Magnum Opus':
National Library of Scotland MSS. 23001–41)

AN INTRODUCTION AND COMMENTARY

edited by

IAIN GORDON BROWN
Assistant Keeper
Department of Manuscripts
National Library of Scotland

Co-published by Pergamon Books Ltd/Aberdeen University Press
in association with the National Library of Scotland

First published 1987
Pergamon Books Ltd/Aberdeen University Press
in association with the National Library of Scotland

British Library Cataloguing in Publication Data

Scott's interleaved Waverley novels: the 'Magnum Opus', National Library of Scotland MSS. 23001–41: an introduction and commentary.
1. Scott, *Sir* Walter, *1771–1832.* Waverley novels
2. Scott, *Sir* Walter, *1771–1832* Manuscripts
I. Brown, Iain Gordon
II. National Library of Scotland
823′.7 JL2811

ISBN 0-08035082-8

PRINTED IN GREAT BRITAIN
THE UNIVERSITY PRESS
ABERDEEN

CONTENTS

Well I can work at something so at the Magnum work I.

Sir Walter Scott, JOURNAL, 27 December 1830

2 Sir Walter Scott by Sir John Watson Gordon. This is a posthumous portrait, dating from perhaps ten years or so after the writer's death. Scottish National Portrait Gallery, Edinburgh.

PREFACE

When in 1986 the National Library of Scotland bought the long-lost Interleaved Set of the Waverley Novels that had been Sir Walter Scott's own working copy in the days of his financial hardship and his most heroic literary effort, the claim was fairly made that perhaps the grandest 'association copy' in English literature had been rediscovered. The Interleaved Set was surely one of the most significant literary treasures still in private hands, and it is an addition of incalculable value to the greatest collection in the world of Scott's literary manuscripts, papers and correspondence.

This book accompanies the microfiche publication of the Interleaved Set by Pergamon Books Ltd and Aberdeen University Press. Although its main purpose is as a companion to and commentary on the Interleaved Set, the book should nevertheless be of wider use to the increasing number of scholars investigating many different aspects of Scott's work and literary world, and of interest to students of the Romantic period in general. It is fitting that both the microfiche publication and the present book should be offered to the public under imprints of companies owned by Mr Robert Maxwell; for it is owing to his generosity, beyond that of any other individual, that the National Library of Scotland was able to secure the Interleaved Set. Our deepest gratitude, and that of scholars everywhere of Scott and Scottish literature, is due to him.

The 'Magnum Opus'—for this is the name that has been attached (however inaccurately) to the Interleaved Set, those printed books containing the manuscript materials written or collected by Scott and forming the author's copy for what he and his circle knew as the Magnum edition published between 1829 and 1833, 'the Magnum as we call it' (*Journal*, 14 April 1829)—is a document of the greatest importance to those interested in the evolution of the text of the Waverley Novels. The articles by Professor Millgate and Dr Alexander discuss these scholarly aspects of the Interleaved Set. Professor Millgate's essay was first published in *Sir Walter Scott's Magnum Opus and the Pforzheimer Manuscripts* (Edinburgh 1986), a booklet produced by the National Library of Scotland to commemorate the acquisition of the Interleaved Set. It is reprinted here largely unaltered. Dr Alexander's contribution has been commissioned specially for the present book. It should be explained that although the Interleaved Set runs to forty-one volumes (NLS MSS. 23001–41), only the first thirty-two of these contain Scott manuscript material in the form of annotations on the original pages, or on the interleaves, or on other papers—'papers apart' as Scott calls them—which were later bound into the volumes. Consequently the decision has been taken not to reproduce on microfiche the final nine unannotated volumes, and so on grounds of strict accuracy it is necessary to state that the two publications—the microfiche package and this conventional book—relate solely to MSS. 23001–32.

Although the Interleaved Set (which preserves what Scott's publisher, Robert Cadell, clearly considered the most important materials for the Magnum edition, and which constitutes such a significant monument to Scott's achievement) is once again in its entirety in Edinburgh, certain other annotated volumes which remain in the United States present a number of problems. In her note on these still rather puzzling interleaved copies in various American libraries, Claire Lamont alludes to the final nine books in the Interleaved Set and discusses the relationship which those volumes in a smaller format may bear to the National Library of Scotland's acquisition. What must be made plain here is simply the fact that the handful of interleaved books at Harvard and in Texas never at any time formed part of the great set now in Edinburgh.

The absence of annotation from the final volumes of the Interleaved Set is itself mute testimony to that other level on which the Set can be appreciated. The volumes are not annotated for the reason that their author was dead before the Magnum edition (of which these titles were to form the final volumes) was complete. To look along the backs of the volumes as they stand on the shelves of the National Library of Scotland strongroom is in itself a moving experience (Plates 1, 2). 'Author's Manuscript Introductions and Annotations 1829–1832' read the stamped letters at the foot of each volume's spine from *Waverley* up to *Woodstock* (XXXII); thereafter all one sees is the date '1833', '1833', '1833' . . . , like the monotone of some literary cardiograph when life has ceased. The interest of the Interleaved Set transcends the purely academic, for it is also a treasure of quite exceptional emotional and sentimental power. As a heritage item it occupies a unique position in the national collection. The 'Magnum Opus' is the most moving relic of one of the immortal episodes of literary history, for it represents Scott's dogged determination to pay off his crippling debts and to re-establish his reputation after his ruin following Archibald Constable's crash in 1826. The years of ceaseless literary labour have their most poignant monument in the Interleaved Set, which is now available to complement the self-revealing record of the incomparable *Journal*. Scott wrote himself out of debt but into the grave (Fig. 22). As a tailpiece to the present group of essays I have compiled from the *Journal* and from Scott's letters an anthology illustrating what the 'Magnum Opus' project meant to Scott in the dark days of bankruptcy and in the succeeding years of mental and physical effort. In both the *Journal* and the Interleaved Set one can see him struggling valiantly and honourably hour by hour, day in day out, in a labour unparalleled in the annals of literature.

How hard Scott worked is clear from the annotations, corrections and additions throughout the Interleaved Set. Professor Millgate and Dr Alexander give many convincing examples of his patient editorial care and remarkable attention to detail when beset by sadness, ill-health, financial anxiety and the ceaseless demands made on his brain by, on the one hand, an inborn need to compose and, on the other, the requests from publishers for him to write yet more. One further example may here suffice. At the end of the first volume of *Ivanhoe* (XIII) a letter to Robert Cadell is bound in, together with an additional last-minute note to the novel. 'I am determined', Scott wrote on 20 April 1830, 'to finish the whole Magnum before beginning anything else. It will be a great job off hand.' This letter (Plate 43) and the additional *Ivanhoe* note (Plate 44) accompanied an interleaved *Quentin Durward* copy for the Magnum edition. Despite all his pressures, here is Scott bothering to expand a note already added on a point of heraldry and the rules of blazon (Plate 45) with a further, much longer, technical discussion of the subject. This second after-thought was inserted by the printer in the Magnum volume twelve pages on from the original passage which had given its author such concern.

The emotional impact of certain parts of the Interleaved Set is indeed considerable. Professor Millgate draws attention to a pathetic letter bound into a *Peveril of the Peak* volume (XXII) (Plate 61), and to the material added in a shaky and failing hand to the proofs of the Magnum *Woodstock* (bound into the Interleaved Set in volume XXXI) (Plates 78, 79) which was the result of information gathered by Scott when in London and on a research visit to the British Museum before his voyage to Malta in October 1831. Even then his concern for 'illustration'—by which he and his publisher meant annotation—was not to be overcome by infirmity. The final note in the interleaved *Woodstock* (XXXII) (Plate 80), in an enfeebled autograph, concerns one of his beloved dogs; and it was of his dogs that he had thought so touchingly—expressing those feelings in perhaps the most memorable page of his *Journal*—when news of his ruin came on 18 December 1825: that disaster which compelled the making of the Magnum edition.

The history of the Interleaved Set in the century or so before its acquisition by the National Library of Scotland is romantic indeed, and one which Scott himself would have enjoyed. It is a tale fully in keeping with the affecting story of the composition of the Magnum edition. This is the subject of my own first contribution, which is a revised and very substantially enlarged version, taking account of much new evidence, of a section of the commemorative booklet mentioned above. It is further to be hoped that my essay sheds light on an interesting episode in bibliophilic taste in the twentieth century, and that it provides some insight both into the changing priorities of libraries in their collecting policy, and into the financial circumstances in which such collecting must be carried out.

The Plates and the commentary on them form an important feature of the book. Never before has so much Scott manuscript material of different kinds been reproduced in one place. The quantity is much greater than that included in the Scott Centenary Exhibition catalogue published in 1872. The present photographic album constitutes indeed one of the most unusual contributions to Scott studies in recent years. It is to be hoped that study of this part of the book will add greatly to the enjoyment and instruction of the reader who should gain from it a special insight into the evolution of the text of the novels.

It would be idle to maintain that the bibliography of the Waverley Novels is anything but complex. The structure of the Interleaved Set, with all its component groups of collected editions, is itself far from simple; and so I have drawn up a concordance which tabulates its contents and indicates the relationship between Interleaved Set and Magnum edition.

A note should be added on the terminology employed in this book. The words *Interleaved Set* refer to the actual interleaved and annotated printed books which form the subject of these essays. '*Magnum Opus*' (always in quotation marks) is used occasionally as a popular name for this set of volumes. *Magnum Opus edition* (without quotation marks), *Magnum edition*, or simply *Magnum*, refer throughout to Robert Cadell's edition of the Waverley Novels published between 1829 and 1833.

The authors of these essays have made individual acknowledgements as appropriate. As editor, I should like to make a general acknowledgement to the Librarian of the National Library of Scotland, Professor Denis Roberts, and to the Keeper of Manuscripts (Acquisitions), Mr Patrick Cadell, for their interest and support. Mr Cadell has throughout been ready to discuss all manner of problems; Mr Alastair Brodie and Mr Steve McAvoy have been, as ever, very helpful in matters connected with the photography of the Interleaved Set; and I am indebted to Dr Janet

Adam Smith, Mr Alan Bell and Dr David Hewitt, as well as, of course, to my fellow contributors, Professor Jane Millgate, Dr J H Alexander and Miss Claire Lamont, for advice on points of detail. Miss Marjorie Leith of Aberdeen University Press has been a 'wizard of the North' in turning the work into an elegant book on such a tight schedule, and Mr Colin MacLean has been an exceptionally patient and considerate publisher. Both they and the editor have had to cope with a book on a subject not yet fully understood, and on which the opinions of the authors were constantly changing as some new fact emerged; as a fresh thought on the genius of Sir Walter Scott, or a telling illustration of his remarkable capacity for annotation or emendation, struck the writer of an essay; or as still another exciting discovery was made in the many thousands of pages that make up the Interleaved Set of the Waverley Novels.

July 1987

Iain Gordon Brown
Department of Manuscripts
National Library of Scotland

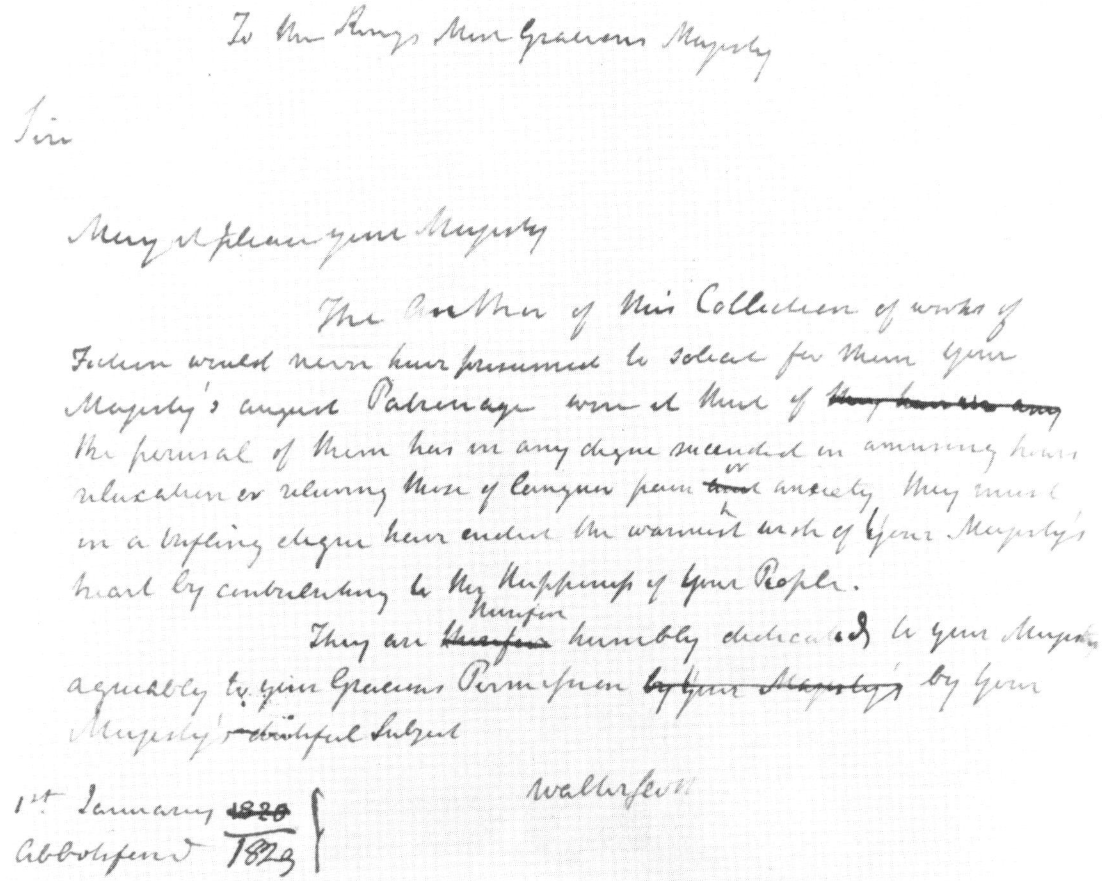

To the King's Most Gracious Majesty

Sire

May it please your Majesty

The Author of this Collection of works of Fiction would never have presumed to solicit for them Your Majesty's august Patronage were it not that the perusal of them has in any degree succeeded in amusing hours of relaxation or relieving those of languor pain or anxiety. They must in a trifling degree have excited the warmest wish of Your Majesty's heart by contributing to the happiness of Your People.

They are therefore humbly dedicated to your Majesty agreeably to your Gracious Permission by Your Majesty's Subject

Walter Scott

1st January 1829
Abbotsford

3 Autograph draft of Dedication of the Magnum Opus edition to King George IV bound into the first volume of the Interleaved Set.

4 Oil sketch of Sir Walter Scott by Sir Edwin Landseer, 1824. National Portrait Gallery, London.

THE INTERLEAVED WAVERLEY NOVELS

Jane Millgate

The original editions of Walter Scott's novels were all published anonymously and without any attempt at extensive introductions or annotations. Scott strenuously resisted attempts by his friends to persuade him to acknowledge authorship of *Waverley* and its numerous successors: if Walter Scott had once been the most famous poet in Europe, it was left to someone called simply the Author of Waverley to become the most famous novelist. In the years from 1814, when *Waverley* first appeared, to 1827, when Scott acknowledged in public for the first time that he had written the twenty-two novels and tales so far published, an elaborate identity game developed in which author and readers seem to have participated with equal relish. Each successive title was seized upon avidly for the clues—whether genuine or deliberately misleading—that it might provide as to the identity of the Author of Waverley.

Although Scott does not seem seriously to have entertained the possibility of revealing his authorship at any time before he, his publishers, and his printer were all ruined following the default of the London booksellers Hurst, Robinson and Co. at the beginning of 1826, he had been persuaded late in the preceding year to embark on some kind of annotated edition of the works of the Author of Waverley. The idea seems to have been first mooted three years earlier by Archibald Constable, Scott's 'Prince of Booksellers',[1] in response to the gift in March 1823 of Scott's surviving novel manuscripts. The only condition Scott attached to the gift was that the manuscripts should 'be scrupulously conceald during the Authors life and only made forthcoming when it may be necessary to assert his right to be accounted the writer of these novels'.[2] Constable's letter of 25 March 1823 not only expressed his gratitude, but made a publishing suggestion. Since others would be only too eager to supply annotations to the novels, why not forestall the attempt: 'it is the Author only who could do anything at all acceptable in the way of genuine illustration [by which he meant annotation]—the Characters Incidents and descriptions in which all of [the novels] so fully abound have either originated in what may

5 Archibald Constable (1774–1827), the 'Prince of Booksellers' and 'the Napoleon of the publishing world', by Andrew Geddes. Scottish National Portrait Gallery, Edinburgh.

be termed reality or are drawn from sources but little known.'[3] Constable offered to prepare an interleaved set of the novels in which Scott might enter the notes as they occurred to him, but Scott was quick to decline this offer, commenting the next day, 'I think your interleaved Copy of the Novels would fright me'. He did not, however, reject the annotation proposal out of hand but promised Constable: 'Such notes as are worth making I will either insert in my memoirs of my own life and literary history or in a separate blank paper book . . . [T]he paper book shall be yours if I go before you.'[4]

There the matter apparently rested until late in 1825, at which time Constable, reluctant to settle for Scott's preference for a posthumous publication, seems finally to have won his point. On 24 December 1825 Scott noted in his journal that Constable had a scheme for publishing the works of the Author of Waverley 'in a superior stile at £1.1. volume'. Not only would this mean employment for the Ballantyne printing works, in which Scott was a partner, but Constable anticipated a profit of £20,000, of which Scott, in return for contributing the annotations, was to have any sum he cared to name. In prospect the task looked to Scott like 'light work',[5] and he embarked on it straight away, only to be interrupted by the financial disaster of January 1826. While the bad news was still coming in Scott had pressed on—recording on 19 January, 'Even yesterday I went about making notes on *Waverley* according to Constable's plan.'[6] But once it became clear that the ownership of the actual copyrights of the novels was in dispute there seemed no point in continuing with the annotations, and all his energies for the next two years were devoted to other literary tasks.

Scott had sold the copyrights of his novels to Constable in a series of transactions commencing in 1819, but the legal position was complicated by the fact that at the time of the crash Constable still owed Scott £7,800 of the purchase price of the fifteen titles up to and including *Quentin Durward*. Arbitration subsequently assigned the disputed copyrights to Constable, but in the meantime Scott's trustees agreed jointly with Constable's trustees that the copyrights should be auctioned and the proceeds held in trust pending a final disposition. At the December 1827 sale buyers 'came on briskly four or five bidders abreast',[7] but in the event the successful purchasers were Scott's trustees in partnership with Robert Cadell for £8,500.

Cadell, who had been Constable's son-in-law and partner, but who had hastened to put as much distance as possible between himself and Constable after the 1826 disaster, had managed by the assiduity with which he helped Scott and his trustees with business advice to become Scott's sole publisher by 1827. He had also resurrected the scheme for an annotated collected edition of the novels, and it was precisely to make such an edition possible that it had been necessary to buy in the copyrights of the first fifteen titles. Cadell's proposal differed in notable respects from that put forward by Constable in 1823. Where Constable has envisaged something grand and expensive—large paper, fine printing, a price of a guinea a volume—Cadell wished to capture a mass market. His much smaller volumes were to be issued monthly, a strategy previously associated only with the lesser forms of publishing life, and at a cost of only five shillings each. The latest technology of stereotyping and, as the edition progressed, of machine printing was to be employed, and well-known artists were to be sought for the engraved frontispieces and title-page vignettes. Costs were to be tightly controlled, and no energy was to be spared in promoting the edition. It was originally planned to print 4,000 copies of each volume, but by publication date this had been increased to 10,000, and by the time the last of the forty-eight volumes appeared more than 30,000 copies of each of the early titles had been produced. Publication began 1 June 1829 and concluded 3 May 1833, almost eight months after Scott's death. From its early stages this edition was referred to by author, publisher, and printer as the *Magnum*

6 Robert Cadell (1788–1849), from a photograph of the painting by Sir John Watson Gordon, 1832. Reproduced from *The Scott Gallery* (1903): National Library of Scotland.

Opus, or simply the Magnum. For its preparation Scott made use of interleaved volumes of several earlier collected editions; and these volumes Cadell subsequently had rebound so as to preserve not only all the revisions Scott made to the texts of the novels and the notes he added on the interleaves, but also all the introductions, appendices, and other supplementary materials the author had sent to Cadell on separate sheets over the course of the Magnum edition's preparation.

It would be pleasant to think that Cadell was so careful to protect the materials connected with the creation of the Magnum edition because of the unique status of these documents in the genesis of the final version of Scott's text, but the truth seems to have been more mundane. The Waverley Novels had been for Constable a matter of pride, his association with their author a source of deep personal pleasure that was quite distinct from the satisfaction associated with the money they generated. Cadell too was proud of his connection with Scott, and of his rôle as publisher both of the individual novels from *Chronicles of the Canongate* onwards and of the new collected edition, but he was much more aware than Constable of the long future Scott's collected works might have as a piece of literary property and of the need to protect that property from predatory assaults by other publishers. Among the papers he left to his family Cadell included the following note on the Interleaved Set:

> The Annotated Edition of the Waverley Novels in 41 volumes octavo, which is not only curious but valuable; the additions in Sir Walter Scott's hand carry down the copyright (so far as these alterations go) to a period of forty-two years from the appearance of each volume of the duodecimo, commencing in 1829 and reaching to 1833.[8]

7 James Ballantyne (1772–1833), who printed not only most of the volumes in the sets of collected editions which make up the Interleaved Set, but also of the Magnum Opus edition itself; from a photograph of the painting at Abbotsford by an unknown artist. Reproduced from *The Scott Gallery* (1903): National Library of Scotland.

What this statement makes clear is that the Interleaved Set was preserved primarily because it provided evidence of the continuation of the copyright in the Waverley Novels—a copyright which had become, through a series of transactions with Scott and subsequently with Scott's family, the sole property of Robert Cadell.

Cadell died in 1849, and in 1851 his family sold the Waverley Novels copyrights to the firm of A & C Black. As part of this transaction Blacks received the Interleaved Set, and it was as their property that it was exhibited in the Scott Centenary Exhibition in Edinburgh in 1871, where the volumes were described as 'specimens of the Copyright text'.[9] Blacks used the volumes in preparing the Centenary Edition of 1871, and a few of Scott's notes not included in the Magnum itself appeared in print for the first time in that edition. (See part III of Dr Alexander's contribution below.)

With all forty-one volumes available for examination, it is now possible to produce a somewhat more accurate account of their contents than that contained in a descriptive pamphlet written by J H Isaacs, a New York bibliophile, in 1930. It is simply not true, for example, that the 'set of printed sheets used by Scott for the purpose of preparing this definitive text, was a SPECIAL IMPRESSION made for him alone, by Cadell, of the First Collected Edition, begun in 1817 and completed in 1833'.[10] The sheets used in the Interleaved Set are not, in fact, a special impression, nor do they come from a collected edition begun in 1817. Collected editions of Scott's novels began to appear in 1819 with the twelve-volume large octavo edition of *Novels and Tales of the Author of Waverley*, consisting of the novels from *Waverley* to *A Legend of Montrose*. Subsequent collections of later groups of novels first appeared in 1822, 1824, 1827, and 1833, and were eventually published in three formats, large octavo, duodecimo, and 18mo. The Interleaved Set was made up of volumes in the large octavo format of these collected editions. The first twelve volumes derived from the 1822 second edition of the large octavo *Novels and Tales of the Author of Waverley*, volumes XIII to XVIII from the 1822 first edition of *Historical Romances of the Author of Waverley*, volumes XIX to XXV from the 1824 first edition of *Novels and Romances of the Author of Waverley*, and volumes XXVI to XXXII from the 1827 first edition of *Tales and Romances of the Author of Waverley*. These thirty-two volumes were the only ones to be collected during Scott's lifetime. The remaining volumes in the present set consist of the first edition of the 1833 seven-volume continuation of the *Tales and Romances* series, and the two volumes which Cadell issued in 1833 to supply owners of the earlier collections with the introductions and annotations Scott had prepared for the Magnum Opus edition. Needless to say, these final nine volumes of the National Library's set are not interleaved and do not contain Scott manuscript material; and (as Dr Brown has made clear above) these volumes, therefore, have not been included in the microfiche edition.

When the volumes were originally prepared for Scott's use they would have had blank interleaves between each pair of pages, and the binding was probably simple boards. Scott recorded the revisions he wished to have made to the novels on these interleaves and in the margins of the printed texts. He also used the interleaves for the newly composed annotations to the novels, continuing the longer notes over several interleaves and sometimes onto the white space in the printed text (Plates 4–8). Very long notes, or notes that were composed subsequent to Scott's original preparation of the Magnum copy, were written on individual sheets of paper of various sizes and sent off separately to Cadell (Plates 44, 46, 75). The introductions and appendices were composed for the most part on separate sheets of the kind of paper Scott customarily used in writing his novels (Plates 24, 40).

Some time after the publication of the final group of *Tales and Romances* and the two volumes of collected Magnum notes in 1833, Cadell had all forty-one volumes rebound in Russia leather and the ascription 'Author's Manuscript Introductions and Annotations 1829–32' stamped on the spine of each interleaved volume, as well as his own crest on the front covers of all the volumes (Plates 1–2; Fig 14). At the time of this rebinding, blank interleaves were removed and the separate sheets containing introductions, appendices, extra notes, etc, were carefully folded and bound in at the appropriate places—sometimes on stubs, or, where margins allowed, sewn directly into the binding (Plates 3, 20, 21, 22, 25, 29, 48). These inserted sheets contain by far the most substantial portion of Scott manuscript material in the volumes; in some cases they also include passages in other hands—usually transcriptions of long quotations, or sections from letters Scott had received containing background information about characters, events, or locations in the novels (Plates 25, 29, 47, 48, 50, 66, 75). The binding job seems to have been done with great care and there are only a very few places where a blank interleaf has escaped notice or a marked one has been bound in at the wrong point. It is typical of Cadell's rage for order that he should have decided to include the nine unmarked volumes at the end so as to make the uniformly bound set complete; but it is to that same temperament, coupled with shrewd commercial

NOVELS AND TALES

OF

THE AUTHOR OF WAVERLEY

VOL. IV.

THE ANTIQUARY.

EDINBURGH;

PRINTED FOR ARCHIBALD CONSTABLE AND C° EDINBURGH;

AND HURST ROBINSON AND C°

LONDON.

1822.

8 Title-page of *The Antiquary* in the collected edition of *Novels and Tales of the Author of Waverley* (1822). Actual size. National Library of Scotland.

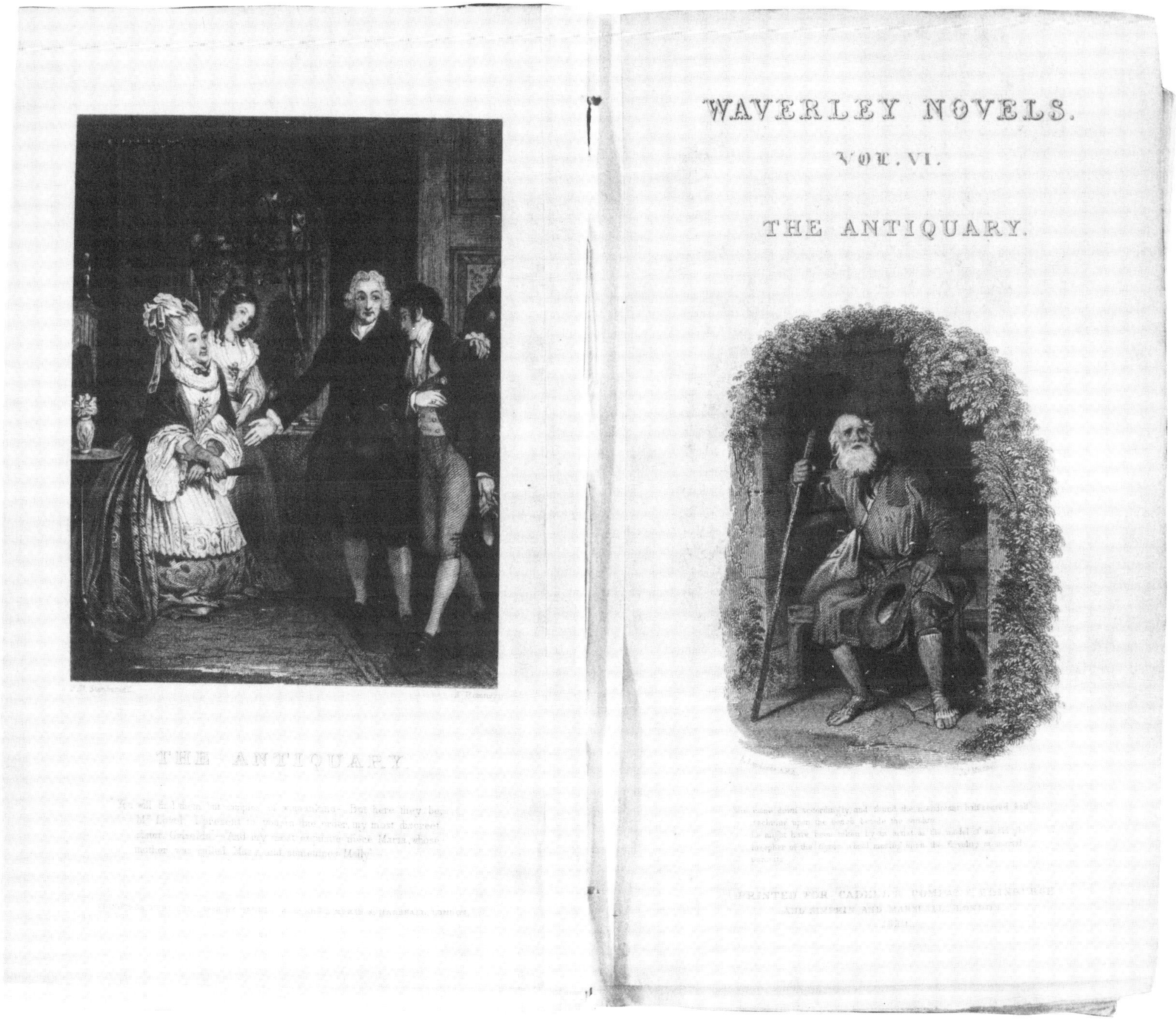

9 Title-page and frontispiece of the second volume of *The Antiquary* in the Magnum Opus edition (1829). Actual size. National Library of Scotland.

sense, that we owe both the Magnum Opus edition itself and this near-complete record of the new material which Scott provided for the volumes up to and including *Woodstock*.

It is not possible to determine an exact date for the preparation of the interleaved volumes, but it is conceivable, from the consistency of the interleaving throughout and the fact that 1821 is the only date to appear in the watermarks of the standard interleaves, that the first twelve volumes (*Novels and Tales*) were prepared by Constable for Scott's use in that first abortive attempt at an annotated edition at the end of 1825, and that some of the notes to *Waverley* may therefore date from this period. The remaining volumes have interleaves of more than one paper stock and show watermarks of 1822 and 1824; all twenty may have been prepared at the same time at Cadell's behest, but they were not in any case sent off to Scott in one batch, since in April 1830 he reminded Cadell that he still needed interleaved copies of the seven volumes of *Tales and Romances* as well as of his three most recent titles, *Anne of Geierstein* and the two series of *Chronicles of the Canongate*, which had not yet been included in a collection.[11] The sheets bearing supplementary material, which were subsequently bound into the thirty-two volumes, bear watermarks ranging from 1795 to 1830, but inscriptions in Scott's own hand—as opposed to transcriptions by others, extracts from letters, etc—appear mainly on paper watermarked 1827, 1828, and 1829, thus tending to confirm the evidence we have from external sources that Scott's major spells of work on the edition occurred between 1828 and 1831.

Bound into the first volume is the set's earliest item in Scott's hand, the fragment of a prose romance entitled 'Thomas the Rhymer' which was composed by Scott in the late 1790s. In preparing copy for the Magnum Opus edition Scott used the original manuscript of this fragment written in the large hand of his early days as a lawyer; in adding certain minor stylistic improvements and clarifications he naturally employed the more economical script he had developed over thirty years of authorship. The document is eloquent both of Scott's youthful ambitions in the realm of prose fiction and of the older Scott's conception of his editorial rôle (Plate 3).

The different types of paper used by Scott for additional notes provide fascinating evidence of the process by which the edition was put together. Late sheets are inserted in volumes whose copy had clearly been completed at an early point in Scott's work; for example, although Scott had finished the basic revision of the text of *The Heart of Mid-Lothian* in 1828, the cover sheet for the transcribed Memorial Concerning the Murder of Captain Porteous, bound into Chapter 9, is written on paper watermarked 1829. Again, an extract from a 31 March 1829 letter from Joseph Train about Robert Paterson—the original of Old Mortality—is inserted in the introduction to that novel both in Train's original and in a transcription, and in the Magnum introduction to *Old Mortality* Scott prefaces the extract with the information that it came to hand 'While these sheets were passing through the press'.[12] This is only one of many examples identifiable in the Interleaved Set of Scott's determination to include right up to the last possible moment any scrap of antiquarian fact or anecdote he thought would enhance the attractiveness of the new edition. Scott's markings on the Train letter have their own interest: he not only indicates the omissions and elisions he wants made but adds a few minor improvements to Train's style (Plate 25). No matter how pressed Scott was for time as he desperately sought to write and publish himself out of debt, very little escaped his editorial scrutiny.

Further evidence of the detailed attention given by Scott to the supplementary material for the Magnum is supplied by the presence in the interleaved set of a small number of proofs: these consist of one page of text for *Peveril of the Peak*, with corrections by Scott that involve the cancellation of a note (Plate 67); and twenty pages, extensively corrected by Scott, for the Introduction to *Woodstock* (Plate 78). The additions on this latter set of proofs probably constitute Scott's last contribution to the material in the Interleaved Set, including as they do information he gathered on a visit to the British Museum during a brief stay in London in October 1831, just before his departure on the voyage to Malta which he hoped would restore his failing health. Apart from one other small group of proofs for Magnum notes, these are the only proofs for the edition which are known to have survived.

Work on the edition did not always proceed smoothly. An interleaved copy prepared months ahead sometimes went missing, and Scott, troubled by the effects of the series of strokes he suffered in 1830 and 1831, could not always remember whether it had been sent off to Cadell or was still somewhere at Abbotsford. The addition of late material to annotations or introductions could also cause confusion, and long delays in the printing of an individual title could impede Scott's determined attempt to keep revisions and annotations consistent and free of repetition. Bound into volume XXII of the Interleaved Set is a previously unpublished open letter from Scott to all those associated with the production of the edition (Plate 61); in it he pleads for special attention to *Peveril of the Peak*, and it provides, with its stumblings and omissions, a moving testament to Scott's determination, no matter what the accidents of the publication process or the limits imposed by his own condition, to make the edition as accurate as possible:

> The printer & publisher must be aware that Peveril of the Peak is under very particular circumstances which unless attended to will occasion great and peculiar errors in printing the effect of which may extend very far. The author therefore calls upon them thus formal to be kind enough to remember that this novel & its notes preface &c has been written rewritten lost and supplied till the whole is a confused in the authors It is unavoidably that there must be repeated passages. The author therefore while he desires to see the proofs as usual will be

greatly obliged to the printer to send *running copy* that he may see what has been done when settling what we are to day It will be also extremely necessary that this work is carried on without delay and not after long intervals so that the whole may be kept in view at the same time.

Abbotsford 19 Nov 1830

Scott's own labours on the edition were immense: he not only revised the text, composed the new introductions and notes, and sought out the information and documentation required for the notes, but he also wrote out the vast majority of these new materials in his own hand. The introductions and notes in these volumes provide therefore a considerable addition to the original manuscript material available to students of Scott's late career. It is true that what is here corresponds in general terms to what appeared in the Magnum Opus edition as published—there seem to be only about thirty uncancelled notes which did not find their way into it in some form, and most of these were later included in the Centenary Edition. But the numerous small differences of phrasing or syntax which occur in every note and on each page of introduction, the sheer mass of material in Scott's hand, the numerous physical evidences of the way in which the editorial apparatus was put together and modified over time—these constitute important new data both for determining the genesis and importance of the Magnum Opus edition and for understanding Scott's habits of composition in general.

The fascination of the Interleaved Set lies not so much in the totality of what it contains and the degree to which that corresponds to the published Magnum, as in its detail. The information it offers to scholars is enormous, revealing as it does not only Scott's first thoughts as to the content, phrasing, and organisation of that elaborate editorial apparatus which was to transform the way in which all subsequent generations read his novels, but also the kinds of changes he wished to see made in what he knew would be the final version of the texts of those novels. The Interleaved Set represents a separate stage in the development of Scott's text, one which scholars will have to take into account in seeking to establish the authority of the published Magnum Opus. The detailed evidence available here about Scott's methods of composition and revision—as about the relationship he wished to achieve with his readers through the new framing material—will take years of examination to exhaust. The volumes also have another kind of importance, related to but separate from their scholarly significance. They constitute one of the most moving of literary documents, revealing on almost every page the enthusiasm, dedication, and sheer hard work which Scott devoted to this final recension of the works of the Author of Waverley. Given his desperate financial situation and failing health it would have been very easy for him to skimp on the editorial labour, to reject a piece of information that came late to hand, to rest content with the most obvious kind of note, or to allow simple autobiographical reminiscence to serve the purposes of introduction. That was not Scott's way. The act of editing perhaps came to him even more naturally than the act of writing novels, and he brought to this last and greatest of his editorial tasks all of his creative as well as his antiquarian powers.

REFERENCES

1 *The Journal of Sir Walter Scott*, ed W E K Anderson (Oxford, 1972), p.331.
2 *The Letters of Sir Walter Scott*, ed H J C Grierson, 12 vols (London, 1932–37), VII. 353.
3 *Letters*, VII. 354.
4 *Letters*, VII. 360.
5 *Journal*, p.48.
6 *Journal*, p.62.
7 *Journal*, p.400.
8 Quoted in *The Scott Exhibition MDCCCLXXI. Catalogue of the Exhibition.* (Edinburgh, 1872), p.130.
9 *Catalogue*, p.130.
10 *Sir Walter Scott's 'Magnum Opus'* (New York, 1930), p.6.
11 *Letters*, XI. 340.
12 *Waverley Novels*, 48 vols (Edinburgh, 1829–33), IX. 228.

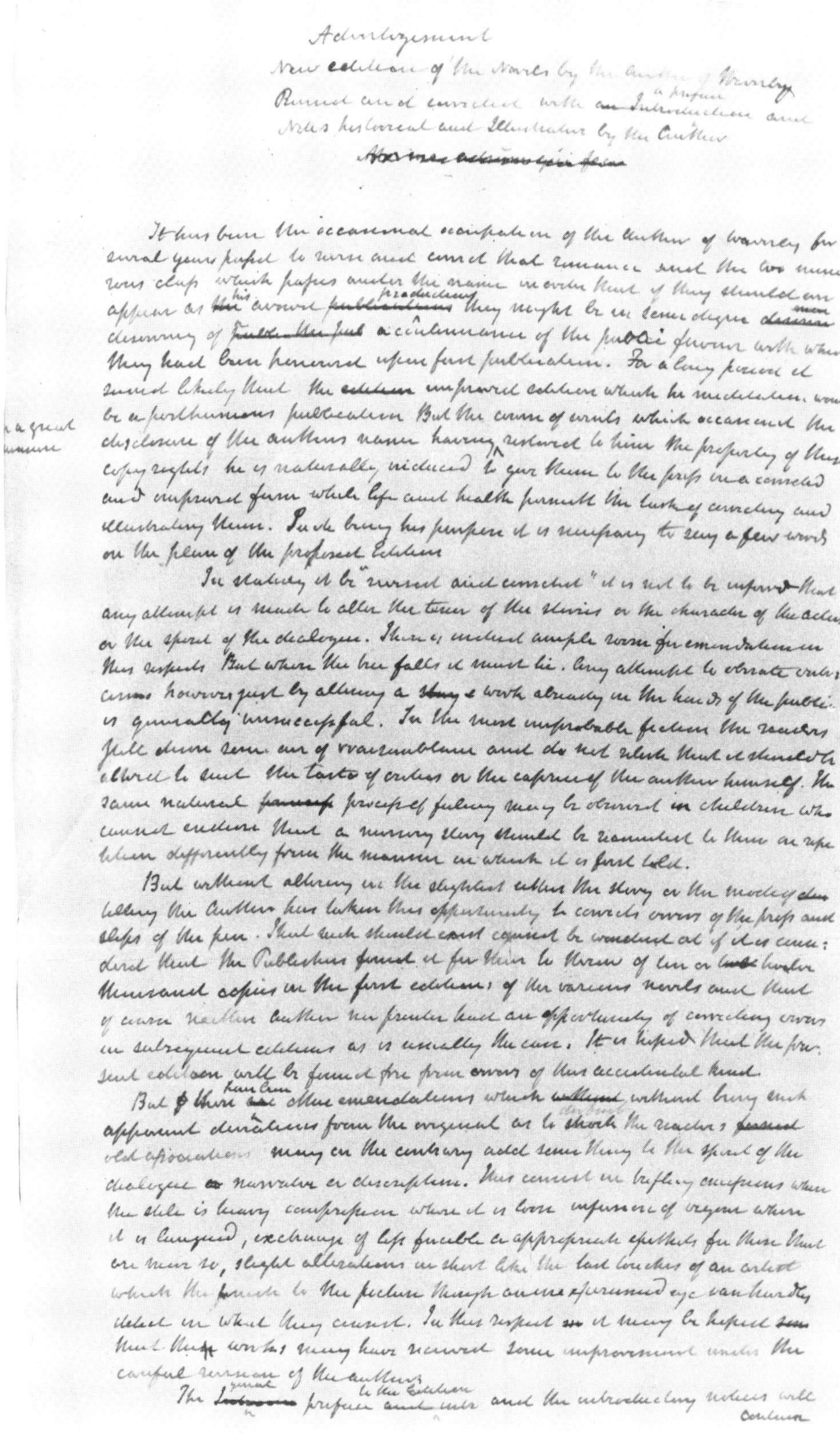

Advertizement

New edition of the Novels by the Author of Waverley
Revised and corrected with a preface Introduction and
Notes historical and Illustrative by the Author

It has been the occasional occupation of the Author of Waverley for several years past to revise and correct that romance and the numerous class which passes under the name in order that if they should ever appear as his avowed production they might be in some degree deserving of a continuance of the public favour with which they had been honoured upon first publication. For a long period it seemed likely that the improved edition which he meditated would be a posthumous publication. But the course of events which occasioned the disclosure of the authors name having in a great measure restored to him the property of these copyrights he is naturally induced to give them to the press in a corrected and improved form while life and health permit the task of correcting and illustrating them. Such being his purpose it is necessary to say a few words on the plan of the proposed edition

In stating it to be "revised and corrected" it is not to be inferred that any attempt is made to alter the tenor of the stories or the character of the actors or the spirit of the dialogue. There is indeed ample room for emendation in these respects But where the tree falls it must lie. Any attempt to obviate criticisms however just by altering a work already in the hands of the public is generally unsuccessful. In the most improbable fiction the reader still desires some air of vraisemblance and does not relish that it should be altered to suit the taste of critics or the caprice of the author himself. The same natural principle of feeling may be observed in children who cannot endure that a nursery story should be repeated to them in a different manner from the manner in which it is first told.

But without altering in the slightest either the story or the mode of telling the Author has taken this opportunity to correct errors of the press and slips of the pen. That such should exist cannot be wondered at if it is considered that the Publishers found it for their interest to throw off ten or twelve thousand copies in the first editions of the various novels and that of course neither author nor printer had an opportunity of correcting errors in subsequent editions as is usually the case. It is hoped that the present edition will be found free from errors of this accidental kind.

But there have been other emendations which without being such apparent deviations from the original as to disturb the reader's old associations may on the contrary add something to the spirit of the dialogue narrative or description. These consist in trifling compressions where the style is heavy compression where it is loose infusion of vigour where it is languid, exchange of less forcible or appropriate epithets for those that are more so, slight alterations in short like the last touches of an artist which the finish to the picture though an unexperienced eye can hardly detect in what they consist. In this respect it may be hoped that the works may have received some improvement under the careful revision of the authors

The general prefaces to the Edition and the introductory notices will continue

10 Initial folio of the Advertisement to the Magnum Opus edition bound into the first volume of the Interleaved Set. (1. Advertisement i–iii.)

DESCRIPTIVE GUIDE TO THE INTERLEAVED SET*

J H Alexander

I. SCOTT'S TEXTUAL EMENDATIONS

Whatever else the Interleaved Set may be, it is an exercise in bookmaking. Scott adds a good deal to his octavo texts and modifies them by substitutions, but he hardly ever deletes anything. Examples of rare deletions, ranging from a sentence to a word or two, can be found at XVIII: 289, XX: 328, XXII: 143, and XXV: 81, 244. Scott's emendations are, with the notable exception of the political alterations in *The Bride of Lammermoor*, unsystematic and patchy. Detailed study may reveal reasons for this, but at this stage it can only be noted that while *Waverley* and especially *Guy Mannering* are very fully revised (Plates 4–15), subsequent novels do not show a regular diminution in emendatory activity: early on in the series *Rob Roy*, *The Bride of Lammermoor*, and *The Heart of Mid-Lothian* already have up to fifty pages without a single alteration, whereas much later on *Quentin Durward* is heavily revised (Plates 68–70). *The Bride* again excepted, it is not immediately obvious that any individual novel attracted a particular type of emendation.

The insertions and modifications fall into three main categories: (1) the introductory material for each novel, varying greatly in length from work to work; (2) the notes, whether short notes intended to appear as footnotes, or longer notes which Scott wished to be placed at the end of chapters; and (3) the host of additions and alterations, mostly very small, scattered unevenly throughout the text.

The first two categories are covered in the two lists which follow this essay: one of material bound into the volumes, excluding that which appears on interleaves but noting the few examples of misbindings; the other of notes not published in the Magnum but mostly picked up in the Centenary Edition of 1871.

The third category is here dealt with by means of a description of some of the main types of smaller alteration. A full analysis of these must wait until the Interleaved Set has been studied in detail, but when taken along with Professor Millgate's essay above and her more extended description in *Scott's Last Edition*[1] the remarks that follow, taken in conjunction with Dr Brown's Illustrated Commentary later in the present volume, should give the reader an idea of what to expect.

It should be stressed at the outset that although the Interleaved Set is of very great interest, and many of the emendations are noteworthy, much of what Scott does is workaday tidying up of the text. The primary purpose of the present essay is description rather than evaluation, but some evaluation is inevitable, recognising that in very many cases there are likely to be contrasting opinions as to the merit of particular types of revision.

One of the most frequent types of revision is intended to clarify the original version: perhaps Scott felt that the new readership envisaged for the Magnum needed rather more help than his original readers had done. Sometimes clarification affects a description. In *Guy Mannering* a sentence is emended thus: 'At first sight he seemed to have perished by a fall from the rocks, which [there] rose \above the spot on which he lay/, in a \perpendicular/ precipice of a hundred feet above the beach.' (II: 367 [3: 93–4]. See also II: 377; XXV: 17; XXVIII: 65). Often narrative details are filled in or otherwise clarified, notably in concluding narratives (see III: 477; VI: 474; X: 134; XIII: 179; XV: 110). One such emendation is in another hand, probably Cadell's: in *The Monastery* Mysie 'led the way to the door of the apartment, \having first carefully extinguished her lamp/' (XV: 319 [19: 174]). Characters' motives and feelings are spelt out, not usually in an unexpected sense. A pleasant example is the addition in *The Antiquary* of the sentences explaining Oldbuck's attachment to Lovel: 'The riddle was notwithstanding

*Deletions are indicated in square brackets, insertions by \.../, and editorial matter by {...}. Unless otherwise stated, all insertions which were included in the Magnum edition are given in their final Magnum form rather than as literal renderings of Scott's usually unpunctuated manuscript additions in the Interleaved Set. Upper case Roman numerals refer to volumes of the Interleaved Set; Arabic numerals refer to volumes of the Magnum edition (1829–33).

easily solved. Lovel had many attractive qualities, but he won our Antiquary's heart by being on most occasions an excellent listener.' (IV: 244, where Scott wrote 'qualities worthy to attract regard' [cf. 5: 216]; see also II: 379; III: 365.) A useful clarification occurs in *Quentin Durward*, where Louis finds 'how differently he \now/ considered his {Quentin's} deportment and features \than he had done at their first interview/' (XXIV: 348 [31: 147]), but others in the same novel will strike many readers as unnecessary word-spinning (XXIV: 376, 377). One finds Scott filling in the historical and sociological background (VI: 399; XVI: 27, 61), clarifying a process (III: 225), replacing pronouns with names or descriptive phrases indicating the character in question (X: 311, 321; XVI: 87; XXI: 364), and spelling out concepts and images rather pedantically (XVIII: 97, 106; XIX: 265; XXIII: 341). The addition of detail is most attractive, though, when it has nothing to do with clarification, but springs from Scott's old zest for particulars. Jane Millgate has noted several examples of comic expansion in *Guy Mannering*.[2] In *Ivanhoe* Scott takes the opportunity to fill out the tournament with several vivid details: 'All stood astonished at his presumption, but none more than the redoubted Knight whom he had thus defied to mortal combat, \and who, little expecting so rude a challenge, was standing carelessly at the door of the pavilion/. (XIII: 141 [16: 131]) '\Fair and true he hit the Norman on the visor, where his lance's point kept hold of the bars./' (XIII: 144 (after some stumbling) [16: 134]; see also the clutch of details added on XIII: 209) (Plate 42).

Probably the commonest sort of filling-in involves the addition of 'said so-and-so' and similar formulas to speeches. Formulas, mostly plain, are sometimes used throughout an exchange, which certainly slows down the reading somewhat and makes the effect less dramatic (III: 130–1, 140–1, 193–6) (cf. Plates 13, 17). Scott is by no means consistent in this, as in other matters, and many exchanges remain in their original states. The formula is often expanded with an explanation of the thought underlying the speech: there are few surprises. Thus in *The Monastery* a speech of Sir Piercie Shafton is glossed: '"Nay, but speak plain, most generous damsel,\" said the knight, who, for once, was puzzled as much as his own elegance of speech was wont to puzzle others, "/for I swear to you that I comprehend nought by the extension of thy fair digit."' (XV: 328 [19: 182]) One such insertion in *Peveril of the Peak* was not caught by Magnum or later editors: '"Think but an instant, silly girl—\answered Christian obviously embarassd but trusting to the flattery which he had found a master-key to the female heart/"' (XXIV: 96 [cf. Magnum 30: 297]). Perhaps most helpful to the reader are indications of the tone in which a speech is delivered. In *The Antiquary* a speech of Oldbuck is glossed thus: '"Indeed? well, young man,\" replied his visitor, in a tone of seriousness very different from his affected gravity, "/be comforted . . .' (IV: 252, where Scott wrote 'replied his friend in tone real seriousness . . .' [5: 224]; see also III: 313). An interesting addition alters the effect of Morton's speech in *Old Mortality*: '"Burley must have deceived me—craft as well as cruelty is permitted by his creed.\" Such was his inward thought; he said aloud, "/I cannot stay, Mrs Wilson, I must go forward directly."' (VIII: 208 [10: 281]) Redgauntlet delivers part of a later speech 'with hypocritical formality' (XXVIII: 437 [36: 306]).

Although Scott frequently pins his characters down more firmly, and sometimes introduces an authorial or narrative opinion (e.g. X: 199; XII: 413), many of his emendations introduce a tentative note. In *The Bride of Lammermoor* when Lucy encounters the wild cattle 'it was not then, as \it may be/ now, a necessary part of a young lady's [education] \demeanour/, to indulge in causeless tremors of the nerves' (XI: 79 [13: 321]); later in the same novel the feuars '"could not say;" the universal refuge of a Scottish peasant, when pressed to admit a claim which his conscience owns\, or perhaps his feelings/, and his interest inclines him to deny' (XI: 221, which has 'feeling' [14: 52]). Even when more information is given, the tentative note may still be present. Of Reuben in *The Heart of Mid-Lothian* the narrator is made to say for the first time in the Interleaved Set: 'On these subjects, however, he was habitually silent, perhaps from modesty, perhaps from a touch of pride, or perhaps from a conjunction of both.' (IX: 159 [11: 310]. For further tentative emendations see X: 299; XII: 23; XX: 14.)

A large group of emendations may be described as corrections. From the manuscript to the Interleaved Set, and probably on to the final proofs of the Magnum, Scott is anxious to eliminate ugly repetitions of words in close proximity (II: 374; V: 349 (possibly by another hand); X: 26, 311; XIV: 79; XIX: 134; XXIX: 159). One correction of this sort was overlooked, so that in *The Bride of Lammermoor* Caleb Balderstone appears as 'the old man' twice in one paragraph, where the first occurrence should have been emended to result in the reading 'The domestic retired, not to rest, but to prayer' (XII: 96 [cf. 14: 365]); once, an insertion gave rise to an ugly repetition, and the insertion had to be changed in proof (XXV: 158 [32: 91 replaces 'appalling' with 'alarming']). At least once Scott was anxious to avoid an ugly echo: in *Quentin Durward* 'tell' becomes 'decide' because of the proximity of 'tolling' (XXIV: 333 [31: 133]). *Mots justes* are often substituted for less appropriate words, as in the same novel (XXIV: 344, 345), in *The Betrothed* where 'fear' becomes 'apprehension' (of future horrors: XXIX: 152 [37: 113]), and in *Woodstock* where Bevis '[hungered] \slobbered/ and whined for the duck-wing' (XXXII: 145 [40: 66]). Grammatical corrections and improvements are fairly frequent (II: 378; VI: 466; XII: 88; XIX: 495). On occasion these corrections may seem pedantic. Of Brian-de-Bois-Guilbert in *Ivanhoe* Scott writes, diminishing the passage: 'His general appearance was grand and commanding; but, looking at him with attention, men read that in his dark features, from which [we] \they/ willingly withdr[a]\e/w [our] \their/ eyes.' (XIV: 280 [17: 368]). Stylistic improvement sometimes involves changing the rhythm or movement of a passage. One of

Burley's speeches in *Old Mortality* was emended thus: '"... Think ye," he continued, "to touch pitch and remain undefiled? to mix in the ranks of malignants, papists, papa-prelatists, latitudinarians, and scoffers; to partake of their sports, which are like the meat offered unto idols; to hold intercourse, perchance, with their daughters, as the sons of God with the daughters of men in the world before the flood \—Think you, I say, to do all these things, and/ yet remain free from pollution?..."' (VII: 351 [9: 321–2]; cf. XVI: 46). Scott also makes his narrative less abrupt on occasion (V: 368; VII: 350; XXIV: 393; XXX: 66, 328). He often divides his longer paragraphs by indicating 'N.L.' (XII: 369, 384; XIV: 9; XVI: 59; XVIII: 136) (cf. Plate 51), and long sentences are also split (XXIX: 221; XXX: 392). There are of course a number of simple corrections of obvious misreadings and misprints in the octavo edition (XVI: 301, 305, 375, 389; XVIII: 132, XIX: 190; XXVII: 425, 461; XXX: 31), Latin presenting particular problems to the printer (XXVII: 283, 291).

Scott takes advantage of the new edition to help the reader with additional glosses of Scottish and other difficult words (III: 70–1 (Plate 12); IX: 424; XXVII: 72 (German)), and on one occasion of an obscure English phrase (XXIV: 324). He took considerable pains to emend the glossary at the end of the original *Novels and Tales* (XII: 509–27), but little use was made of these emendations in the full glossary which appeared at the end of the Magnum after his death (Plate 39). Linguists will be particularly anxious to analyse the occasions on which he adds Scots vocabulary (II: 389; III: 50; IV: 356 (possibly another hand); VI: 193, 258; VIII: 220; IX: 91, 224, 226; X: 232, 234, this last not taken up in the Magnum) or when, less often, he deletes the Scots element (V: 133; II: 316, 318, 322; (these four conceivably deleted by another hand) VI: 137, XIX: 474).

It is of interest to observe that Scott sometimes makes alterations in his own verse, always for the better. The tenth chapter of *The Black Dwarf* is prefaced with a stanza attributed to 'Old Ballad', which read in the *Novels and Tales*:

> I left my ladye's bower last night—
>   It was clad in wreaths of snaw,—
> I sought it when the sun was bright,
>   And sweet the roses blaw.

Scott altered the third line to read 'I'll seek it when the sun is bright' (VII: 135 [9: 106]). The most famous of these alterations is in 'County Guy' in *Quentin Durward*, where Scott substituted 'confess' for 'they know' in the first stanza, to the great improvement of the sound (XXIV: 265 [31: 66]; see also XV: 203; XIX: 414; XX: 109; XXX: 339). In *The Betrothed* an interesting rejected emendation to 'Soldier, wake' appears at XXIX: 335, and in the same novel Scott composes a spontaneous, though hardly distinguished motto, '*Hymn to the Virgin*' as Magnum's attribution has it (XXIX: 108 [37: 74]).

On a number of occasions, especially in the later novels, Scott indulges in a practice familiar in his narrative poems of introducing a 'peg' into the text on which he can hang a note. The most striking example of this occurs in *Peveril of the Peak*, where additional material was needed.[3] Scott inserts into the text several sentences on the amusements of the Manx, and appends a long note at the end of the chapter (XXII: 339 [28: 192–3, 208–11] (Plate 62); see also III: 120, XII: 292; XX: 51 (Plate 54); XXIII: 73–7 (Plate 65); XXIV: 49, 73).

It is, as Jane Millgate remarks, rare for Scott to change the meaning of his original text. The celebrated example of *The Bride of Lammermoor* is the most striking exception.[4] Other much smaller examples can occasionally be observed. Grandmother Mucklebackit's speech in *The Antiquary* was emended thus: '"... And it was thought a proud word o' the family, and they aye stickit by it—and the mair in the latter times, because in the night-time they had mair freedom to perform their popish ceremonies by darkness and in secrecy than in the daylight—at least that was the case in my time—they wad hae been disturbed in the day-time baith by the law and the commons of Fairport—they [hae mair freedom now] \may be owerlooked now/, as I have heard..."' (IV: 435 [6: 71]). In *The Black Dwarf* Ratcliffe's description is altered: '"... But freedom, and wealth were unable to restore the equipoise of his mind; [the first he despised, the last] \to the former his grief made him indifferent—the latter/ only served him as far as it afforded him the means of indulging his strange and wayward fancy.' (VII: 221 [9: 183]) The tone of the beginning of a late chapter of *Guy Mannering* is altered in the interleaved copy: 'As Mr Sampson crossed the hall with a bewildered look, \Mrs Allan,/ the good housekeeper, who\, with the reverent attention which is usually rendered to the clergy in Scotland,/ was on the watch for his return, sallied forth to meet him...' (III: 339 [4: 225] The words 'to meet' were changed from 'upon' to complete the mutation, but at a stage subsequent to the annotation of the Interleaved Set volume). In *Quentin Durward* Louis says to Quentin 'I like thee', rather than 'I love thee' (XXIV: 385 [31: 182]).

Apart from the example in *Peveril of the Peak* mentioned above, unusually long insertions in the text not noted elsewhere in this essay occur in: *Old Mortality* (a strengthening of the description of the royalist forces assembling at VIII: 245 [10: 315]); *The Heart of Mid-Lothian* (a fine piece of legal characterization at IX: 408 [12: 128–9]) (Plate 34); *The Pirate* (Zetland toasts incorporated in the text rather than entirely relegated to a note at XIX: 262 [24: 235]) (Plate 52); and *St Ronan's Well* (a characteristic expansion of a speech by Mrs Blower, and a delightful description of the young Puck in the amateur production in that novel of *A Midsummer Night's Dream*: XXVI: 377, 395 [34: 10–11, 27]) (Plate 71).

Finally, having had occasion to observe that many of the emendations in the Interleaved Set tend to the pedantic or may be thought unnecessary by some readers, it is a pleasure to note a number of examples where Scott's imaginative vigour is evidently at work. In the description of the battle of Prestonpans in *Waverley* he adds a telling detail: 'The clansmen on every side stript their plaids, prepared their arms, and there was an awful pause of about three minutes, during which the men, pulling off their bonnets, raised their faces to heaven, and uttered a short prayer\; then pulled their bonnets over their brows, and began to move forward at first slowly/.' (I: 514 [2: 167]) In *Guy Mannering* besides the Wasp addition (III: 318) noted by Jane Millgate,[5] there is a well-judged contrast in the emended opening sentence of a later chapter: 'When the several by-plays, as they may be termed, had taken place among the individuals of the Woodbourne family, as we have intimated in the preceding chapter, the breakfast party at length assembled\, Dandie excepted, who had consulted his taste in viands, and perhaps in society, by partaking of a cup of tea with Mrs Allan, just laced with two tea-spoonfuls of Cogniac, and reinforced with various slices from a huge round of beef. He had a kind of feeling that he could eat twice as much, and speak twice as much, with this good dame and Barnes, as with the grand folk in the parlour. Indeed, the meal of this less distinguished party was much more mirthful than that in the higher circle, where/ there was an obvious air of constraint on the greater part of the assistants.' (III: 416 [4: 299]) (Plate 15). There is a telling addition at the end of *The Black Dwarf*, not adopted in the Magnum or the Centenary Edition: Willie of Westburnflat 'died in his bed, and is recorded upon his tombstone at Kirkwhistle, (still extant,) as having played all the parts of a brave soldier, a discreet neighbour, and a sincere Christian \being epithets which the village sculptor had at command of any person who ordered a *tombstone* of his manufacture/' (VII: 258 [cf. 9: 215]). The ride from Tillietudlem to Hamilton in *Old Mortality* is atmospherically strengthened by the indications of dawn and sunrise (VIII: 234, 240 [10: 305, 311]). Scott adds a vivid and haunting detail at the execution of Porteous in *The Heart of Mid-Lothian*: 'Butler, then, at the opening into the low street called the Cowgate, cast back a terrified glance, and, by the red and dusky light of the torches, he could discern a figure wavering and struggling as it hung suspended above the heads of the multitude\, and could even observe men striking at it with their Lochaber-axes and partisans/.' (IX: 128 [11: 270]) (Plate 32). In *A Legend of Montrose* Allan is made to remark of the envisaged slaughter: 'they dropped like the dry leaves in autumn' (XII: 217 [15: 89]). The Grand Master's characterisation of his order in *Ivanhoe* is strengthened: ' "... They are forbidden to read, save what their Superior permitted, or [what] \listen to what is read, save to/ such holy thing\s/ [was] \as may be/ recited aloud during the hours of refection\; but lo! their ears are at the command of idle minstrels, and their eyes study empty romaunts/" ' (XIV: 115 [17: 215, inserting 'such', and substituting 'recited' for a repeated 'read']). In *Kenilworth* William Hamper's information (and some of his suggested words) are used to add richness to the description of the Castle: it is instructive to see how Scott handled Hamper's original (XVIII: 317 (paper apart), 340: cf. the letter at 350) (Plates 49–51). In the same novel the Queen's judgement of Blount is improved by adding 'he may be a good soldier in the field, though a preposterous ass in a banqueting-hall' (XVIII: 340 [23: 225]) (Plate 51). Triptolemus's flight in *The Pirate* is vividly reinforced by the added sentence: 'His very mode of running seemed to be that peculiar to his fleecy care, for, like a ram in the midst of his race, he ever and anon encouraged himself by a great bouncing attempt at a leap, though there were no obstacles in his way.' (XX: 160 [25: 257]) One short but telling addition adds lustre to the end of *The Fortunes of Nigel*, as Mistress Bride is made to say to the King: ' "There are fools, sire," replied she, "who have wit, and fools who have courage \—aye, and fools who have learning/, and are great fools notwithstanding..." ' (XXII: 104 [27: 387–8]). Felicitous additions also play prominent parts at the end of *Quentin Durward* and *Redgauntlet* (XXV: 476; XXVII: 505). In *St Ronan's Well* Touchwood endears himself to Meg Dods by remarking of the spa: 'no well in your swamps tenanted by such a conceited colony of clamorous frogs' (XXVI: 277 [33: 257]), and in *Redgauntlet* a legal touch lends humanity to Mr Fairford as Scott adds 'alas! he was both a father and an agent. In the one capacity, he looked on his son as dearer to him than all the world besides; in the other, the lawsuit which he conducted was to him like an infant to its nurse' (XXVII: 505 [35: 266, with slight emendations as given here]). A happy expansion of an image occurs in *The Betrothed* when Wilkin 'gave a yawn so wide, as if he had proposed to swallow one of the turrets at an angle of the platform on which he stood \as if it had only garnished a Christmas pasty/' (XXIX: 149, where the Interleaved Set's printed text has 'turrets that garnished an angle' [37: 110]). Finally, in *Woodstock* Joliffe's voice is not only like a saw but, with a felicitous expansion, like an 'ungreased and rusty' one (XXXI: 234 [39: 69]).

The Interleaved Set is only the first stage in the production of the Magnum edition. In the opening third of *Kenilworth* (up to the end of the text in volume XVII) there are some 750 variations between the octavo *Historical Romances* text on which Scott set to work and the final text of the Magnum. Approximately 150 of them are verbal variants, and of these only sixty or so were made by Scott in the Interleaved Set. It is difficult to imagine that most of the rest were not also introduced by Scott at proof stage, for they are exactly the sorts of emendations which this essay has sketched, but we have at the moment no unambiguous external evidence to confirm this. Nevertheless the Interleaved Set is a precious document: most moving as a personal testament, and of inestimable value for all those interested in the extraordinarily complex textual evolution of the Waverley Novels.

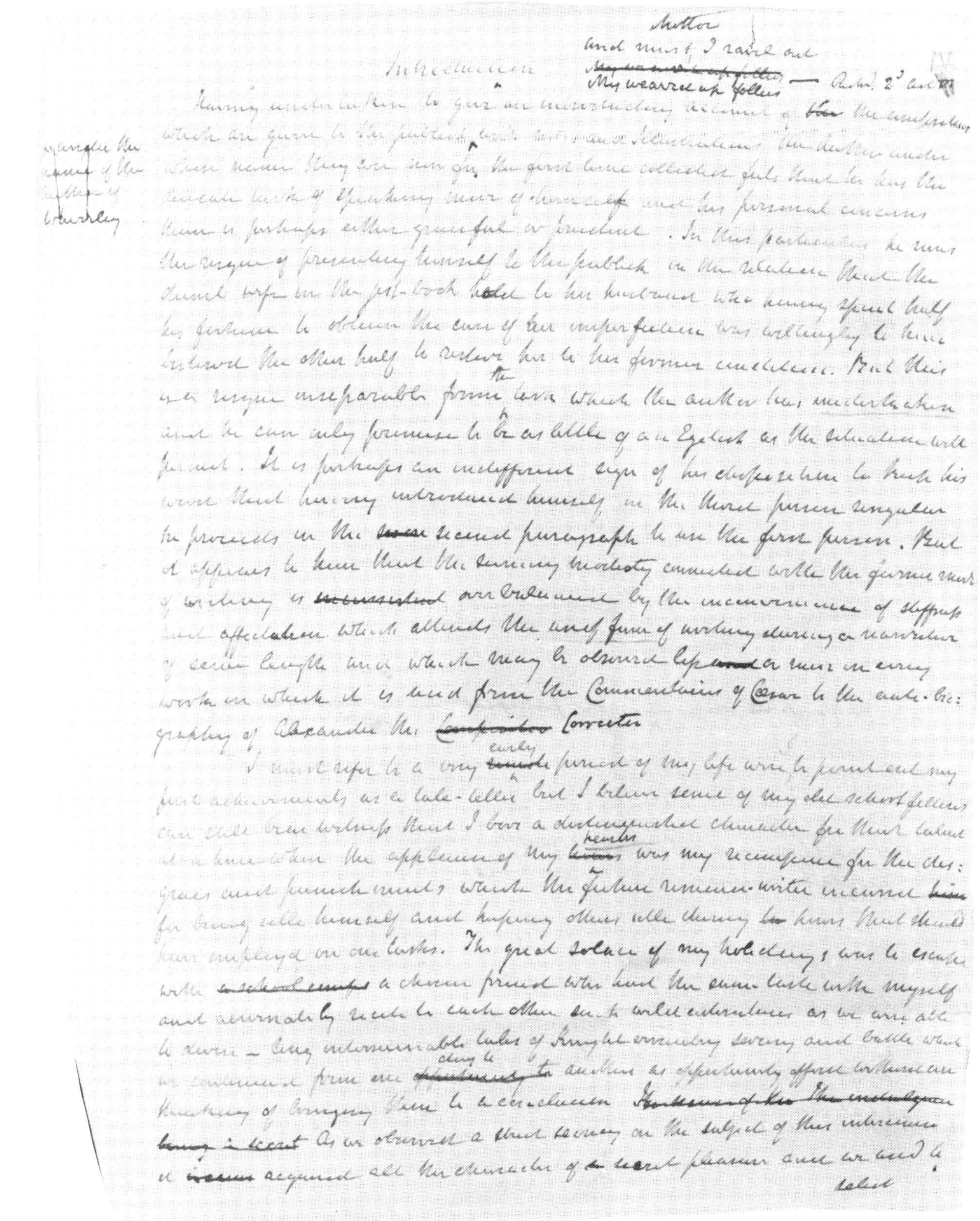

11 The initial folio of the Introduction to the Magnum Opus edition bound into the first volume of the Interleaved Set. This was in fact called the 'General Preface' when the first volume of the new edition was published in 1829. (1. General Preface i–iii.)

II. LIST OF MATERIAL, EXCLUDING STANDARD INTERLEAVES, BOUND INTO THE INTERLEAVED SET (WITH A NOTE OF MISBINDINGS)

Scott employed a number of amanuenses to copy material for the Magnum notes. It is possible to identify the four most frequent contributors to the Interleaved Set:

JOHN BUCHANAN 'a young man from the Register office',[6] who worked for Scott in 1829 and 1830;

WILLIAM LAIDLAW Scott's old factor, who resumed his rôle as amanuensis in 1831;[7]

ANNE SCOTT Scott's daughter, who managed the household after her mother's death in 1826; and

ANNE RUTHERFORD SCOTT Scott's niece, who stayed at Abbotsford for a year in 1828–29.

In addition, Robert Cadell's hand is much in evidence in miscellaneous material, mostly notes destined, usually after re-copying, for the printer's attention.

The material in this list is in Scott's late hand unless otherwise stated. Bound-in material is identified by the numeral of the preceding printed page, but it should be noted that it often follows a standard interleaf, and that it frequently continues notes begun on standard interleaves and printed pages.

VOLUME I (MS. 23001)

Following title page (46 ff.):

1 f. (No WM) Scott's specimen signature, Cadell note, and Scott's court signature.

1 f. (WM n.d.) Dedication (Fig. 3).

2 ff. (WM n.d.) Advertisement [Magnum 1: i–iv] (Fig. 10).

1 f. (WM n.d.) Direction: 'continuation of Introduction with three articles of appendix'.

10 ff. (WM n.d.) 'Introduction' [Magnum 1's General Preface: i–xl] with numerous corrections and additions, some of them probably made rather later than the main period of composition. The corresponding part of the text (ff. 8–9) differs substantially from Magnum 1: xxxv–xxxvi (Figs 11–12).

11 ff. (WM 1795) Fragment 'Thomas the Rhymer', in Scott's early hand, with alterations in his late hand [Magnum 1's Appendix No. I: xli–li] (Plate 3).

2 ff. (WM n.d.) Continuation of Appendix No. I [Magnum 1: xlix–liv]. Printer's ink marks prominent.

12 ff. (WM n.d.) Continuation of Appendix No. I, 'The Lord of Ennerdale' [Magnum 1: lv–lxiv]. In Scott's early hand, with alterations in his late hand.

(Appendix No. II [Magnum 1: lxv–xc] is not present.)

3 ff. (WM n.d.) Appendix No. III: a very clean copy with little alteration [Magnum 1: xci–xcvi].

1 f. (WM 1825) 'Memorandum for the Preface to Waverly as a separate work', i.e. the Introduction [Magnum 1: xcvii–civ]. The printer is directed to take material from the *Quarterly Review*. Endorsed on verso by Cadell: 'Introduction to Waverley'.

1 f. (No WM) List of proposed illustrations and artists up to *Rob Roy*, in Cadell's hand. Pencil notes on verso in another hand.

1 f. (No WM) Covering sheet for the preceding item, addressed by Cadell on verso 'Sir Walter Scott Bart'. On the recto, a different list of illustrations up to *Rob Roy*, in Scott's hand, with names of additional artists in another hand as preceding item.

VOLUME II (MS. 23002)

At beginning of Guy Mannering (*on fly-title and interleaves*):

Introduction to *Guy Mannering* [Magnum 3: i–xxxi], directing printer to take in the passage from *Blackwood's Magazine*. A slip (no WM) pasted to p.273 bears an observation dated 19 December 1828 on contemporary astrological practice: most of this appears in the Magnum Introduction [xviii–xix] (Plate 10).

VOLUME III (MS. 23003)

Following p.26 and interleaf:

1 f. (No WM) Conclusion of note begun on interleaf, from 'I trust I shall not' to the end [Magnum 3: 242–3].

(Only the second paragraph of Note II is on the interleaf facing p. 50: the first paragraph is in place at the end of the chapter, facing p. 56.)

At end of volume (4 ff.):

4 ff. (WM 1827) Additional Note to *Guy Mannering* [Magnum 4: 374–8].

VOLUME IV (MS. 23004)

Following p.70: Interleaf with cancelled draft of part of Introduction, numbered 6. This should be bound with the interleaf following p.8.

VOLUME V (MS. 23005)

Attached to p.152: Slip with note [Magnum 6: 243] (Plate 19).

Following p.236:

3 ff. (WM n.d.) Note [Magnum 6: 338–40].

Following p.252:

2 ff. (WM 1827) 'Additional Note to Antiquary end of Volume I', beginning 'It may be worth while to mention although omitted at the proper place that the incident of the supposed Praetorium actually happend to an Antiquary of great learning and acute Sir John Clerk of Pennycuik'. Not in Magnum, but published (slightly altered) in Centenary Edition, 3: 421–2 (Plate 20).

At beginning of Rob Roy (*44 ff.*):

34 ff. (WM 1827 and 1825) Introduction to *Rob Roy* [Magnum 7: vii–cxviii]. The long quotations are in Anne Scott's hand, except for that on the first of the two folios both numbered 32 which is in the hand of Anne Rutherford Scott. A few illegible or nonsensical words have been underlined in pencil, and on p.cxviii 'Ite, conclamatum est' has been carefully copied for the printer (or transcriber) also in pencil. There are many differences in the Magnum text. Scott has made substantial deletions on p.liv, and there is some unpublished material.

1 f. (WM n.d.) Appendix V [Magnum 7: cxxxii–cxxxiv].

1 f. (WM with date incomplete) This is a small slip, with many printer's fingermarks, bearing Appendix VI [Magnum 7: cxxxiv–cxxxv], the first paragraph on the verso, the rest on the recto. Also on the verso is the following beginning of a letter: 'My dear Lord / The enclosed letter from David / Laing the Secretary of the booksellers / has', and an endorsement by Cadell (Plates 21, 22).

1 f. (WM n.d.) Appendix III [Magnum 7: cxxviii–cxxx].

2 ff. (WM 1827) Appendix IV [Magnum 7: cxxx–cxxxii], in Anne Scott's hand. Second folio blank except for Scott's endorsement on verso.

4 ff. (WM 1825) Appendix II [Magnum 7: cxxi–cxxvii], the quotations in Anne Rutherford Scott's hand.

1 f. (WM 1827) (after interleaf with endorsement and figures) Appendix I [Magnum 7: cxix–cxx].

VOLUME VI (MS. 23006)

Following p.240:

1 f. (WM n.d.) Note with quotation in Anne Rutherford Scott's hand [Magnum 8: 179–80].

At end of volume:

1 f. (WM 1829) Postscript to *Rob Roy*: the quotation is absent. Endorsed on verso: 'This to be taken in at / the end of 2 vol / of Rob Roy like a flyleaf.'

VOLUME VII (MS. 23007)

Following title page (19 ff.):
(The Introduction to *Tales of My Landlord* [Magnum 9: iii–xiv] is not present.)

5 ff. (WM 1827) Introduction to *The Black Dwarf* [Magnum 9: xvi–xxix] (Plate 24). The quotation [xx–xxiii] is in Anne Rutherford Scott's hand, with alterations in Scott's hand. Printer's fingermarks, pencil marks, and one pagination numeral (not that in Magnum) present.

14 ff. Introduction to *Old Mortality* [Magnum 9: 221–38], defective, made up as follows:

- 2 ff. (WM 1827) Beginning of Introduction, to Magnum p.229 'talents and worth', followed by a sentence and six words not used in Magnum because of the arrival of the next item.
- 2 ff. (WM 1821) Transcript in an unidentified hand of Joseph Train's account of Robert Paterson (as edited by Scott: see below) [Magnum 9: 228–30]. This insert is imperfect, beginning at 'of Gatelowbrigg' [Magnum 9: 230]. It is followed by Scott's resumption of the Introduction [Magnum, 236] which is dovetailed with the following item.
- 1 f. (WM 1827) Scott's conclusion of the Introduction [Magnum 9: 236–8].
- 1 f. (WM 1828, the same paper as the following item) Scott's paragraph introducing Train, in red ink: 'While . . . source' [Magnum 9: 228].
- 8 ff. (WM 1828) Train's original ALS of 31 March 1829 containing the account of Paterson, partly transcribed above, edited in Scott's hand in red ink [Magnum 9: 230–6] (Plate 25). (The notes on Magnum 9: 232 and 233 are actually by Scott.)

Following p.294:

2 ff. (WM 1825) Note, with quotation in Anne Rutherford Scott's hand [Magnum 9: 268–9] on first folio; second folio blank except for Scott's endorsement on verso.

Following p.314:

1 f. (WM 1824) Note [Magnum 9: 296–7].

VOLUME VIII (MS. 23008)

Following p.54 (3 ff.):

1 f. (WM 1824) First four paragraphs of Note III [Magnum 10: 140–1, where the beginning is different].

1 f. (No WM) *Bellum Bothuellianum* quotation to complete Note III, in Scott's young hand [Magnum 10: 141–2] (Plate 27).

1 f. (No WM) Quotations for Note II in Anne Rutherford Scott's hand, with ascriptions in Scott's hand [Magnum 10: 140].

Following p.68:

2 ff. (WM 1829) Quotation for note, transcribed in a large bold hand, from a letter in the Duke of Buckingham's library [Magnum 10: 157–8]. These folios have heavy printer's fingerprints (Plate 29).

2 ff. (WM 1825) Quotation, in hand of Anne Rutherford Scott, with linking material in Scott's hand, for note continued from interleaf and p.69 [Magnum 10: 156–7]. (The second complete paragraph on Magnum p.157 is not present.) (Plate 29).

The note on p.217 refers to p.211 [cf. Magnum 10: 284].

Following p.246:

1 f. (WM 1827) Quotation in Anne Rutherford Scott's hand, with end of note in Scott's hand [Magnum 10: 319].

Following p.253:

1 f. (No WM) Quotation for note, in Anne Scott's hand [Magnum 10: 341].

VOLUME IX (MS. 23009)

Following p.10 is a paper apart with an insertion for the note beginning on the interleaf [Magnum 11: 157–61]. An extra interleaf with an amendment slip stuck to the verso follows with quotations [Magnum 11: 158–60] in the hand of Charles Kirkpatrick Sharpe. All these inserts are without WM.

Following title page (6 ff.):

(The rest of the introductory matter to *The Heart of Mid-Lothian* is bound in the wrong order: Magnum 11: 151–7 as printed in the Interleaved Set precedes the inserted Introduction 141–9, for which the quotations are also in the wrong order. The 'Postscript' [Magnum 11: 151★–152★] is not present.)

2 ff. (WM 1815) The first folio is blank except for Scott's endorsement on the recto. The second carries on its recto a quotation for the Introduction in an unidentified hand (Hand A) [Magnum 11: 147–9].

4 ff. (WM 1822) Quotation in Hand A, with linking material in Scott's hand [Magnum 11: 142–7].

(The last paragraph of the Introduction [Magnum 11: 149] is not present.)

Following p.130 (10 ff.):

2 ff. (WM 1829) First two paragraphs of note to Chapter 7 [Magnum 11: 274]. The second folio is blank except for Scott's endorsement and Cadell's correction on the verso.

8 ff. (WM n.d.) Packet in eighteenth-century copperplate hand, endorsed on final verso 'Memoriall / Concerning The / Murder of Captain / Porteus— / 1737' [Magnum 11: 275–82, partly modernised] (Plate 33).

(The rest of this note [Magnum 11: 282–3] is on the interleaves and on a paper apart (1 f. WM 1824) following p.132.)

Following p.196:

1 f. (WM n.d.) Quotation for note, in Anne Rutherford Scott's hand; Scott finishes the note in his own hand [Magnum 11: 344–6].

Following p.290:

2 ff. (WM 1801) Quotation for note, in Anne Scott's hand [Magnum 12: 19–20].

(Note III on 'Child Murder' [relocated on Magnum 12: 21] appears after p.96 in this volume of the Interleaved Set.)

VOLUME X (MS. 23010)

Following p.265:

2 ff. (No WM) ALS from Joseph Train to Scott, PM 12 November 1818, including quotation used in note on interleaves and text [Magnum 13: 36–9].

Following p.314:

1 f. (WM 1827) Quotation for note, in Anne Rutherford Scott's hand [Magnum 13: 83–4].

VOLUME XI (MS. 23011)

Following title page:

9 ff. (WM 1827) Introduction to *The Bride of Lammermoor* [Magnum 13: 237–55]. The quotations [Magnum 13: 250–3] are in Anne Rutherford Scott's hand, with connecting material in Scott's.

VOLUME XII (MS. 23012)

At beginning of A Legend of Montrose (*6 ff.*):

(The Introduction [Magnum 15: [iii]–xix] begins on the fly-title verso, and continues on interleaves, which are interrupted by the six folios, themselves bound in the wrong order.)

2 ff. (WM 1829) Quotation for note, in John Buchanan's hand [Magnum 15: xiv–xvii], and connecting paragraph in Scott's hand. Printer's fingerprints prominent.

1 f. (WM 1829) Final quotation in hand A [Magnum 15: xviii–xix], endorsed by Cadell. Printer's fingerprints prominent.

(Appendix I is not present.)

2 ff. (WM 1801) Appendix II: First paragraph not present. Quotation, including all the comments, in Anne Rutherford Scott's hand [Magnum 15: xxii–xxiii]. Second sheet blank except for endorsement on verso.

1 f. (WM 1829) Postscript: first and last paragraphs, as in Magnum 15: xxv, xxxi, but the letter is not present.

Following p.106:

1 f. (WM 1801) Quotation in Anne Rutherford Scott's hand [Magnum 15: xi–xii]. Note continues in Scott's hand.

(The two paragraphs that follow this last insertion, which ends with two short paragraphs deleted, are taken from the note on Dalgetty, the first part of which has been deleted, at pp.146–7 in this volume of the Interleaved Set.)

(The paper apart referred to on p.417 is not present.)

VOLUME XIII (MS. 23013)

Following title page:

7 ff. (WM 1829) Introduction to *Ivanhoe* [Magnum 16: [iii]–xxii] (Plate 40).

Following p.360:

10 ff. (WM 1829) Quotations for note, in hand A [Magnum 16: 330–2, 333–5].

(The linking paragraphs [Magnum, 332–3] are in the body of the note on interleaf. Of the conclusion [335] only the penultimate paragraph is present, on the penultimate folio after the second quotation. The final folio is blank except for Scott's endorsement and a false start, or interrupted continuation, or endorsement, by the transcriber: 'The erle of Callis'. A few printer's fingerprints are present.)

At end of volume:

2 ff. (WM 1827) Addition to *Ivanhoe* note on p.481 [Magnum 17: 111]), with attached ALS from Scott to Cadell, dated from Abbotsford 20 April 1830, and cover endorsed by Cadell (Plates 43–44).

VOLUME XIV (MS. 23014)

Following p.248 (*5 ff.*):

2 ff. (WM 1829) Note on Coningsburgh [cf. Magnum 17: 335–9] (Plate 46).

1 f. (WM 1829) A different version of the Coningsburgh note, not used in Magnum.

2 ff. (WM 1825) Quotation for note, in John Buchanan's hand [Magnum 17: 338–9].

Following p.280:

11 ff. (WM 1829) Introduction to *The Monastery* [Magnum 18: [iii]–xxxi].

The interleaf following p.384 should be bound after p.368 [cf. Magnum 18: xcvii–xcviii].

Following p.446:

1 f. (WM 1829) Quotation for note, in unidentified hand [Magnum 18: 72].

VOLUME XV (MS. 23015)

Following p.308:

4 ff. (WM 1828) Quotation for note, in Anne Scott's hand [Magnum 19: 163–4] (Plate 47).

Following p.434:

4 ff. (WM 1827) Latin quotation in careful copperplate hand on lined paper [Magnum 19: 282–3].

Following p.496 (*2 ff.*):

1 f. (WM n.d.) Note II, beginning in Scott's hand, continued in John Buchanan's hand [Magnum 19: 354–5].

1 f. (WM n.d.) Note I [Magnum 19: 353–4].

VOLUME XVI (MS. 23016)

Following title page:

7 ff. (WM 1829) Introduction to *The Abbot* [Magnum 20: [iii]–xv].

Following p.216 (4 ff.):

1 f. (WM n.d.) Quotation for Note II in John Buchanan's hand [Magnum 20: 209–10].
1 f. (WM 1829) First quotation for Note III in Anne Scott's hand [Magnum 20: 210–11] (Plate 48).
2 ff. (after interleaf) (WM 1825) Second quotation for Note III in unidentified hand [Magnum 20: 211–12]. Note ends in Scott's hand (Plate 48).

Following p.220:

4 ff. (WM 1829) Note I, from 'The reader' to the end, in Hand A [Magnum 20: 207–8]. (The first part of this note is on interleaves; the quotation extends further than in the printed text.)

Following p.254:

2 ff. (WM 1829) Quotations for note, in Anne Scott's hand [Magnum 20: 237–8].

VOLUME XVII (MS. 23017)

Following p.189:

1 f. (WM 1829) Quotations for note I, in Anne Scott's hand [Magnum 21: 293]. Linking material in Scott's hand.

Following p.192:

1 f. (WM n.d.) Quotation for Note II, in Anne Scott's hand [Magnum 21: 294–5].

Following p.244:

2 ff. (WM 1829) Quotation for note, in Anne Scott's hand [Magnum 21: 340–1]. Conclusion of note in Scott's hand.

Following p.262:

2 ff. (WM 1827) Latin quotation in the same hand as at XVI: 434, on the same lined paper [Magnum 21: 358].

At beginning of Kenilworth:

7 ff. (WM 1825) Introduction to *Kenilworth* [Magnum 22: [iii]–xv]. The correct order of the folios is: 1, 6, 7, 5, 2–4. The quotations are in John Buchanan's hand.

Following p.490:

1 f. (WM n.d.) Paper apart with note 'Legend of Wayland Smith' [found, with two additional sentences, in Magnum 22: 246].

Following p.564:

1 f. (WM 1829) Paper apart with paragraphs 2 and 3 of Note II [Magnum 22: 258].

VOLUME XVIII (MS. 23018)

Following p.120:

2 ff. (WM n.d.) Quotations for note, in John Buchanan's hand [Magnum 23: 26–7].

Attached to p.317:

1 f. (No WM) Slip with addition to text (Plate 49).

Following p.334:

1 f. (WM n.d.) Note on paper apart [Magnum 23: 220].

Following p.350:

2 ff. (WM 1822) ALS dated 2 June 1829 from William Hamper with material about Kenilworth Castle. Mostly quoted in note [Magnum 23: 237–41] (Plate 50).

Following p.522:

2 ff. (first folio WM 1827) Final note to *Kenilworth*: the second folio is a scrap bearing Leicester's epitaph in an unidentified hand [Magnum 23: 396].

VOLUME XIX (MS. 23019)

Following title page:

3 ff. (WM n.d.) Introduction to *The Pirate* [Magnum 24: [iii]–xi].

Following p.294 (7 ff.):

1 f. (WM n.d.) First quotation for note, in Anne Scott's hand [Magnum 24: 266]. Linking material in Scott's hand.
6 ff. (WM n.d.) Second quotation, in John Buchanan's hand [Magnum 24: 267–71]. The last folio is blank except for Scott's endorsement on verso.

Following p.420:

1 f. (WM n.d.) Note (including paper apart slip stuck to the inserted sheet) [Magnum 25: 21–3] (Plate 53).

VOLUME XX (MS. 23020)

Following p.290:

6 ff. (WM 1822) Preface to *The Fortunes of Nigel* [Magnum 26: [iii]–xvii].

Following p.355:

2 ff. (WM 1828) Quotation for note, in Anne Scott's hand [Magnum 26: 19–20].

VOLUME XXI (MS. 23021)

Following p.398:

1 f. (WM 1829) Quotation for Note III; in John Buchanan's hand (Magnum 27: 203–4].

(Note I [Magnum 27: 202] is on the interleaf verso following p.398. Note II [202–3] follows p.390. Note IV [204–5] follows p.394. Note V [205] follows p.398.)

Following p.492:

1 f. (WM n.d.) Quotation for note, in John Buchanan's hand [Magnum 27: 291–2].

VOLUME XXII (MS. 23022)

Following title page of Peveril of the Peak (*part of pamphlet, interleaf, and 8 ff.*):

pp. 41–42 of pamphlet [*Historical Notices of Edward and William Christian; Two Characters in Peveril of the Peak*], bearing pencilled and ink printers' marks and names, and ink fingerprints, with connecting paragraph on final blank leaf corresponding to part of the Introduction [Magnum 28: xxxi–l]. Not all of the pamphlet as used in the Introduction has been preserved here. Scott continues the Introduction [Magnum 28: l] on the verso of the final blank leaf of the pamphlet.

Interleaf (with endorsement)

2 ff. (WM 1824) Quotations in unidentified hand [Magnum 28: l–liii]. Stanzas 1–5 are on the recto of the first sheet, 6–11 on the verso of the second, and 12–18 on the recto of the second. The verso of the first sheet is a copy of part of the Manx comments, probably from John Christian, in a different hand. Printer's fingerprints prominent.

(Magnum 28: liv–lxi is not present.)

1 f. (No WM) Letter from Scott to the printers, dated from Abbotsford 19 November 1830 [quoted above by Millgate pp 8-9] (Plate 61).

5 ff. (WM 1829) Introduction to *Peveril of the Peak* [Magnum 28: [iii]–xiv].

Following p.208:

1 f. (WM n.d.) Continuation of note from following interleaf [Magnum 28: 65–6].

Following p.338:

1 f. (WM 1828) Paper apart containing insertion in text [Magnum 28: 192–3] (Plate 62).

Following p.444:

4 ff. (WM 1829) Quotation for note, in John Buchanan's hand [Magnum 29: 24–8, which has an additional concluding paragraph, not present here].

VOLUME XXIII (MS. 23023)

Following p.34:

2 ff. (WM 1829) Note, all in John Buchanan's hand [Magnum 29: 130–1].

Following p.222:

2 ff. (WM 1821) The actual ALS quoted in Magnum 29: 309–10, PM 20 June 1823, bearing printer's fingerprints (Plate 66).

VOLUME XXIV (MS. 23024)

Following p.24:

1 f. Page proof of Magnum 30: 229, on which Scott has inserted three sentences. The note originally supplied on the interleaf verso was deleted for Magnum, but it is not so marked here. Endorsed in another hand (or hands) 'Proof', and 'Page 25 of Copy'. The page has been roughly trimmed and folded small, either by itself or as the outer leaf of a very small packet (Plate 67).

Following p.138 (20 ff.):

13 ff. (WM 1829) Note II, all in John Buchanan's hand [Magnum 30: 337–52). Part of this note (on the last folio recto) used for Magnum 30: 145 was copied by Scott at XXIII: 416–17 above.

At beginning of Quentin Durward:

7 ff. (WM 1827) Introduction to *Quentin Durward* [Magnum 31: [iii]–xxi, but lacking the Fénélon passage xv–xvii].

VOLUME XXV (MS. 23025)

The interleaf between pp.48 and 49 should be bound between pp.64 and 65 [cf. Magnum 32: 7–9].

VOLUME XXVI (MS. 23026)

Following p.376:

4 ff. (WM 1827) Introduction to *St Ronan's Well*, curiously misbound in this position [Magnum 33: [iii]–ix: the last two paragraphs (p.x) are not present in this version].

VOLUME XXVII (MS. 23027)

At beginning of Redgauntlet:

10 ff. (WM 1829) Introduction to *Redgauntlet* [Magnum 35: [iii]–xxiii], begun in Scott's hand, but mostly in William Laidlaw's.

VOLUME XXIX (MS. 23029)

Following title page:

10 ff. (WM 1829) Introduction to *The Betrothed* [Magnum 37: [iii]–xx] in William Laidlaw's hand, with a few additions and emendations in Scott's hand. The portion corresponding to page xiv is in John Buchanan's hand, with a pencil sketch of the engraving and directions in Laidlaw's and Scott's hands (Plate 75). The last short paragraph of the Introduction [xx] is not present at this stage.

Following p.252:

2 ff. (WM n.d.) Quotation for note, in William Laidlaw's hand [Magnum 37: 202–3]. The second folio is a mere slip.

VOLUME XXX (MS. 23030)

At beginning of The Talisman:

16 ff. (WM 1829) Introduction and Appendix to *The Talisman* [Magnum 38: [iii]–xxii]. Lacks the first two folios, beginning with one numbered 3. (The missing folios are in the Sir Hugh Walpole Collection at the King's School, Canterbury.) First folio in Scott's hand, beginning on Magnum p.vi 'that at which the warlike character'; blank contiguous folio; then from 'A principal incident' [Magnum, viii] to end of Appendix in Laidlaw's hand. Printer's fingerprints prominent on some later folios.

VOLUME XXXI (MS. 23031)

At beginning of Woodstock (*6 ff., proofs, 45 ff.*):

6 ff. (WM 1830) Appendix I [Magnum 39: [xxiii]–xxxv] in an unidentified hand.

Page proofs of Introduction to *Woodstock* with corrections by Scott and comments in another hand (Plate 78).

26 ff. (WM 1829) Introduction to *Woodstock* in Laidlaw's hand, with two proof page numbers (in ink) and one set of printers' initials (in pencil) added [Magnum 39: [iii]–xx]. The last folio is a revised conclusion of the note in Scott's hand, further revised in Magnum 39: xx–xxi (Plate 79).

6 ff. (WM n.d.) Letter on Mr Lenthal's death transcribed by Laidlaw with endorsement by Scott on final verso asking for *Woodstock* to be sent to Abbotsford if Cadell has trouble placing the illustration. He apparently had, for it does not appear in the Magnum, but it is printed as Appendix III in Centenary Edition 21: 499–500.

13 ff. (WM 1830) Appendix II in the same hand as Appendix I [Magnum 39: xxxvi–[lxiv]], and final partly deleted endorsement in Scott's last hand.

(These 45 folios have printer's fingerprints.)

VOLUME XXXII (MS. 23032)

Following p.122:

1 f. (WM n.d.) Beginning of note, continued on interleaf [Magnum 40: 43–5].

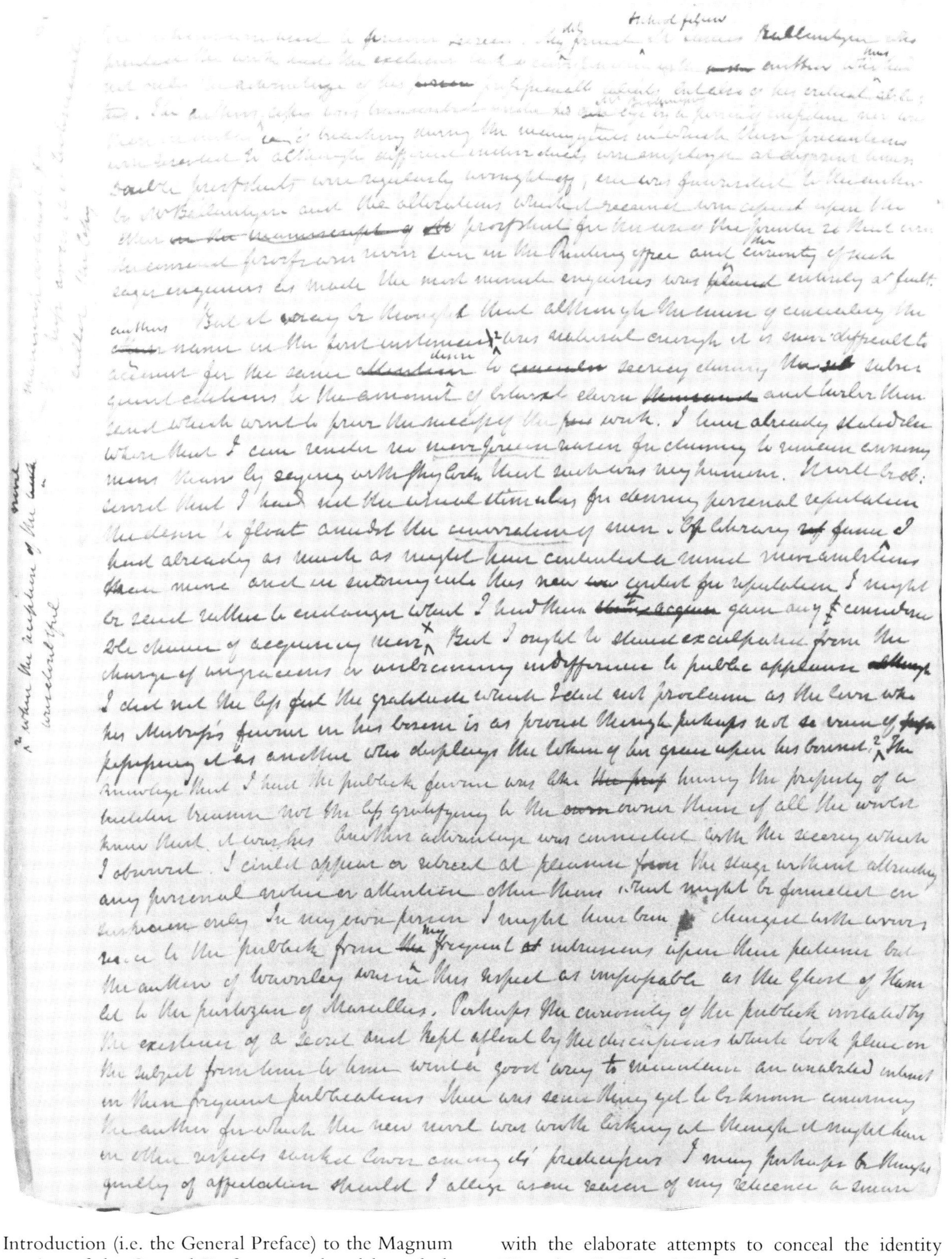

12 A folio of the Introduction (i.e. the General Preface) to the Magnum Opus edition. The section of the General Preface reproduced here deals with the elaborate attempts to conceal the identity of the Author of Waverley. (1. General Preface xx–xxv.)

III. LIST OF NOTES IN THE INTERLEAVED SET OMITTED FROM THE MAGNUM EDITION

I: 14	On the date 1745 Partly printed in Centenary Edition 1: 25
I: 180	*sidier roy* Printed in Centenary Edition 1: 117
I: 273	'See Don Quixote' Printed in Centenary Edition 1: 170
I: 299	Conan the Jester Unpublished (Replaced by note in Magnum 1: 241)
II: 21	Simplicity of the Highland insurgents Printed in Dryburgh Edition 1: 482
II: 352	Sapling branch Printed in Centenary Edition 2: 65 ('reise' is defined as 'twig' in Magnum glossary)
III: 72	'darkmans' glossed as 'Nights' Unpublished
III: 188	High Jinks Printed in Centenary Edition 2: 433–4
V: 252	Praetorium Printed in Centenary Edition 3: 421–2 (Plate 20)
VII: 30	'Keb' glossed as 'Miscarry of their lambs' Printed (varied) in Centenary Edition 6: 237 (Defined as 'to cast lamb' in Magnum glossary)
VII: 88	Ball-play Printed in Centenary Edition 6: 269
VII: 91	Willie of Westburnflat Printed in Centenary Edition 6: 372
VII: 97	The Brouze Printed in Centenary Edition 6: 274
VII: 98	'scouther' glossed as 'A singing bout' Unpublished (Defined as 'Scorch' in Magnum glossary)
VII: 99	Jeddart (expanded version) Printed in Centenary Edition 6: 276
VII: 104	Borderers in Flanders Printed in Centenary Edition 6: 278
VII: 117	Catrail Printed in Centenary Edition 6: 286
VII: 124	Cat Printed in Centenary Edition 6: 290
VII: 125	King's keys Printed in Centenary Edition 6: 290
VII: 132	Border lintels First and last sentences printed in Centenary Edition 6: 294; all printed in Dryburgh Edition 5: 365
VII: 197	Border Jacobites Printed in Centenary Edition 6: 372–3 Captain Green Printed in Centenary Edition 6: 373 Invasion by the Chevalier Printed in Centenary Edition 6: 373
X: 31	'lauch' glossed as 'Law' Magnum mis-reads as 'land-law', in text, but 'lauch' appears in its glossary defined as 'law'; Centenary Edition has 'landlaw' in text; Dryburgh has 'lauch' in text and 'law' *inter alia*. in glossary, correctly
X: 236	Duncan Forbes, Lord Advocate Printed in Dryburgh Edition 7: 403
X: 245	Expulsion of the Scottish bishops (continued on interleaf following p.246) Printed in Centenary Edition 7: 556
XVIII: 316	Final paragraph of note not used in Magnum 23: 203 Printed, with emendations, in Centenary Edition 12: 472
XX: 18	'spae-women' glossed as 'Sorceresses and fortune-tellers' Printed in Centenary Edition 13: 306 (Magnum's glossary defines 'spae-wife' as 'prophetess')
XXIV: 86	Old French song Printed in Dryburgh Edition 15: 612
XXIV: 341	Louis' tryannic conduct Unpublished [cf. Magnum 31: 172]
XXVIII: 381	Ten additional lines of note added by Scott, but in a different pen, dealing with George II's calm reaction to the Jacobites, not used in Magnum, which adds to the beginning of the note and deletes the end [36: 254–5]. The deleted passage is printed in Centenary Edition 18: 455 (abandoning Magnum's version).

The surviving single page proof of *Peveril of the Peak* (XXIV: 24) (Plate 67) shows Scott in the act of deleting (by implication) a note on Venner's insurrection which he had earlier written in the Interleaved Set (printed in Centenary Edition 15: 506–7), so as to expand the text (or conceivably expanding the text so as to cover the deletion of the note). This may help to account for some of the omissions in this list. The large number of omitted notes in *The Black Dwarf* may suggest a general desire to save space in the volume containing that novel and the beginning of *Old Mortality*. In the body of the Interleaved Set Scott occasionally had second thoughts about notes or attempts at notes (VII: 21; VIII: 247; XXII: 168; XXVIII: 144), and there are of course, as throughout the insertions, examples of deletions and other alterations made during or after composition.

NOTES AND REFERENCES

I would like to thank my colleagues on the executive editorial team of the Edinburgh Edition of the Waverley Novels for their help in compiling this description: Dr David Hewitt (editor-in-chief), Dr P D Garside, Miss Claire Lamont, Dr Douglas Mack, and Mr G A M Wood. Professor Jane Millgate has been generous with her penetrating comments. The Department of Manuscripts of the National Library of Scotland has made its facilities available with even more than its usual cordial liberality.

1 Jane Millgate, *Scott's Last Edition* (Edinburgh, 1987), Chapters 5 and 6.
2 *Scott's Last Edition*, pp.79–80.
3 *Scott's Last Edition*, pp.73–4.
4 *Scott's Last Edition*, pp.74–5.
5 *Scott's Last Edition*, p.80.
6 *The Letters of Sir Walter Scott*, ed H J C Grierson, 12 vols (London, 1932–37), XI. 240
7 *The Journal of Sir Walter Scott*, ed W E K Anderson (Oxford, 1972), p.624.

13 Sir Walter Scott by Andrew Geddes, 1818. This sensitive portrait is a study for a painting of the discovery that year of the Scottish Regalia in Edinburgh Castle. The finished picture is now destroyed. Scottish National Portrait Gallery.

THE EXILE AND RETURN OF THE 'MAGNUM OPUS':
Episodes in the Life of a Literary Wanderer

IAIN GORDON BROWN

A romantic might be forgiven for likening the vicissitudes between the later 1920s and 1986 of Sir Walter Scott's own annotated set of the Waverley Novels to the fate of some Jacobite family of the Scotland of Edward Waverley, Cosmo Bradwardine and Flora MacIvor, and of the times in which are set *Guy Mannering* and *The Antiquary*: passage on a French ship, exile in a foreign land, and subsequent attainder, are followed at length by the restoration of honours, titles and estates. For ''tis sixty years since' (almost) that the volumes began their wanderings. But long before a fateful day in 1929 the life of the books had been a troubled one. This essay looks at the history of the Interleaved Set from the time it left Scotland until the hour of its homecoming to the country and the city of its author's birth.

Robert Cadell's collection of the literary manuscripts, letters and papers of Sir Walter Scott was the most important assemblage outside the writer's own family circle of material relating to Scott's literary affairs in general, and to the publication of the Waverley Novels in particular. The Interleaved Set was part of this collection; and when in 1851 Cadell's trustees sold the novel copyrights, together with the existing stock of printed books and sheets, stereotyped plates and steel- and wood-engravings, to the Edinburgh publishers Adam and Charles Black for a total of £27,000, the Set formed part of the bargain.[1] The forty-one volumes had been described by Cadell as 'not only curious but valuable'; and twenty years after their purchase the new owners praised the set as 'the valuable interleaved copy . . . containing the Author's latest manuscript corrections and notes . . .'[2] The whole property—copyrights, Interleaved Set and the rest—had been bought by Blacks at Hodgson's in London in the spring of 1851. Literary circles in Edinburgh viewed with pleasure the return of what was then—in marked contrast with the attitude some seventy years later—seen as an important part of the Scottish national heritage. Welcoming the successful bid by Messrs A & C Black, *The Scotsman* observed:

> It is most creditable to the commercial and publishing enterprise of our city that we have thus been enabled to retain amongst us the works of our great national author; and the circumstance must be gratifying to all Scotsmen, not only as it tends to sustain the reputation of our northern metropolis as a seat of letters and learning, but as preserving unbroken in the strictest sense the connection between Scott and Scotland—the country of which he was proud, and which may well be proud of him. The lustre that Sir Walter Scott's writings have shed upon his native land will thus continue, so to speak, emanating from his own loved 'romantic town'.

A selection of the volumes of the Interleaved Set was lent to the important Scott Centenary Exhibition in 1871 (listed as being from the 'Author's Annotated edition'). In 1901 volumes I and VII were shown in the Fine Art and Scottish History section of the Glasgow International Exhibition (no. 944). Then in 1911 the two volumes of *Waverley* (evidently the first two volumes of the Interleaved Set, the second containing also part of *Guy Mannering*) were lent by Blacks to the remarkable Scottish Exhibition of National History, Art and Industry which was also held in Glasgow.[3] As Professor Millgate has shown above, shrewd commercial sense underlay the veneration paid to the volumes; and indeed the 'Magnum Opus' was to serve the publishers well, right up to the production by Blacks of the Dryburgh Edition of the Waverley Novels in the 1890s.

The Interleaved Set was kept in the A & C Black office in Edinburgh (6 North Bridge, and subsequently 22 Hanover Street). The firm moved to London in 1891, and Soho Square became its headquarters. The books were very probably removed to London then, but at any rate they were certainly taken south when the Edinburgh premises were given up in 1894. Thereafter, apart from short outings to Glasgow for the exhibitions already mentioned, the interleaved volumes were to remain in Soho Square until 1929.

Mr Colin Inman's researches into the A & C Black records have filled in some fascinating details of the history of the Interleaved Set during the years it remained in London.[4] Despite the fine words first of Robert Cadell and then of A & C Black on the importance of the Set, it seems clear that by the early years of the twentieth century its value was reduced to that of mere antiquarian curiosity. And it appears, moreover, that sentimental attachment to the Set might be overcome by an acceptable cash offer from some suitable quarter.

Late in November 1900 two contrasting letters were written by members of the staff of A & C Black. One was to a New York publishing executive, Mr D D Merrill. Here mention was made of the 'Magnum Opus' as 'Sir Walter's own annotated press copy which has been a cherished possession of the firm ever since it took over Scott's Works'. Mr William Callender of Blacks went on to say that 'only a few privileged people have ever seen the annotated copy at all'. The offer was made to reproduce in facsimile some twenty-five sections of manuscript from volumes of the Interleaved Set which Merrill's firm might use to illustrate its edition of the novels, an edition, of course, founded on Blacks own Centenary text in which the great majority of Scott's notes had been included. It was pointed out that the annotations and the other papers bound into the Set was the only Scott manuscript material which A & C Black owned, and that it would be impossible to let the American publishers have any of the actual manuscript material. However, only three days later, a cryptic note was dispatched from Soho Square to William Brown, the well-known Edinburgh bookseller. The second of its two sentences reads: 'We have decided not to dispose of the interleaved Scott in the meantime.' If this indicates that a sale was being contemplated—though the somewhat schizophrenic attitude of Blacks to their heritage item (or 'relic' as they called it) is indeed remarkable—nothing more appears in the records until 1904. On 28 January of that year the firm wrote to J Pierpont Morgan junior to offer his bibliophile father a unique collector's item which can only be the Interleaved Set. In a letter of extraordinary reticence the goods in question were never mentioned by name:

> 'Knowing how great a lover Mr Pierpont Morgan, your father, is of rare books we have for some considerable time past had the intention of approaching him with regard to an unique work now in our possession. We unfortunately missed him during his last stay in this country, & as we do not hear any report of an approaching visit, we venture to ask if we may submit the volumes to you in order that you may report to Mr Pierpont Morgan. The price is £5,000 & full particulars can, of course, be given.'

There is no evidence to chart the progress of any further negotiations with the Pierpont Morgans; but the very mention of the name is of the greatest interest, and causes those in Scotland now entrusted with the care and augmentation of the national collection of Scott manuscript material to start in surprise. For to what was even then the largest assemblage by far of Scott novel manuscripts—by 1904 the Morgan collection included *Anne of Geierstein*, *The Black Dwarf*, *Guy Mannering*, such fragments of *Ivanhoe* as are extant, *Old Mortality*, *Peveril of the Peak*, *St Ronan's Well*, fifteen leaves of *Waverley*, and *Woodstock*; *The Monastery* was to be bought later that same year[5]—might well have been added the Interleaved Set. Eighty years after this original offer to the Morgan family, the superb library which J P Morgan junior had established in 1924 was to be thought of by worried men in Edinburgh as a possible competitor for the prize of the 'Magnum Opus'.

In 1904, however, A & C Black appear to have been making strenuous efforts in several directions to dispose of their 'cherished possession'. In April they wrote to one Mr J Douglas at the Hotel Bristol, Paris. This is perhaps to be interpreted as a reply to an enquiry about the Set's availability for sale, for news that the firm was prepared to part with the volumes will have spread rapidly through the book-collecting world. 'Sir Walter Scott', wrote Messrs A & C Black,

> kept beside him for many years an interleaved set of the Waverley Novels in which he jotted down all the corrections and improvements that occurred to him & in which are bound up all the MS introductions and notes which were afterwards published in the Author's Favourite Edition . . . We believe this to be the finest relic of Scott extant but rather than expatiate on its merits we should prefer that you inspected it personally. We should be happy to submit it to you at any time or place.

May 1904 saw A & C Black in further negotiation with William Brown of Edinburgh. The bookseller was keen to buy the Interleaved Set. Blacks declared that they should not care to accept less than five thousand pounds. Brown evidently thought this too high, but the vendors replied curtly that 'the price is the same now as at the time the question was first opened'. Other enquiries after the Interleaved Set followed. In reply to one such of March 1905, Blacks observed that 'it has twice been offered for sale by third parties, once to Mr Pierpont Morgan and once to a gentlemen in Scotland, whose name we do not know. We shall be happy to show the volumes at any time'. But it appears that such private negotiations with potential purchasers or with their agents were all unsatisfactory to the owners, for in June and July 1905 Sotheby, Wilkinson & Hodge entered the lists. 'May we ask', wrote A & C Black to the auctioneers, 'if the prices received for the documents you were good enough to sell for us the other day have affected our estimate of the value of the set of the Waverley Novels, which was formerly in your hands? In any case will you kindly let us know what you think you could get for it now?' A week later Blacks asked: 'Do you think you could get £3,000 net for us for the volumes? We have always valued the set at £5,000, but are willing to be guided by you in the matter.' The next summer the owners made an unsolicitied offer of the Set to a party who had just bought a first edition of *Waverley* in Sotheby's rooms.

At this point efforts to realise the (declining) commercial value of the Interleaved Set seem to have ceased. Perhaps Blacks decided after all to retain their relic. three yards of handsomely bound Scott has never looked out of place as board-room furniture. And so after exhibition in Glasgow in 1911 the 'Magnum Opus' gathered dust in Soho Square, and for the firm that published *Who's Who* the historic association copy became rather a candidate for some bibliographic *Who Was Who*.

No further mention of the Interleaved Set has been noted in any of the A & C Black letter-books, or in minute-books of company board meetings. There is, however, evidence that the publishing firm was maintaining its historic interest in Scott and his works throughout the first three decades of the century. Blacks had a particular concern; and they were, indeed, keeping a close watch on Scott manuscript prices in the auction houses of the world, and an eye on likely collectors who might some day, perhaps, step forward as purchasers of their great association copy. Cuttings-books were compiled of material relating to Sir Walter Scott, and to sales of his manuscripts or to acquisitions by libraries. It may be that hope of a sale to the Morgan family was not quite extinguished, for an article in *The Times* of 4 December 1908 on the Morgan collection was marked by Blacks for its references to the Scott holdings in New York. An observation by *The Times* apropos Scott's *Journal* as the jewel in the Morgan crown—'how this was ever allowed to leave the United Kingdom is incomprehensible'—was highlighted in red ink in the cuttings-book. A number of papers on the Interleaved Set were prepared: one about 1910, another in April 1912, and a third in October 1920. This last, a high-flown production by C W Home McCall, late of the Ballantyne Press in London, referred throughout to Scott's 'personal "Magnum Opus"', that relic 'which was in a literary sense Sir Walter Scott's closest companion during the years of his grim fight against adversity'. It was, moreover, claimed by McCall that the books contained evidence that Scott 'was making corrections on this personal interleaved set of volumes up to the last few hours before he died'.

In the later 1920s A & C Black began to take note of the impending centenary of Scott's death. In 1926 William Callender had retired from the firm. He had been presented with his portrait by W R Brealey in recognition of his long service as employee and as partner. For this painting Callender had chosen to hold a volume of the 'Magnum Opus', eloquent testimony to its status as the primary relic of the house. The next year a further memorandum on the Interleaved Set was drawn up. Articles on the firm in different trade and professional journals in these years mention the existence of the Interleaved Set in Soho Square as late as December 1928. The writer of a piece in *The Ontario School Teachers' Federation Bulletin* mentioned in an article on A & C Black (one of a series of notes on publishers in Canada) that the 'Magnum Opus' had 'always remained the chief treasure of the firm'. But it seems that hopes of a sale had been revived, although no record whatsoever of any negotiations has been preserved. In retrospect one is struck by the absence from the consciousness of Messrs A & C Black of any thought that the young National Library of Scotland might be interested in acquiring the Interleaved Set. Though the Library was a new national institution, it was one established on an old foundation, and it had the proud tradition of the Advocates' Library as a collector of literary manuscripts to maintain and develop. The National Library had already shown its interest in Scott material, and handsome gifts of highly important Burns and Scott manuscripts had received some publicity. One can only speculate that it may have been Constable & Co's communication in *The Times* of 10 January 1929 about the projected Centenary Edition of Scott's letters, which would have had the effect of making owners of Scott manuscripts take notice of their interesting and potentially valuable literary property, that prompted Blacks to settle finally on a sale. Anyway, it must be assumed that at last they received a tempting offer for this museum-piece shelf of books because in 1929, exactly a century after the publication of the first titles in the Magnum edition, the Interleaved Set, which preserved the materials collected for that edition, was sold, and the monument to the most heroic labour in literary history slipped quietly and apparently unnoticed across the Atlantic.

The arrival of the Interleaved Set in America was announced in *The New York Times* of 8 January 1930. It had been bought by, or at any rate through the agency of the bibliophile and adviser to collectors, J H Isaacs, who, as a prolific miscellaneous writer himself, had adopted the pseudonym of 'Temple Scott'. According to the newspaper report, Temple Scott put a value of $150,000 on the

14 Robert Cadell's crest and motto, from the binding of a volume in the Interleaved Set (enlarged).

Set, and to stimulate interest in his acquisition he published a descriptive booklet. This inaccurate production has been, until now, the chief source of information on the Interleaved Set. In his enthusiasm, Isaacs mistook Cadell's crest (a stag's head proper with the motto 'Vigilantia') which is stamped on the bindings of the Set, for Scott's (Fig. 14). He revealed nothing of the circumstances of purchase, nor, naturally enough, what price he had paid; just as, indeed, the A & C Black official history twice mentions the Interleaved Set and stresses its value to the firm, yet passes over the sale in silence. However a copy letter of 30 August 1929 has been identified among the Temple Scott papers in the Harry Ransom Humanities Research Center of the University of Texas.[6] Writing to George Wilson of A & C Black, Isaacs gives the purchase price as £5000. The Interleaved Set was shipped to the United States on board the *Ile de France* in October 1929. Isaacs's sense of surprise that he had actually pulled off this bibliographical coup is evident. 'Nor is it necessary', he wrote, in a passage which gives a somewhat distorted view of what we now know to be the facts of the case,

> to enlarge on the sentiment in which these volumes are steeped. For a century they have been kept in the strong rooms of the Edinburgh publishers, prized as a treasure of outstanding importance in the literary history of Great Britain. Students and book-lovers the world over, eager to view so intimate an association heritage of the world's greatest writer of romance, made pilgrimages to Edinburgh to examine it; some even making offers to purchase it for a more public appreciation in America; but the owners, while willingly permitting free access for reference, held it sacred.

It was, however, in the United States (Isaacs supposed) that the books would find 'their final fitting home'.[7]

That the Interleaved Set should have left Great Britain precisely when it did, and in a manner (so it seems) totally unrecorded by any involved in the world of Scottish literary scholarship, is odd indeed. For 1929 was the year that saw the start of work on Sir Herbert Grierson's edition of Scott's letters. The editor recalled how it was the presentation to the National Library in 1928 of the Law collection of Scott letters, themselves already used by Davidson Cook, which had first suggested to Messrs Constable & Co the idea of a collected edition. Such a project could be linked to the approaching centenary of Scott's death, which would fall in 1932.[8] Grierson's coadjutor, W M Parker, was a man with an eye for Scott letters and documents in unlikely places. His scrapbooks, now in the National Library, contain no mention of the Interleaved Set; nor do the Library's own files indicate that staff in either the Departments of Printed Books or Manuscripts knew anything about the loss to the cultural patrimony of the nation.

In the years immediately preceding the centenary in 1932, many commemorative books and articles were in gestation.[9] One would have imagined that this resurgence of domestic interest might have led to some realisation of the potential threat posed to the Interleaved Set by transatlantic bibliophiles, and indeed that some attempt might have been made by amateurs of Scott to save the set for a British library. Some time before, in a letter to *The Scotsman* of 29 November 1923 which had been occasioned by the sale of the manuscript of *Redgauntlet* and the subsequent saving of that volume for the nation, W S Crockett had drawn attention to the lamentable escape of Scott's *Journal* to the United States. As has been shown, A & C Black were well aware of the interest generated by the impending hundredth anniversary. In 1934 Grierson lamented the fact that so much of Scott's correspondence had 'wandered afar'. On a visit to America in the centenary year he had looked at a wide range of Scott material; and in alluding to rising prices for Scott manuscripts he praised Sir Walter Maxwell-Scott of Abbotsford for accepting less money than he might have obtained from American buyers so that the papers in the great family collection might find 'their proper home' in the National Library of Scotland.[10] Wilfred Partington's invaluable selections from Scott's incoming correspondence appeared in 1930 and 1932. Grierson was again in America in 1938—the preface to his life of Scott published that year is signed and dated from Columbia University Library—and yet in mentioning the additions of Scott material to public collections in Britain during the 1930s he gave no indication of any knowledge of the treasure then for sale in New York. John Buchan and the rest wrote their Scott books and magazine articles, Buchan in his referring to Sir Walter's 'Opus Magnum', which classical precision makes one think of Scott poking fun at the 'pedantry of former times'—but then Buchan was, after all, a greater devotee of the 'most capital of the ancients' and hardly a man (unlike Scott) to class himself as 'one of the unlearned'.[11] But in all the centenary writing there was a remarkable lack of curiosity about the Interleaved Set.

The organisers of the Scott exhibition held at the National Gallery of Scotland in the summer of 1932 seem to have had no concern to establish the Set's whereabouts, or even to confirm the continued existence of such a potent Scott relic. Dr W K Dickson, first Librarian of the National Library (1925–31), spoke at the exhibition opening of the spirit of enthusiasm aroused by the centenary:

> The Exhibition is a small part of the great manifestation of gratitude and affection to the memory of Sir Walter Scott which is taking place in Scotland this summer. He is being commemorated as the most eminent Scotsman of his generation, as the founder of the Romantic Movement in European literature, and as the interpreter of Scotland to the world. But to most of us he is simply the great purveyor of human happiness, the man to whom we owe countless hours of pleasure.[12]

The organising committee assembled a very fine collection of portraits, and a representative and imaginatively chosen selection of memorabilia and book and manuscript exhibits. However of the

Interleaved Set—present in Britain or absent abroad—there was no mention. It had gone, if indeed the centenary writers and exhibitors knew of its survival, and there was an end of it.

Isaacs did not sell the 'Magnum Opus' to a private buyer. The financial climate of the 1930s, the time of the Great Depression following the Wall Street crash of 1929, was hardly conducive to book-collecting in the United States on that grand scale possible in earlier years—the age in which princely collections such as the Huntington, the Folger, the Pierpont Morgan and the Carl H Pforzheimer Libraries were built up. Certainly in 1929 the Morgan Library had bought the manuscript of *The Antiquary*. A centenary Scott exhibition was held at Columbia University Library, and to this Carl Pforzheimer lent his manuscript of *Quentin Durward*. But even this local display of Scott material did not enable the new owner of the Interleaved Set to make a sale.

We hear no more of the Interleaved Set until 1939, by which time it was being offered by James F Drake of New York. The evidence suggests that Drake *may* have bought it from Isaacs as early as 1930: at least by the end of the decade Marston E Drake, president of the firm, was claiming that he had bought it *direct* from A & C Black, and certainly by that time copies of the Temple Scott pamphlet of 1930 bore the Drake trade label on the cover. At some time in the 1930s, too, the books were dressed up in the eyecatching quarter bound red leather boxes in which Cadell's less showy volumes are kept today. (Beneath their inner cloth linings the boxes have a layer of newspaper, and this material bears dates early in the decade.) The idea that such a striking item could lie for nine years in a New York bookshop, unsold and—even more improbably—unreported to literary scholars in America or in Britain, is almost too unlikely for words. Yet that is precisely what seems to have happened. The Wizard of the North would have thought his spell was broken: 'It is possible no doubt that the works may lose their effect on the public mind but this must be risqued . . . Perhaps those who read this prophesy may shake their heads and say "Poor fellow! he little thought how he should see the publick interest in him and his extinguished. . . ." '[13]

Early in April 1939 a Canadian lawyer from Halifax, Nova Scotia, Mr J McG Stewart, KC, wrote to a friend in London, Lord Macmillan of Aberfeldy. 'Whenever I come to New York', Stewart announced,

> I make the rounds of the bookshops, and today came across an item that was so important to all people of Scotch origin that I felt I should bring it to your attention. It is the original Magnum Opus of Sir Walter Scott . . . In 1930 this unique set changed hands for around £20,000. Today it can be had for $30,000 US funds—and even that figure might be slightly shaded. The library at Edinburgh seems to be the only place in the world fit for it, and it occured to me that you might know the right man (or men) to furnish the funds. I only wish I had the money to do it. . . .[14]

Hugh Macmillan, Lord of Appeal in Ordinary, was a good man to have approached. A noted bibliophile, he was then Chairman of the Pilgrim Trust and a Trustee of the British Museum, and had been President of the Scottish Text Society. More important still, he had, when Lord Advocate in Ramsay MacDonald's government in 1924, played the leading part in pressing for the creation of the National Library of Scotland on the foundation of the Advocates' Library collections, to which he had already presented the MS. of *Redgauntlet*. Subsequently he had served as a Trustee of the new institution. However nearly two months elapsed before Macmillan vouchsafed this intelligence to the National Librarian, Dr Henry Meikle:

> I expect you know of the treasure to which he [Stewart] refers. I share his wish that it should find a home in Edinburgh under your care, but I cannot think of anyone whom I could approach in the matter, now that Sir Alexander Grant [who had donated substantial funds to establish the National Library] is no longer with us, and I fear you may be in the same position. It is too big a transaction for the Friends of the National Libraries. Can anything be done, do you think?

Henry Meikle was on a fishing holiday on Loch Morar. In his absence, Marryat Dobie, Keeper of Manuscripts, replied to Lord Macmillan:

> It would be magnificent if we could get it, for its sentimental value is certainly very great and its usefulness to the student is probably so. The price is, of course, enormous—£150 a volume at least. We should also have to know more about the MS. alterations. If they merely represent the difference between the Magnum and the previous editions, without showing intermediate changes of mind, etc, they are less interesting. The Lord President [Lord Normand, Convener of the Standing Committee of the Board of Trustees, and himself a great Scott enthusiast] has suggested that we might obtain information from a correspondent in New York. Mr [William] Beattie, the Keeper of Printed Books, says that the Librarian of the Pierpont Morgan Library (which possesses a great collection of Scott MSS. and therefore presumably some experts on the subject) might help.

Dobie also wrote to Lord Clyde, Chairman of the Board of Trustees, 'in case [he thought] that anything could, or should, be done' and giving the sterling price as £6,400 which he hoped might be 'shaded' down to £6,000. 'This seems rather much', was Dobie's opinion, given the uncertain nature of the 'corrections' and the unknown quantity of their possible interest; and it was 'quite probable that a student would gather all that he wanted to know on the subject by comparing the Magnum with the original editions of the works'. Meikle was disturbed in the middle of his country pursuits by the news from Edinburgh: 'It would be nice to have such a set, but it is far too dear', he told Dobie on 7 June 1939. Like the Keeper of Manuscripts, he doubted the value to scholarship, and he drew comparisons with prices realised in recent sales of Scott material. 'Time passes quickly and pleasantly here', Meikle concluded. 'Yesterday we had a glorious day on the loch. Total catch 3 trout, for 2 of which Jessie was responsible, 1 weighing $\frac{1}{2}$ lb.'

Lord Clyde felt that the 'Magnum Opus' was 'a very tempting proposition—but temptations lose their force when the cost of yielding to them is beyond one's purse. I don't myself see any mode of financing a transaction in the neighbourhood of £6,000...'. Dr James Maclehose, Convener of the Books and Manuscripts Committee of the Trustees confessed to Dobie that he did not known that the annotated set was still in existence. Writing from holiday in Brittany he offered to make enquiries through business contacts in New York about 'this MS. or its pedigree'. Everyone seemed to have forgotten the treasure of A & C Black's publishing house.

In the end Henry Meikle decided to ask two members of the academic staff of Columbia University to examine the Interleaved Set to see how the corrections and annotations corresponded to the printed Magnum edition. 'Unless Scott made further alterations in the final proofs, which would therefore not be contained in the set now for sale, the set would appear to be a "museum piece" of little value to students of the evolution of Scott's text.' The men selected were Gilbert Highet, the distinguished classical scholar late of Glasgow and Oxford, and Hellmut Lehmann-Haupt, Professor of Book Arts in the School of Library Service. (The latter was, in fact, the son-in-law of Sir Herbert Grierson.) Lehmann-Haupt quickly established that what he was looking at in Drake's shop was nothing other than A & C Black's 'valuable interleaved copy'. It took a German in America to tell the Scots what they had forgotten. He established, too, the relationship between the annotated set and the 1870–71 Centenary Edition. For his part James H Drake worked hard to supply Lehmann-Haupt with detailed information on the standing of his merchandise in relation to both the Magnum and the Centenary Editions. 'From what I have seen', he reported,

> I am sure that this is one of the interesting phases of this work in that it will furnish students of Scott with opportunities for research for years to come... Its interest, its value, its importance will never diminish, but [will] grow in consequence as succeeding editors of Scott's works, as they have done before, consult its pages for the author's own final revisions... It contains sufficient unused and unpublished matter to provide the basis for work of considerable interest on Scott's literary methods, or possibly for a variorum edition of the text.

Drake concluded thus, with genuine feeling that transcends mere sales-talk:

> As an association item, it is without a peer. I do not recall as great a set of books which stand out as a monument to one of the greatest literary labors... The 'Magnum Opus', from an historical, sentimental, association and collector's view-point, is undoubtedly one of the greatest monuments of English literature, and it is my fervent wish, entirely aside from a business view-point, that the 'Magnum Opus' finally finds its way home to Scotland, where it so rightfully belongs.

'Under which King...?' The choice now had to be faced. On the one hand, sentiment, and the possibility of real literary and academic value; on the other, the more mundane question of finance. The textual scholarship of the day was very different from that climate in which the new Edinburgh Edition of the Waverley Novels is now being undertaken. Grierson's imperfect edition of Scott's letters was the product of that time. The general belief in Edinburgh was that the 'Magnum Opus' would be comparatively uninteresting to literary scholars. The National Library did not see Temple Scott's pamphlet until late August or early September 1939. Sentiment certainly had its price, but Lord Clyde was right about yielding to temptation. Then, as now, if an institution were to spend all its funds on one exotic purchase, it might put itself in the position of having to forego something else of interest or importance were that to come on the market unexpectedly. The Interleaved Set was just far too expensive.

In 1939 the National Library depended very largely on its trust funds for money to buy manuscripts. At the Standing Committee meeting of the Board of Trustees on 7 July the Convener of the Finance Committee reported on the state of those funds: the Reid, Rosebery and Keppie Funds. Together these produced a total income of £3,610. Of this figure, the Reid Fund (the bequest of Mr & Mrs William Robert Reid of Lauriston Castle) accounted for £3,292; and it was from this income that most manuscript purchases were made. The Government grant-in-aid for book purchase was tiny. The Standing Committee minutes for 17 March record that in response to a Treasury appeal for economy, it had been agreed to reduce this annual sum from £200 to £100. (By 15 December the minutes record a further reduction to £75.) Certainly major purchases had been made, and the biggest of all by far were in the field of Scott manuscripts. In May 1931 and June the following year the Library had bought large parts of the Abbotsford collection from Scott's descendants for £2,000 and £1,600 (MSS. 851–938). Yet more Abbotsford Papers were acquired in 1934 and 1935 for £1,200 and £550 (MSS. 1549–1634). Much of this correspondence came indeed from Scott's very desk, and the celebrated letters to his wife had been found in a secret drawer. This was material of great 'sentimental' and 'associational' interest, and the price had been an enormous one for an institution with limited resources. Four volumes of the Cadell collection of Scott's correspondence chiefly with Archibald Constable and Robert Cadell (MSS. 742–45) had been bought in 1932 for £1,680. (The Library had to wait until 1970 to acquire the fifth volume of this series, when it paid about the same amount for one single tome as it had for the other four together; and this was bought, too, from the Reid Fund.) But these splendid Scott acquisitions were exceptional. They do, however, form the nearest parallel to the 'Magnum Opus' in terms of major outlay for material of, on the one hand, literary importance, and on the other, 'heritage' and historical value.

In general, purchases in the 1930s were much more modest. Some Scott examples may be given. The papers of Sir Walter's kinsfolk, the Scotts of Raeburn were bought in 1936 for £175. Nine Scott letters cost £50. 7*s*. 3*d*. in July of the same year. In December 1938, Scott letters were bought at £1. 15*s*. and £2. 5*s*. each, and in January and February 1939 two were added to the collection at £10 and £7. 10*s*. So Scott was never cheap in comparison with other purchases, many of which in 1939 still cost under a pound in the case of individual letters. Other literary and historical manuscript acquisitions help to set the price of the Interleaved Set in context and perspective. A sonnet and notes by Drummond of Hawthornden were bought for £105 in July 1936; a collection of poems and prose pieces by Allan Ramsay cost £100 in July 1938; a Boswell letter came in February 1938 for £22, and a Flora Macdonald letter, with associated memoranda of 1789, for £180 later the same year; a Raeburn letter was added for £5 in August 1939; Thomas Carlyle letters in 1938 and 1939 were costing between £2 and £5; and David Livingstone letters were never very cheap for the time at £8, £22 and £16 in December 1938 and August 1939. The Library paid £175 for the Erskine Murray Papers (MSS. 5070–138) in June 1939.

There is no record in the Minutes of the Standing Committee of the Trustees (or for that matter of the full Board) for meetings in the second half of 1939 to the effect that the question of the 'Magnum Opus' was ever discussed. Sir Herbert Grierson remained a Trustee until the autumn. But September saw events much graver than the problems of finding £6,000; and by the time the Board next met, three of the Library staff were already in the Forces, the Keeper of Manuscripts was waiting to be called up, and eight members of staff had been transferred to other Government Departments. Two hundred and seventy-two volumes of manuscripts, together with the catalogues, had been sent for safety to houses in the country. As James Maclehose pointed out, this was not the moment 'to purchase expensive rarities when we are trying to find safe places for those we have'. Meikle wrote to New York to say that the Library could take no action. James H Drake replied, and incidentally conveyed the news of Temple Scott's recent death, which—ironically enough—had occurred in Edinburgh. 'Let us hope', Drake wrote, 'this war will not be of long duration and that events will transpire which will enable [the Interleaved Set] to find its way back home.' We may think of Scott writing in 1829: 'So on the whole I have only to pray for quiet times for how can men mind their serious business, that is according to Cadell's views buying Waverley novels, when they are going mad. . . .'[15]

For forty-five years nothing was heard of the 'Magnum Opus'. All trace of the volumes vanished, and although Drake was said to have sold them to a private collector, the buyer—presumably American—remained by his or her own wish anonymous. Students of Scott debated the problem of where the Interleaved Set might be. Writing his entry on Scott for the *New Cambridge Bibliography of English Literature*, Dr James Corson, doyen of Scott scholars, stated confidently that the 'interleaved copy of the novels, with his MS. corrections . . . is now in private hands in the USA';[16] but neither he nor any other specialist had definite knowledge beyond the fact that the Set did not appear to be in an open or accessible collection. The Department of Manuscripts of the National Library kept to hand its 'Magnum file', and joined in the bemused speculation. Like its author, the 'Magnum Opus' was also itself 'the Great Unknown'.

The mystery was solved on 28 August 1984. On that day Mr Patrick Cadell, Keeper of Manuscripts in the National Library of Scotland, received a telephone call from Messrs Bernard Quaritch, the London booksellers. Did the words 'Magnum Opus' mean anything in connection with Sir Walter Scott? The question was

15 Miss Doris Benz's bookplate from the first volume of the Interleaved Set.

16 'The Great Unknown': from a cartoon published in 1825, some two years before Scott acknowledged in public his authorship of the Waverley Novels. National Library of Scotland.

being posed because a set of books, apparently with autograph annotations by Scott, had turned up in a private library which Christie's New York were preparing for sale. The owner of this library, which (as Christie's were then discovering) was rich in fine bindings and association copies, was Miss Doris Louise Benz, a shoe-leather manufacturer's heiress, of Lynn, Massachusetts. She had died in April 1984, and under an arrangement made three years previously she had directed that Dartmouth College Library should be the beneficiary of the sale of her book collection. Dartmouth was not to have her actual library, but rather the proceeds of its dispersal at auction by Christie's: Miss Benz had evidently decided, in a manner reminiscent of Edmond de Goncourt, whose celebrated will directed the sale of his own collections, that she should prefer to think of her cherished books bringing pleasure to another generation of collectors. Miss Benz's library—'a buried treasure' was the way Christie's described it in the sale catalogue of 16 November 1984—was wholly unknown to any in the bibliographical world save only the dealers from whom, between the 1930s and the early 1960s, she had quietly bought her superb-quality standard English literary sets and sophisticated copies.

Miss Benz's principal suppliers had been James F Drake, and the Interleaved Set had been sold to her, probably in 1941—by which time it had been in exile for over eleven years. The opulent New York boxes which had been made in an effort to sell the books perhaps ten years earlier will have appealed to Miss Benz's taste, and this expensive work must, in her eyes, have rendered the Interleaved Set a worthier shelf-companion for her other finely-bound treasures, which included (in the field of Scott bibliophily) an elegant and profusely extra-illustrated set of the Waverley Novels (25 vols., A & C Black, Edinburgh, 1852–53) and an interesting set of proofs with autograph corrections and revisions of the first volume of the *History of Scotland* (London, 1830).

But even then, 'buskit braw' in its bright boxes, the life of the 'Magnum Opus' was still unsettled; for each spring the most valuable of Miss Benz's books were stowed in large trunks and loaded into two vintage Rolls-Royces to be taken from her seaside house in Lynn to her other property in North Sandwich, New Hampshire, where she liked to spend a large part of the year. And so on Miss Benz's death the Interleaved Set seemed destined to wander once more—not that her trustees nor the auctioneers even knew that she had owned it; but when the great relic came to light, by a fine twist of fate only fourteen out of what Christie's and Quaritch's soon realised should be forty-one volumes could be found. The delay in locating the remaining twenty-seven volumes was to prove vital for the National Library of Scotland.

The first fourteen volumes of the Interleaved Set were not included in the catalogue for the November sale. Instead advertisements were placed in the international press offering a reward for information leading to the recovery of the missing books: to continue the Jacobite analogy of exile and dispossession, the volumes were wanderers now with a price on their heads. Meanwhile, on the other side of the Atlantic, when the National Library learned that the 'Magnum Opus', or a part of it at any rate, had been found, the result was akin to that recorded by Lord Cockburn of the effect of *Waverley* on the Edinburgh of 1814: the Department of Manuscripts experienced an 'electric shock of delight'.[17] The decision was taken to attempt to buy the Interleaved Set for the nation, and negotiations with Christie's New York and the Benz trustees were begun through the agency of the Earl of Perth, chairman of the Finance and General Purposes Committee of the Board of Trustees of the National Library.

At first it had been assumed that the Library would have to bid at auction for the Interleaved Set, and the stiffest competition was expected from North American libraries and private collectors. But when the full set could not be found in time for the Benz auction, the possibility of arranging a private-treaty sale was actively investigated. Through its contacts the Library was able to move more quickly and successfully in this direction than any of its possible rivals, and the determination to succeed was always strong. In due course the missing volumes turned up in circumstances still unsatisfactorily explained: the books mysteriously appeared one day in the spring of 1985 in a room in the Benz house which had already been thoroughly searched.

By the time that the two parts of the Interleaved Set had been reunited, and Christie's, the Benz trustees and Dartmouth College had been persuaded to agree to a private sale to the National Library, a further very remarkable and wholly coincidental development had taken place. The Carl H Pforzheimer Library in New York had decided to divest itself of all its Scott literary manuscripts—novels, poetry, criticism and various proof sheets—and to offer the whole collection to the National Library of Scotland. Not one but two major purchases had to be faced.[18]

The problems of raising the $250,000 asked for the Interleaved Set paled into insignificance beside the sum needed to secure the Pforzheimer manuscripts—$670,000. It seemed sensible to combine the two groups of Scott material in a single fund-raising campaign in order to gather the total of $920,000. The enterprise itself attracted publicity, for cultural repatriation of literary material on this scale is rare indeed, and the bringing back of heritage items already lost is harder by far than campaigning to prevent them leaving the country in the first place. Nevertheless the idea of a British national institution being able to reverse the flow of such material across the Atlantic was one that appealed to donors. Had either collection gone to auction, the outcome for Scotland would almost certainly have been very different; for it would have been difficult or impossible to raise money by public appeal if the actual sum needed were dependent on the vagaries of the sale-room. Without the fixed target which a private-treaty arrangement provides, how much does one need to raise, and can the bidding even be opened at all if it is not known whether one has the

17 Dominie Sampson in Colonel Mannering's library at Woodbourne: 'Pro-di-gi-ous!'. Frontispiece by C R Leslie to the first volume of *Guy Mannering* in the Magnum Opus edition, 1829.

resources, in fact or by guarantee, to outbid any potential opponent? And if one fails, what does one do with donations in hand . . . ?

However the National Library did not fail. Thanks to the generosity of trusts, companies and private individuals, and through the Library's willingness to commit a very large sum from its own resources, the Scott collections were secured. On 5 March 1986 the 'Magnum Opus' returned to Edinburgh, to be followed less than 24 hours later by the Pforzheimer manuscripts. It was the most remarkable day in the history of the Library, and an occasion such as might have delighted that perfervid would-be librarian, Dominie Sampson himself. Those who that day enjoyed the life he so much coveted were tempted to exclaim, with him, 'Pro-di-gi-ous!' No one involved will forget the experience of unpacking the air-freight boxes, nor the sight of volume after volume piling up beneath the gaze of the Department of Manuscripts copy of the Chantrey bust of Scott. More moving still was the presence across the room of Scott's death-mask, bearing mournful witness to the mental and physical effort so eloquently represented by these very volumes.

In the General Preface to the Magnum edition of the Waverley Novels, written in 1829, Scott described his early experiments in prose romance which were the forerunners of the long procession of published novels, tales and romances which followed—the 'inundation' as he self-mockingly called it. He told the story of his abortive attempt—just one of many literary avocations—to write and publish *Waverley*, the first chapters of which he 'threw together' in 1805.[19] The manuscript of this he had put aside in an old writing-desk, which itself was forgotten among his other 'gabions' at Abbotsford. Almost a decade later he wanted to find some fishing-tackle for the use of a guest. Scott searched the old desk: 'I got access to it with some difficulty; and, in looking for lines and flies, the long-lost manuscript presented itself.'[20] The discovery led, as all the world knows, to Scott the poet and antiquary becoming Scott the novelist, the Author of Waverley. The finding of the Interleaved Set has led without doubt to a greater interest than ever in Scott and his work. The return of the 'Magnum Opus' may well herald a new age in Scottish literary studies, and the investment offers the prospect of its greatest return in the scholarship of the new Edinburgh Edition of the novels. The National Library of Scotland has landed a bigger fish than ever Henry Meikle caught on Loch Morar.

NOTES AND REFERENCES

1 *Adam & Charles Black 1807–1957* (London, 1957), pp.22–3.

2 NLS MS. 23063, f.29v, grangerised copy of *The Scott Exhibition MDCCCLXXI. Catalogue of the Exhibition* (Edinburgh, 1872), II.130; A & C Black's preliminary Advertisement in the Centenary Edition *Waverley* (Edinburgh, 1870).

3 *Scottish Exhibition. Official Historical Catalogue* (Glasgow, 1911), p.158.

4 I am greatly indebted to Mr Inman for allowing me to make use of information which he has collected in the course of a thorough examination of the A & C Black letterbooks. Several of the quotations which follow have been supplied by Mr Inman, who has gone far out of his way to assist me in attempting to unravel the mystery of the sale of the Interleaved Set. I am also grateful to Mrs Rosemary Shepherd of Messrs A & C Black (Publishers) Ltd for guiding me in my own investigation of the firm's records.

5 These details may be established by study of Gillian Dyson, 'The Manuscripts and Proof Sheets of Scott's Waverley Novels', *Transactions of the Edinburgh Bibliographical Society*, IV, pt.i for 1955–56 (1960), pp.15–42.

6 Jane Millgate, *Scott's Last Edition* (Edinburgh, 1987), p.133 (n.3).

7 *Sir Walter Scott's 'Magnum Opus'* (New York, 1930), p.8. There is a copy of this in NLS, press-mark 1939.30.

8 *The Letters of Sir Walter Scott*, ed H J C Grierson, 12 vols (London, 1932–37), I.v.

9 For the vast outpouring of commemorative and critical writing occasioned by the centenary see James C Corson, *A Bibliography of Sir Walter Scott: a classified and annotated list of books and articles relating to his life and works 1797–1940* (Edinburgh, 1943); and Jill Rubinstein, *Sir Walter Scott: a reference guide* (Boston, Mass., 1978).

10 H J C Grierson, 'Sir Walter Scott as correspondent: experiences in editing Scott's letters', *Glasgow Herald*, 22 November 1934.

11 John Buchan, *Sir Walter Scott* (London, 1932), p.315; Grierson, *Letters*, VIII.415, 148; IV.139.

12 NLS MS. 9483, f.18: volume of papers relating to the 1932 exhibition collected by W K Dickson.

13 *The Journal of Sir Walter Scott*, ed W E K Anderson (Oxford, 1972), p.398.

14 This and subsequent quotations from correspondence of 1939 are taken from letters in the 'Magnum file' in the records of the Department of Manuscripts.

15 *Journal*, p.529.

16 *NCBEL*, ed George Watson: III (Cambridge, 1969), col.671.

17 Henry Cockburn, *Memorials of his Time*, new edn (Edinburgh, 1909), p.270.

18 For accounts of the National Library's activities in connection with the acquisitions, and for brief comments on the material in question see [A S Bell], 'Scott for Scotland', *The Book Collector*, XXXV (Autumn 1986), pp.281–92); I G Brown, 'The Annus Mirabilis for Scott Manuscript Acquisition', *Books in Scotland*, 21 (Summer 1986), pp.4–5; and P M Cadell, 'The Pforzheimer Scott Manuscripts', in *Sir Walter Scott's Magnum Opus and the Pforzheimer Manuscripts* (Edinburgh, 1986), pp.25–6.

19 Sir Walter Scott, *Waverley Novels*, 48 vols (Edinburgh, 1829–33), I.ix–xii.

20 *Ibid.*, pp.xvii–xviii.

18 The splendid freestone statue of Scott by the Lanarkshire stonemason and self-taught sculptor John Greenshields was perhaps commissioned by Robert Cadell, who bought this masterpiece on its completion in 1835. Greenshields had seen Scott but twice, in 1829 and 1831; but he was able to produce a likeness of extraordinary nobility which seems to catch the very essence of the man.

On Cadell's death the sculpture was presented by his trustees to the Faculty of Advocates (by whose permission it is here reproduced). At Parliament House, Edinburgh, it remained for a century in the Laigh Hall (the 'ancient dark Gothic room', where formerly had met the Privy Council of Scotland, as described by Scott in *Old Mortality*) when that room was occupied by the Advocates' Library and subsequently by the National Library. In 1952 the statue was installed in Parliament Hall itself, where Scott had spent his legal life as advocate and as Clerk of Session. At Lockhart's suggestion Cadell had the inscription from Bacon's effigy at St Albans carved on the plinth: SIC SEDEBAT. Lockhart considered the statue 'a very wonderful performance'; and Thomas Thomson declared at to be a 'petrification of Scott'.

19 Scott's armorial bearings on a panel believed to come from his coach. National Library of Scotland.

RELATED MATERIAL IN AMERICAN COLLECTIONS

CLAIRE LAMONT

This book has described the Interleaved Set of the Waverley Novels now in the National Library of Scotland. It is a set of forty-one volumes of uniform format, uniformly bound. Only thirty-two, however, are interleaved and annotated. The present note is occasioned by the existence of the remaining nine volumes. What is said here is offered very much as an interim report, and as such it is dependent on the work of Professor Jane Millgate in her *Scott's Last Edition: a Study in Publishing History* (1987).

The first thirty-two volumes of the Interleaved Set contain the novels from *Waverley* to *Woodstock*. The other volumes contain Scott's later novels, together with two omnibus volumes of *Introductions, and Notes and Illustrations, to the Novels, Tales and Romances of the Author of Waverley*. These last contain material published in the individual volumes of the Magnum edition. In 1833 Cadell gathered together all this material and republished it in two volumes in large octavo format for those who wished to add the Magnum introductions and notes to existing unannotated large octavo sets of the novels already in their possession. The seven books which form Volumes XXXIII to XXXIX of the Interleaved Set are a collection published in 1833 which continues the *Tales and Romances* series. The novels concerned are: *Chronicles of the Canongate* (first series); *Chronicles of the Canongate* (second series, *The Fair Maid of Perth*); *Anne of Geierstein*; *Count Robert of Paris*; and *Castle Dangerous*. As this collection, used by Cadell to complete the Interleaved Set, came out in 1833—the year after Scott's death—the books are neither interleaved nor annotated. That would be the end of the story, but for the fact that Scott did indeed write introductions and annotations for most of the later novels. Were copies of the later novels, therefore, also interleaved to assist in this task?

On 23 April 1830, Scott wrote to Cadell about his annotation of the novels and he mentions '*Anne of Geierstein* and *Chronicles of the Canongate* of which I would be better of interleavd copy from you'.[1] Cadell interleaved copies of the two sets of *Chronicles of the Canongate* and *Anne of Geierstein* from the editions that he had to hand and took them to Scott on 6 May 1830.[2] For *Count Robert of Paris*, over the writing of which there had been much difficulty, Scott wrote no Magnum introduction, and such notes as are in it were supplied by Lockhart.[3] For *Castle Dangerous* Scott sent an introduction from Naples in February 1832, 'together with some corrections of the text, and notes on localities mentioned in the Novel'.[4] There is no evidence that these last two novels were ever interleaved.

So there were in addition to the thirty-two interleaved volumes of the novels, now in Edinburgh, eight more: two volumes of *Chronicles of the Canongate* (first series), three of *Chronicles of the Canongate* (second series), and three of *Anne of Geierstein*. Where are they now?

To take the eight additional interleaved volumes in turn: Volume II of *Chronicles of the Canongate* (first series) is in the Widener Collection at Harvard.[5] It is an interleaved volume of the first edition of 1827. The first volume of this work was sold at auction in 1939 at the John A Spoor sale, and has not been traced since. The sale catalogue describes it as Volume I of *Chronicles of the Canongate* (1828):[6]

> Sir Walter's copy with his autograph corrections and notations throughout the volume, aggregating about 500 words. Some of Scott's interesting marginalia appears on leaves that are larger than those in the rest of the volume. These have been folded in for protection. A note in Mr Spoor's library states that this volume comes from the library of a Scotch gentleman who had purchased it from Mrs Cadell, the wife of Sir Walter's publisher.[7]

For *Chronicles of the Canongate* (second series), three interleaved volumes are in the Wrenn Library, University of Texas.[8] It is an interleaved set of the second edition of 1828. Interleaved copies of Volumes I and III of *Anne of Geierstein* are in the Houghton Library at Harvard.[9] They are volumes of the first edition of 1829. The interleaved second volume has not been traced.

For some reason that remains unclear, the introductions were not bound into these late interleaved volumes, and if those introductions have survived they have survived separately: that for *Chronicles of the Canongate* (first series) is in the Huntington Library, San Marino, California;[10] that for *Chronicles of the Canongate* (second series) is in the National Library of Scotland;[11] that for *Anne of Geierstein* has not been traced.

There is much that is puzzling about this state of affairs, besides the items still missing. The most obvious question is why did Cadell, who took such care of the interleaved volumes of the earlier novels, allow these others to escape? Unfortunately the little evidence we have for their history after they had fulfilled their task as copy for the Magnum edition does not enable us to answer that question.

The catalogue note about the missing first volume of the interleaved *Chronicles of the Canongate* (first series) says that the volume came 'from the library of a Scotch gentleman who had purchased it from Mrs Cadell, the wife of Sir Walter's publisher'. Professor Millgate observes that pasted inside the front cover of the second volume, at Harvard, is a note signed by Charles J Hargitt stating that it was 'given to me on my leaving Edinburgh by a partner in the firm of Ballantyne & Co, the printers'.[12] It appears from these notes that the two volumes had not been kept together. The probable explanation for this is the treatment of the first series of *Chronicles of the Canongate* in the Magnum edition. The work consists of three tales with a narrative framework, and in the Magnum edition it was split so that the contents of the first volume of *Chronicles* appeared in Volume 41 in October 1832; the contents of the second volume, *The Surgeon's Daughter*, did not appear until the final volume of the Magnum, Volume 48, in May 1833. A pencil note in the front of the interleaved second series of *Chronicles of the Canongate* reads 'Purchased about the year 1850 from Mrs Cadell (widow of the publisher)'.[13] Robert Cadell had died in 1849.

There is evidence, therefore, that some at least of the American volumes came from the Cadell household. Were they there when Robert Cadell had the groups of collected editions of novels, each volume annotated by the author and each carefully preserved by Cadell himself for his own reasons, handsomely rebound as a uniform set? Though the Interleaved Set itself has been found, the riddle of Scott's other interleaved working copies is still not entirely solved.

NOTES AND REFERENCES

1 *The Letters of Sir Walter Scott*, ed H J C Grierson, 12 vols (London, 1932–37), XI.340.
2 NLS MS. 794, f.366; NLS MS. 21043, f.40v.
3 Kurt Gamerschlag, 'The Making and Un-Making of Sir Walter Scott's *Count Robert of Paris*', *Studies in Scottish Literature*, XV (1980), pp.95–123. 'Advertisement' to *Count Robert of Paris* in the Magnum edition, vol.46 (1833), p.[iii].
4 Headnote to the Introduction to *Castle Dangerous* in the Magnum edition, vol.47 (1833), p.[245].
5 Houghton Library, HEW 9.10.3. Jane Millgate, *Scott's Last Edition* (Edinburgh, 1987), pp.58, 134 (n.15).
6 The date is puzzling. It may be a copy of the advertised but hitherto untraced second edition, or issue, of the book.
7 The *Catalogue* of the John A Spoor Sale, Part II, item 734, Parke-Bernet, New York, 3, 4, 5 May 1939. Quoted from *Scott's Last Edition*, p.58.
8 Wn Sco86 828cb. *Scott's Last Edition*, pp.58, 133 (n.12).
9 Lowell EC8. Sco86. 829aa. *Scott's Last Edition*, pp.58, 133–4 (n.13).
10 HM 1982; HM 979.
11 NLS MS. 911, ff.264–71.
12 *Scott's Last Edition*, p.58.
13 *Ibid.*, p.58.

20 During his visit to Italy in the spring of 1832 in the forlorn attempt to restore his failing health, Scott was sketched by Neapolitan, Roman and visiting British artists on a number of occasions. This is to be reckoned the finest and most faithful likeness of that time. It is here reproduced by permission of Mrs Maxwell-Scott of Abbotsford.

The small pencil drawing, only 3 × 2 inches, is by Vincenzo Morani. It was drawn during Scott's visit to the Benedictine monastery of La Trinità di Cava on 11 March 1832. Here Scott was shown some manuscripts, and while he was absorbed in the examination of these he was sketched without his being aware that the portrait was being taken. Sir William Gell, who accompanied him on the visit, considered the sketch an excellent one 'most luckily like', and superior to that taken by Morani the next month at a formal sitting in Naples: 'it represented Sir Walter in his best moment and most natural position, not constrained . . . he being in fact at that time quite unconscious of the painter's presence.'

Gell's memoir of Scott's residence in Italy presents a moving record of these last months before the final journey home to Abbotsford and death. Though tired and ill, Scott nevertheless preserved something of his old vivacity, brilliance, kindness, geniality and delight in natural beauty. Sometimes the landscape of Italy seemed to remind him of Scotland. Gell records how, when gazing on Lake Avernus and while being instructed in the topography of the Phlegraean Fields, Scott was suddenly inspired to repeat aloud lines from a Jacobite song; and how, when driving through the wooded hills at the base of the Sorrento peninsula, he quoted at length from 'Hardyknute' and recited the favourite Border ballad of Jock o' Hazledean.

21 Sketch of Scott at the time he was at work on the Interleaved Set, done in Court by a young advocate, Mark Napier, on the fly-leaf of David Welsh, *The Life and Writings of Thomas Brown, MD* (Edinburgh, 1825). The sketch is inscribed: 'Sir Walter as he was 1829, sitting under the Lords as Clerk of Session, thinking of anything but his business.' National Library of Scotland.

'MY OWN RIGHT HAND SHALL DO IT':

An Anthology of Extracts from Scott's *Journal* and *Letters*, 1825–1831*

compiled by IAIN GORDON BROWN

18 DECEMBER 1825. Ballantyne calld on me this morning. *Venit illa suprema dies.* My extremity is come. Cadell has received letters from London which all but positively announce the failure of Hurst and Robinson so that Constable and Coy must follow and I must go with poor James Ballantyne for company. I suppose it will involve my all . . . Men will think pride has had a fall. Let them indulge their own pride in thinking that my fall makes them higher or seem so at least. I have the satisfaction to recollect that my prosperity has been of advantage to many and that some at least will forgive my transient wealth on account of the innocence of my intentions . . . How could I tread my hall with such a diminishd crest? How live a poor indebted man where I was once the wealthy—the honourd? My children are provided—thank God for that . . . I must end this or I shall lose the tone of mind with which men should meet distress.

19 JANUARY 1826. I feel quite composed and determined to labour. There is no remedy. I guess . . . that we shall not be troubled with visitors and I *calculate* that I will not go out at all so what can I do better than labour? Even yesterday I went about making notes on *Waverley* according to Constable's plan. It will do good one day.

21 JANUARY 1826. Things are so much worse with Constable than I apprehended that I shall neither save Abbotsford nor any thing else—Naked we enterd the world and naked we leave it. Blessed be the name of the Lord.

22 JANUARY 1826. I feel neither dishonourd nor broken down by the bad—miserably bad news I have received. I have walkd my last on the domains I have planted, sate the last time in the halls I have built. But death would have taken them from me if misfortune had spared them. My poor people whom I loved so well!! There is just another dye to turn up against me in this run of ill luck—i.e. If I should break my magic wand in a fall from this elephant & lose my popularity with my fortune. Then *Woodstock* and *Boney* may both go to the paper-maker and I may take to smoking cigars and drinking grog or turn devotee and intoxicate the brain another way. In prospect of absolute ruin I wonder if they would let me leave the Court of Session. I should like methinks to go abroad

And lay my banes far from the Tweed.

But I find my eyes moistening and that will not do. I will not yield without a fight for it. It is odd, when I set myself to work *doggedly* as Dr Johnson would say, I am exactly the same man that I ever was—neither low spirited nor *distrait*. In prosperous times I have sometimes felt my fancy and powers of language flag—but adversity is to me at least a tonic & bracer—the fountain is awakend from its inmost recesses as if the spirit of afliction had troubled it in his passage . . . I will involve no friend either rich or poor—My own right hand shall do it—Else will I be *done* in the slang language and *undone* in common parlance . . . Well—exertion—exertion—O Invention rouze thyself. May man be kind—may God be propitious . . . All my hope is in the continued indulgence of the public.

23 JANUARY 1826. I know not if my imagination has flaggd—probably it has but at least my powers of labour have not diminshd during the last melancholy week. On Monday & Tuesday my exertions were suspended. Since Wednesday inclusive I have written thirty eight of my close manuscript pages of which seventy make a volume of the usual novel size.

Wrote till twelve a.m. finishing half of what I call a good day's work, ten pages of print or rather twelve.

24 JANUARY 1826. I went to the Court for the first time today and like the man with the large nose thought everybody was thinking of me and my mishaps. Many were undoubtedly and all

* The text is that of *The Journal of Sir Walter Scott*, ed W E K Anderson (Clarendon Press, Oxford, 1972), and *The Letters of Sir Walter Scott*, ed H J C Grierson, 12 vols (Constable and Co., London, 1932–37).

rather regrettingly, some obvously affected. It is singular to see [the] difference of men's manner whilst they strive to be kind or civil in their way of addressing me. Some smiled as they wishd me good day as if to say 'Think nothing about it my lad; it is quite out of out thoughts—'. Others greeted me with the affected gravity which one sees and despises at a funeral. The best-bred, all I believe meaning equally well, just shook hands and went on . . .

If I am hard pressd and measures used against me I must use all measures of legal defence and subscribe myself bankrupt in a petition for sequestration. It is the course I would have advised a client to take and would have the effect of saving my land, which is secured by my son's contract of marriage. I might save my library &c. by assistance of friends and bid my creditors defiance. But for this I would in a court of Honour deserve to lose my spurs for—No, if they permit me, I will be their vassal for life and dig in the mine of my imagina[tion] to find diamonds (or what may sell for such) to make good my engagements, not to enrich myself.

15 February 1826. Yesterday I did not write a line of *Wood–k*. Partly I was a little out of spirits—though that would not have hindered—partly I wanted to wait for some new ideas—a sort of collecting of straw to make bricks of—partly I was a little too far beyond the press. I cannot pull well in long traces [in] which the draught is too far behind me. I love to have the press thumping, clattering and banging in my rear—it creates the necessity [which] almost always makes me work best—needs must when the Devil drives—and drive he does even according to the letter. I must work to-day howere.

4 June 1826. I wrote a good task yesterday and to-day a great one, scarce stirring from the desk the whole day except a few minutes . . . I am not sure it is right to work so hard . . . Well but if I lay down the pen as the pain in my breast hints that I should what am I to do? If I think—why I shall weep—and that's nonsense—and I have no friend now—none—to receive my tediousness for half an hour of the gloaming—Let me be grateful—I have good news from Abbotsford.

5 June 1826. Between correcting proofs and writing letters I have got as yet but two pages written and that with labour and a sensation of pain in the Chest. I may be bringing on some serious disease by working thus hard. If I had once justice done to other folks I do not much care, only I would not like to suffer long pain . . . These two interruptions did me good though I am still a poor wretch. After all I have fagg'd through six pages . . . And my head aches—my eyes ache—my back aches—so does my breast—and I am sure my heart aches—And what can duty ask more?

24 September 1827. Workd in the morning as usual and sent off the proofs and copy. Some things of the black dog still hanging about me but I will shake him off. I generally affect good spirits in company of my family whether I am enjoying them or not. It is too severe to sadden the harmless mirth of others by suffering your own causeless melancholy to be seen. And this species of exertion is like virtue its own reward for the good spirits which are at first simulated become at length real.

24 December 1827. . . . I could not have slept as I now can under the comfortable impression of receiving the thanks of my creditors and the conscious feeling of discharging my duty like a man of honour and honesty. I see before me a long tedious and dark path but it leads to true Fame and stainless reputation. If I die in the harrows as is very likely I shall die with honour; if I achieve my task I shall have the thanks of all concernd and the approbation of my own conscience. And so I think I can fairly face the return of Christmas day.

22 'Abbotsford': a cartoon from *The Looking Glass*, 1 June 1831. As the figure of Death watches in amazement, Scott writes himself out of debt but into the grave. National Library of Scotland.

7 JANUARY 1828. . . . write what I will or to whom I will, I am doggedly determined to write myself out of the present scrape by any labour that is fair and honest.

17 JANUARY 1828. I nibbled for an hour or two at *Napoleon* then took handsomely to my gears and wrote with great ease and fluency six pages of the *Chronicles*. If they are but tolerable I shall be satisfied. In fact such as they are they must do, for I shall get warm as I work as has happend on former occasions. The fact is I scarce know what is to succeed or not, but this is the consequence of writing too much and too often. I must get some breathing space. But how is that to be managed? There is the rub.

18 AND 19 JANUARY 1828. Remaind still at home and wrought hard. The fountain trickles free enough. But God knows whether the waters will be worth drinking. However I have finishd a good deal of hard work, that's the humour of it.

25 JANUARY 1828. I went on working sometimes at my legitimate labours sometimes at my bye jobs of Notes etc. but still working faithfully, in good spirits and contented.

10 JANUARY 1829. Every thing else goes off well enough. My cash affairs are clearing and though last year was an expensive one I have been paying debt. Yet I have a dull contest before me which will probably outlast my life. If well maintaind however, it will be an honourable one, and if the Magnum opus succeed it will afford me some repose.

4 MARCH 1829. At four o'clock arrives Mr Cadell with his horn charged with good news—The prospectus of the magnum already issued only a week has produced such a demand among the trade that he thinks he must add a large number of copies that the present edition of 7000 may be increased to the demand—he talks of raising it to ten or 12,000. If so I shall have a powerful and constant income to bear on my unfortunate debts to a large amount yearly and may fairly hope to put my debts in a secure way of payment even if I should be cut off in life or in health and the power of labour. I hope to be able in a year or two to make proposals for eating with my own spoons and using my own books, which if I can give value for them can hardly I think be refused to me.

6 MARCH 1829. There is a stronger gleam of hope on my affairs than has yet touchd on them. It is not steady or certain but it is bright and conspicuous. Ten years may last with me though I have little chance of it. At the end of this time these works will have operated a clearance of debt . . .

7 MARCH 1829. Sent away proofs—This extrication of my affairs, though only a Pisgah prospect, occupies my mind more than is fitting but with[out] some such hope I must have felt like one of the victims of the wretch Burke struggling against a smothering weight on my bosom till nature could endure it no longer. No—I will not be sport of circumstances. Come of it what will *I'll bend my brows/Like highland truis* and make a bold fight of it—

> The best o't the warst o't
> Is only just to die.

6 APRIL 1829. Workd at the Review for three or four hours yet, hang it, I can't get on. I wonder if I am turning dunny in other matters. Certainly I cannot write against time as I used to do. My thoughts will not be duly regulated. My pen declares for itself, will neither write nor spell and goes under independant colours . . .

27 APRIL 1829. This day must not be wasted . . . Accordingly I well nigh accomplishd my work but about three o'clock my story fell into a slough and in getting it out I lost my way and was forced to pos[t]pone the conclusion till tomorrow. Wrote a good day's work notwithstanding.

30 APRIL 1829. Well nobody can say I eat the bread of idleness. Why should I? Those who do not work from necessity take violent labour from choice and were necessity out of [the] question I would take the same sort of literary [labour] from choice—something more leisurely though.

5 JUNE 1829. . . . My head aches cruel. I made a fight at working and reading till eleven and then came sleep with a particolourd [mantle] of fantastic hues and wrapped me into an imaginary world.

6 JUNE 1829. I wrote the whole morning till two o'clock. Then I went into the gardens of Princ[e]'s street to my great exhilaration. I never felt better for a walk; also it is the first I have taken this whole week and more . . . The shrubs and young trees . . . are now of good size and gay with leaf and blossom. I too—old trunk as I am—have put out tender buds of hope which seemd checkd for ever. I may now look with fair hope to freeing myself of obligation from all men and spending the rest of my life in ease and quiet. God make me thankful to so cheering a prospect.

28 MAY 1830. My affairs go on up to calculation and the magnum keeps its ground. If this can last for five or six years longer we may clear our hands of debt but perhaps I shall have paid that of nature before that time come.

27 DECEMBER 1830. Well I can work at something so at the Magnum work I.

To Mrs Thomas Hughes, 9 or 10 October [1828] (XI.7)
. . . About these novels you know my feelings are something like those of Macbeth

> I am afraid to think on what I've done
> Look on't again I dare not—

. . . I have thoughts (though it is a *great secret*) of making a revised edition with some illustrations . . . I beg the favour of you to say nothing about the plan . . . We must try to make the new edition superior by illustrations and embellishments as a faded beauty dresses and lays on [a] prudent touch of rouge to compensate for want of her juvenile graces . . . The thing is really of very considerable importance & if it succeeds will do much to rub off old scores incurd by the bankruptcy of my publishers.

To Robert Cadell [15 October 1828] (XI.12)
. . . I could not think of setting about new studies with all the work of the Magnum before me. Both from choice and necessity I bestow a certain portion of each day upon it & am getting on.

To J. G. Lockhart, 30 October 1828 (XI.29)
. . . I have also twined off a world of not bad balaam in the way of notes, &c. for my Magnum, which if we could but manage the artists decently, might soon be afloat, and will, I do think, do wonders for my extrication.

To Charles Scott, 5 March [1829] (XI.143)
. . . You will see in the bookseller shops that I have been making a Da capo rota of Waverley &c and will [be] happy to learn it promises to be highly successful and if the publick be as kind as I have reason at present to hope will go far to relieve my unhappy embarassments without the labour of constant exertion for which I grow a little too blind and old.

To Robert Cadell, 18 March [1829] (XI.153)
. . . If the novels are to [be] given up as is probable we must think of something else for I cannot afford to be idle . . . Pray let proofs of the Magnum come regularly.

To Sir William Knighton, 18 May 1829 (XI.185–6)
I have the honour of enclosing to your care the first copy of the new edition of the Waverley Novels, inscribed to the King by his Majesty's most gracious permission. As it is a work intended for wide diffusion and a small price, its exterior could not have the splendour which ought to have attended the dedication; but I trust the decorations, which I believe are good,—at least they are executed by the best artists we have,—may be esteemed an apology for the humility of the volumes. We start with a sale of ten thousand, which, in a work which runs to forty volumes, is a very considerable matter.

To Walter Scott, 2 May [recte June 1829] (XI.196)
. . . I write to send you a copy of the Waverley novels . . . The sale is pro-di-gi-ous. If I live a few years it will completely clear my feet of former encrumbances . . . I shall be happy to die a free man and leave a competent provision for my family & I am sure you will all of you [be] kind to poor Anne who will miss me most. I do not intend to die a moment sooner than I can help it for all this but when a man makes blood instead of water he is tempted to think on the possibility of his soon making earth.

To John Wilson Croker, 3 June 1829 (XI.196–7)
I enclose a copy of a book to my son in which he and I are something interested and so I know will you [be] when I tell you it is the new edition of Waverley and that [if] its popularity should *haud it* as John Moody says, [it] will redeem me from the awkward jumble my affairs got when two Houses of Fat Booksellers fell down and well nigh jamd me to pieces between them.

To J. G. Lockhart, 11 December [1829] (XI.275)
. . . I should like to see and hope to see my affairs wound up for which to all appearance five or six years will be sufficient & much less will put them en bon train as the Waverley & its companions go on like whip and spur. I am busied finishing the edition so that you whom I naturally look to as my substitute may have as little trouble as possible . . . My complaint though I suspect it is a signal of breaking up is manageable and gives me neither pain nor anxiety.

To Robert Cadell, 2 January 1830 (XI.283)
. . . I fancy the Almanack is a good hint to me to mind how time passes. To show I am not idle I send you two volumes of the Magnum complete and have more in forwardness . . . I would not begin the printing of the poetry till I look every thing carefully over.

To J. G. Lockhart, 30 May [1830] (XI.192–3)
. . . My Magnum opus as Cadell calls it I mean the new edition of the Waverley novels gets on capitally—12000 copies are disposed of & the demand increases. At this rate we will soon clear off old scores and I shall leave the scene with [the] satisfaction of having paid every man his own & provided for my family.

To Robert Chambers, 7 March 1831 (XI.484–5)
. . . I fear I cannot be of use to you in the way you propose . . . But Dr Abercrombie threatens me with Death if I write so much & die I suppose I must if I give it up suddenly . . . for after all that same dying is a ceremony one would put off as long as they could . . .

23 Scott's last novels, *Count Robert of Paris* and *Castle Dangerous*, were published together on 1 December 1831 under the collective title of *Tales of My Landlord, Fourth and Last Series*. The author drafted an introduction to the series of tales, and a postscript, both of which had a distinct valedictory character and an air of finality. The Author of Waverley could and would write no more, and therefore took leave of his readers. The Introductory Address to these final Tales purports to be the work of Jedediah Cleishbotham: Scott's invented schoolmaster of Gandercleuch prints the last labours of Peter Pattieson, which were in reality the final works of fiction of Sir Walter Scott himself. Speaking through Jedediah, Scott calls this last series of tales 'my youngest literary babe, and, probably at the same time, the last child of mine old age'. By the time that *Count Robert* and *Castle Dangerous* were republished in the Magnum edition, their author was dead, and the intimations of mortality conveyed in the Introductory Address and postscript were fulfilled. However J G Lockhart, James Ballantyne and Robert Cadell had, in co-operation, practically re-written the novels and had radically altered and curtailed what Scott had intended to say in valediction. The collections of the National Library of Scotland contain no less than four sets of proofs of the Introductory Address, each heavily revised: the galleys shown here (MS. 23052) are the earliest, and were corrected by Scott in October 1831. They formed part of the Pforzheimer Collection bought in 1986.

In this illustration several items of Scott memorabilia in the National Library's collection are also displayed. The travelling writing-desk is that on which three of the great narrative poems were written. The open leather box carried manuscripts and proofs between Scott and James Ballantyne's printing house. The pen, a Bramah patent model, was one given by Scott to Maria Edgeworth. This new type of pen had greatly simplified writing. Once when Scott had wanted to write to Lady Abercorn and found himself without a pen he had had to 'sally forth and shoot a crow to procure a quill'. The new Bramah offered the convenience of ready-made nibs. Scott had at first disliked the innovation ('the deil take all new inventions more and less! I have been writing with a patent pen this hour which only scratches the paper without letting down ink!); but later he came to rely on the Bramah. This one is identical to that which he holds in Watson Gordon's portrait reproduced in the present book.

24 The Interleaved Set displayed in the boxes made for the volumes in New York in the 1930s.

AN ILLUSTRATED COMMENTARY ON THE INTERLEAVED SET

Plates chosen and described by Iain Gordon Brown

Photography by S W McAvoy

In this section of *Scott's Interleaved Waverley Novels* an album of plates, each with a short commentary, is offered as a guide to the riches of the collection. The purpose is to provide a companion to what might almost be called the archaeology of the Interleaved Set, for the physical make-up of the volumes is daunting. In many cases the annotation in a volume appears as a complex mass of paper—interleaf upon printed page, bound-in paper apart upon interleaf, paper apart upon paper apart, slips bearing last-minute additions pasted to papers apart. The whole vast edifice of editorial apparatus has, as it were, its own stratigraphy which must be stripped down, examined and recorded layer by layer. It is to be hoped that the plates and commentary will enable a sort of literary excavation to take place.

The selection of plates includes some representation of every novel from *Waverley* to *Woodstock*. The plates have been carefully chosen to illustrate different types and levels of annotation, emendation of the text, alteration of fact and opinion, discursiveness, glossing, integration of information supplied by others, incorporation of autobiographical elements into notes and introductions: every aspect of Scott's editorial rôle is touched upon. To those who have not the opportunity for personal inspection and study of the Interleaved Set, a photograph of a heavily annotated page or an emended portion of the text will explain more than words alone can do; and the passages here selected for illustration and discussion will tell the reader much about the evolution of the text of the Magnum Opus edition, which is the form in which Scott's novels have come down to us today.

References at the end of the commentary on each plate are to the equivalent passages in the volumes of the Magnum edition of 1829–33.

PLATE 1 The entire Interleaved Set in Robert Cadell's Russia leather bindings.

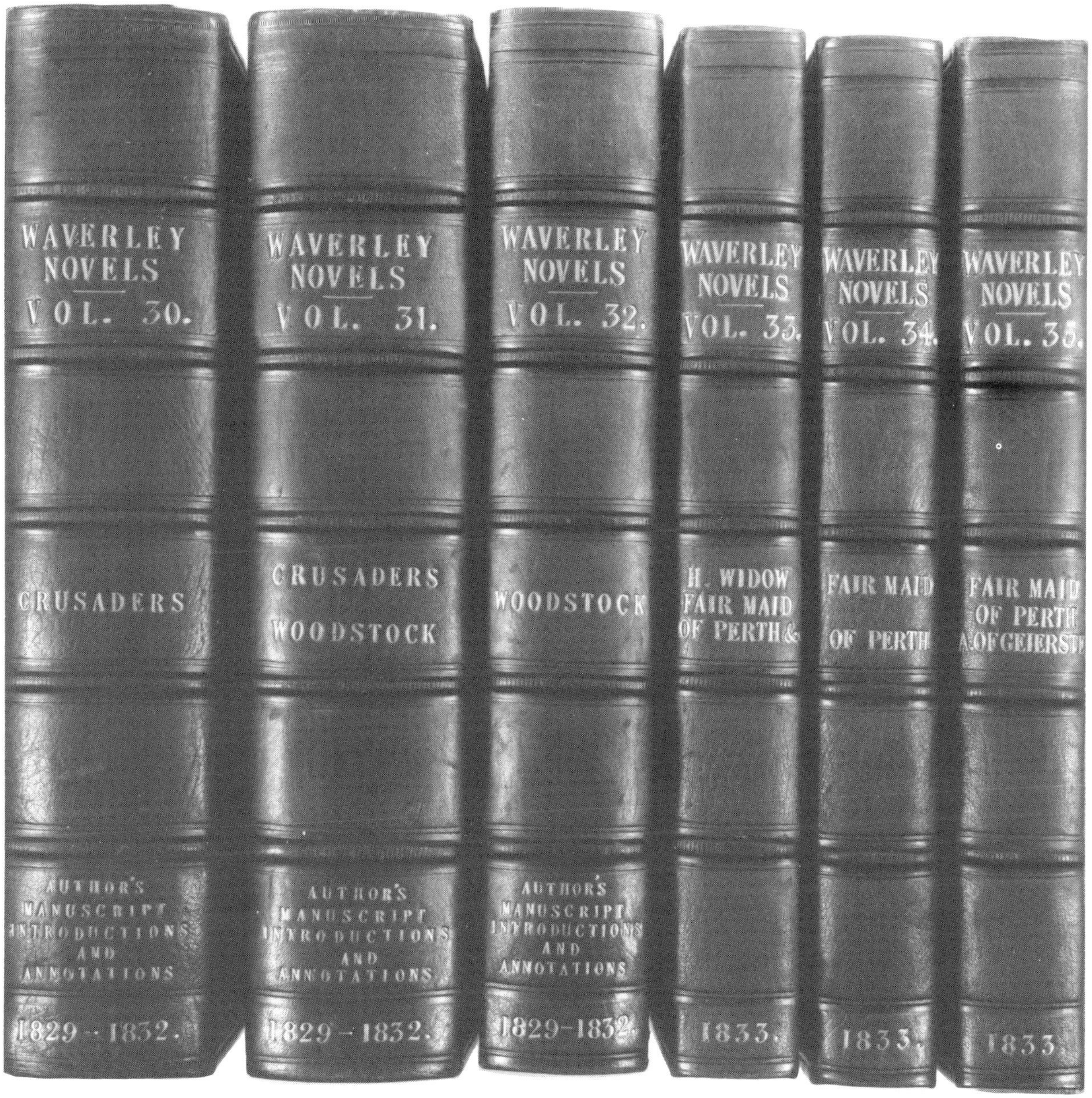

PLATE 2
The spines of six volumes of the Interleaved Set showing the clear difference between the interleaved and annotated volumes used by Scott in the preparation of the Magnum Opus edition, and the supplementary volumes added by Cadell after the author's death in order to complete the set.

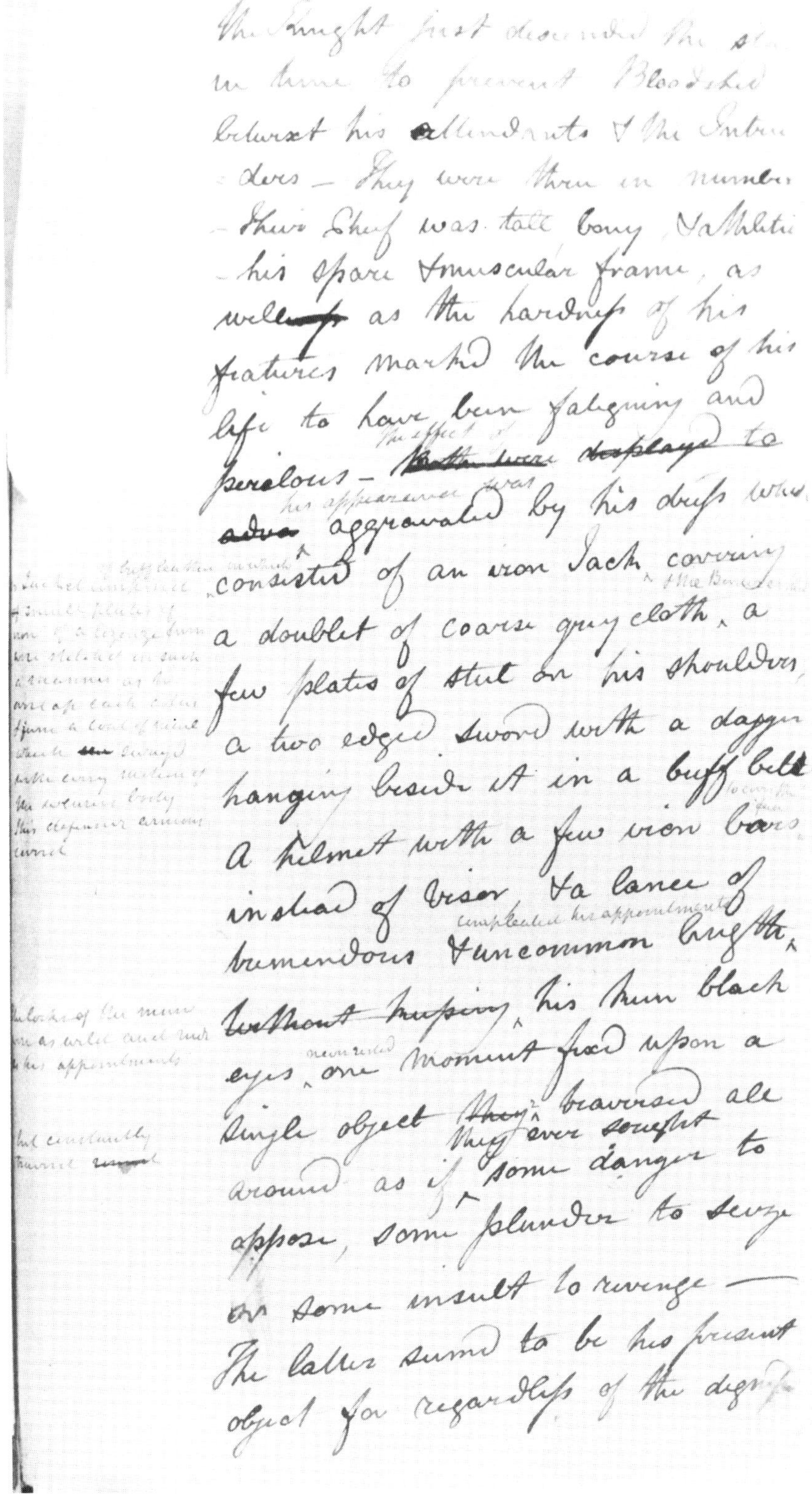
The Knight first descended the s[tair]
in time to prevent Bloodshed
betwixt his attendants & the Intru-
-ders — They were three in number
— Their Chief was tall bony & athletic
— his spare & muscular frame, as
well as the hardness of his
features marked the course of his
life to have been fatiguing and
perilous —
aggravated by his dress which
consisted of an iron Jack covering
a doublet of coarse grey cloth, a
few plates of steel on his shoulders,
a two edged sword with a dagger
hanging beside it in a buff belt
A helmet with a few iron bars
instead of visor & a lance of
tremendous & uncommon length,
without keeping his keen black
eyes one moment fixed upon a
single object they traversed all
around as if some danger to
oppose, some plunder to seize
or some insult to revenge —
The latter seemed to be his present
object for regardless of the dignity

PLATE 3 Vol. I *WAVERLEY*

A leaf of the fragment 'Thomas the Rhymer', in Scott's early hand and with alterations in his later hand, bound into the first volume of the Interleaved Set as part of the general introductory material in that volume. In the General Preface to the Magnum edition, Scott alluded to this, and to another fragment entitled 'The Lord of Ennerdale', as works which might have some interest for the public as 'the first attempts at romantic composition by an author, who has since written so much in that department'. He went on to suggest of these fragments that 'there may be some curiosity attached to them, as to the first etchings of a plate, which are accounted interesting by those who have, in any degree, been interested in the more finished works of the artist'. However, what Scott does not explain, either in the General Preface itself or in its Appendix where the fragment is printed, is that the text given there had been edited upwards of a quarter of a century after its original composition. (1. General Preface xlvi–xlvii)

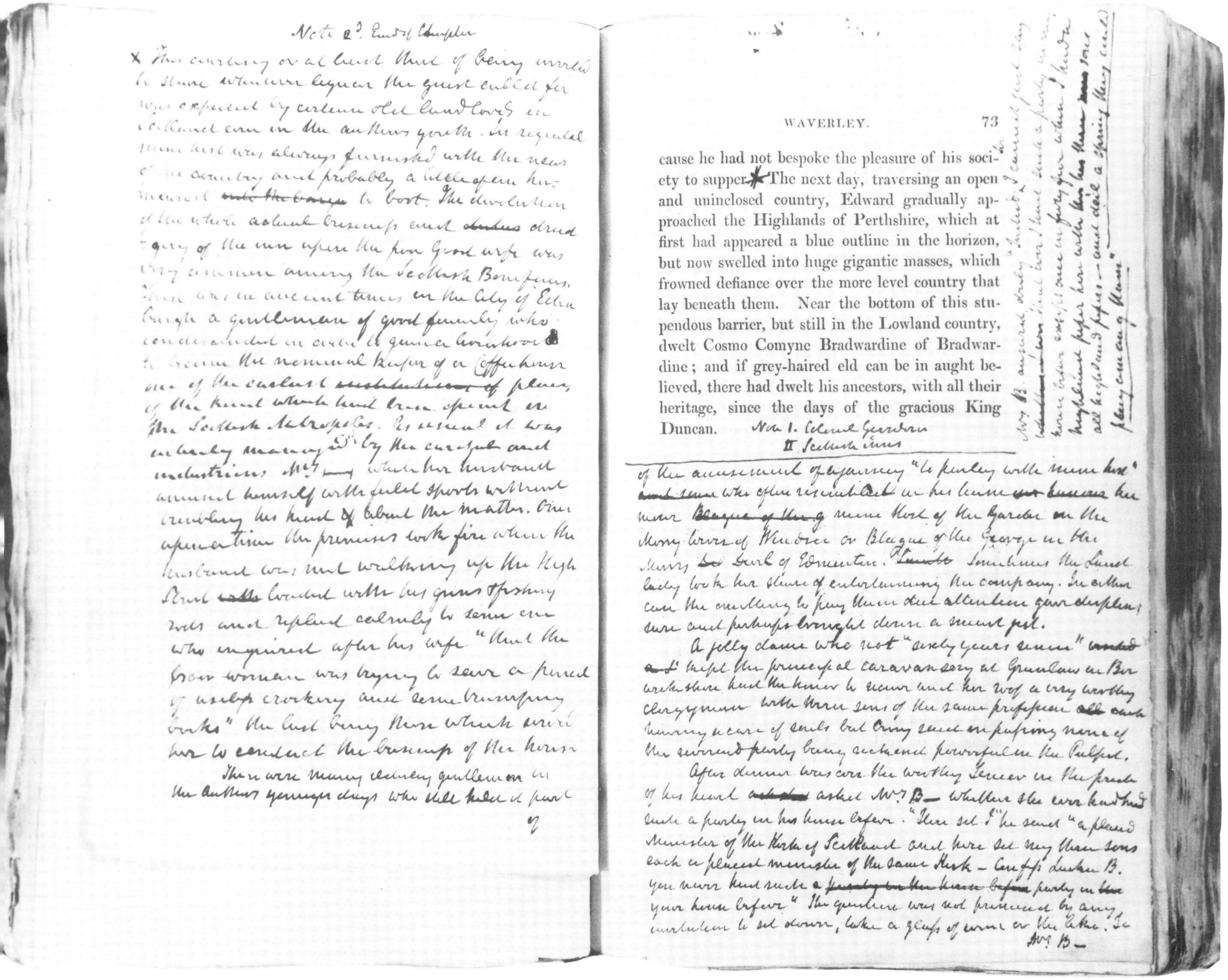

WAVERLEY. 73

cause he had not bespoke the pleasure of his society to supper.* The next day, traversing an open and uninclosed country, Edward gradually approached the Highlands of Perthshire, which at first had appeared a blue outline in the horizon, but now swelled into huge gigantic masses, which frowned defiance over the more level country that lay beneath them. Near the bottom of this stupendous barrier, but still in the Lowland country, dwelt Cosmo Comyne Bradwardine of Bradwardine; and if grey-haired eld can be in aught believed, there had dwelt his ancestors, with all their heritage, since the days of the gracious King Duncan.

PLATE 4 Vol. I *WAVERLEY*

An opening in the first volume of *Waverley* showing Scott's use of an interleaf, the white space on a page at the conclusion of a chapter, and in addition the margin of that page, for a long note on Scottish Inns. Immediately below the text on p.73 is the instruction to the printer to take in at that point material for another note, itself written on an interleaf earlier in the volume. The note illustrated here was therefore to be the second lengthy passage appended to a very short chapter. (1. 71: text; 73–74: note ii)

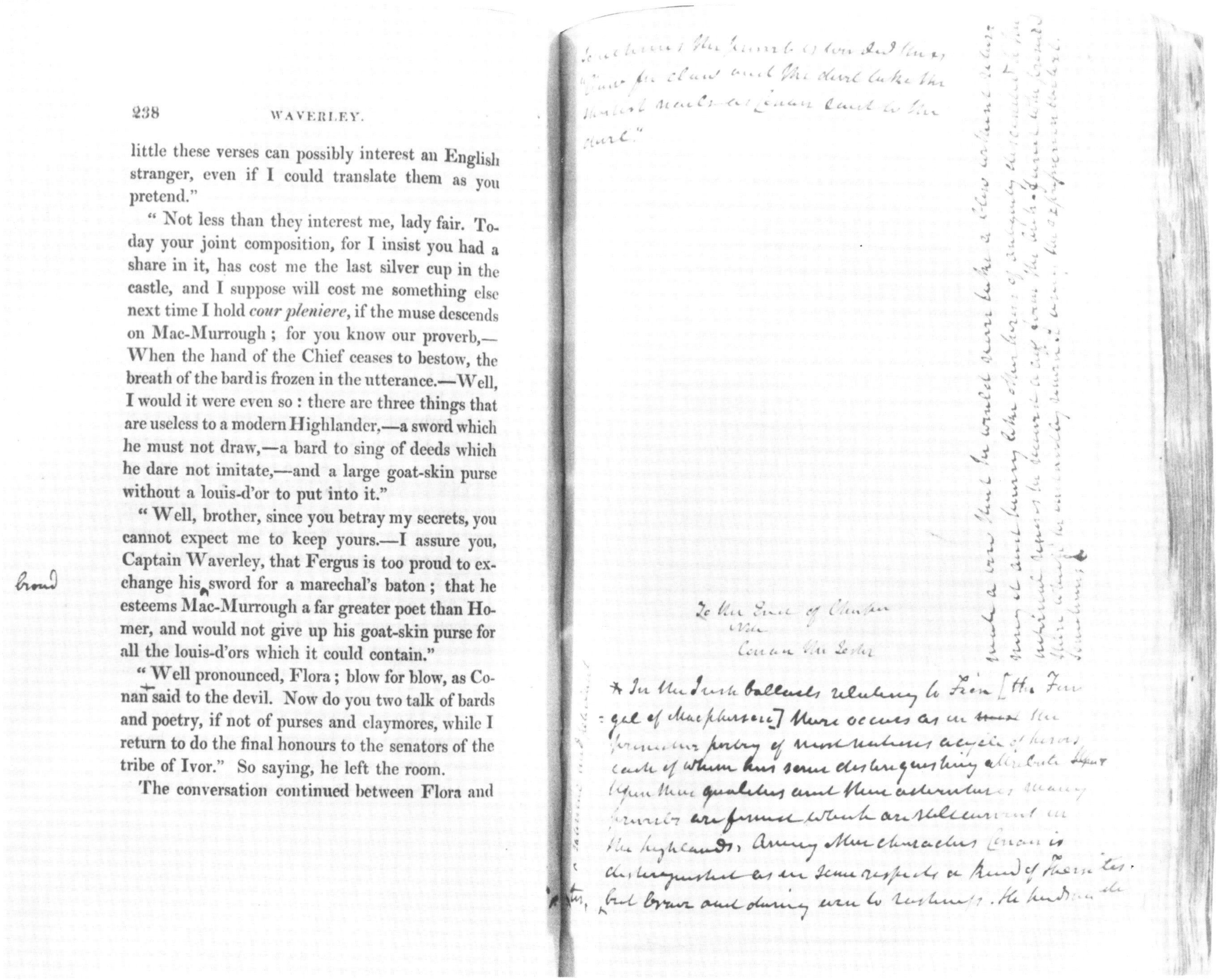

238 WAVERLEY.

little these verses can possibly interest an English stranger, even if I could translate them as you pretend."

"Not less than they interest me, lady fair. To-day your joint composition, for I insist you had a share in it, has cost me the last silver cup in the castle, and I suppose will cost me something else next time I hold *cour pleniere*, if the muse descends on Mac-Murrough; for you know our proverb,—When the hand of the Chief ceases to bestow, the breath of the bard is frozen in the utterance.—Well, I would it were even so: there are three things that are useless to a modern Highlander,—a sword which he must not draw,—a bard to sing of deeds which he dare not imitate,—and a large goat-skin purse without a louis-d'or to put into it."

"Well, brother, since you betray my secrets, you cannot expect me to keep yours.—I assure you, Captain Waverley, that Fergus is too proud to exchange his broad sword for a marechal's baton; that he esteems Mac-Murrough a far greater poet than Homer, and would not give up his goat-skin purse for all the louis-d'ors which it could contain."

"Well pronounced, Flora; blow for blow, as Conan said to the devil. Now do you two talk of bards and poetry, if not of purses and claymores, while I return to do the final honours to the senators of the tribe of Ivor." So saying, he left the room.

The conversation continued between Flora and

Sometimes the proverb is worded thus "Claw for claw and the devil take the shortest nails as Conan said to the devil."

To the End of Chapter

* In the Irish ballads relating to Fion [the Fingal of Macpherson] there occurs as in the primitive poetry of most nations a cycle of heroes each of whom has some distinguishing attribute. Upon these qualities and their adventures many proverbs are formed which are still current in the highlands. Among these characters Conan is distinguished as in some respects a kind of Thersites but brave and daring even to rashness. He had made

PLATE 5 Vol. I *WAVERLEY*

A passing allusion to Conan by Fergus MacIvor allows Scott to include a note on Irish ballads and folklore at the end of a chapter entitled 'Highland Minstrelsy'. The note begins at the foot of the interleaf, continues up the edge, and is concluded at the top. In the text opposite, the word 'sword' in a speech of Flora MacIvor is expanded to read 'broadsword', thus providing a better balance for the 'marechal's baton' which follows. (1. 229: text; 241: note i)

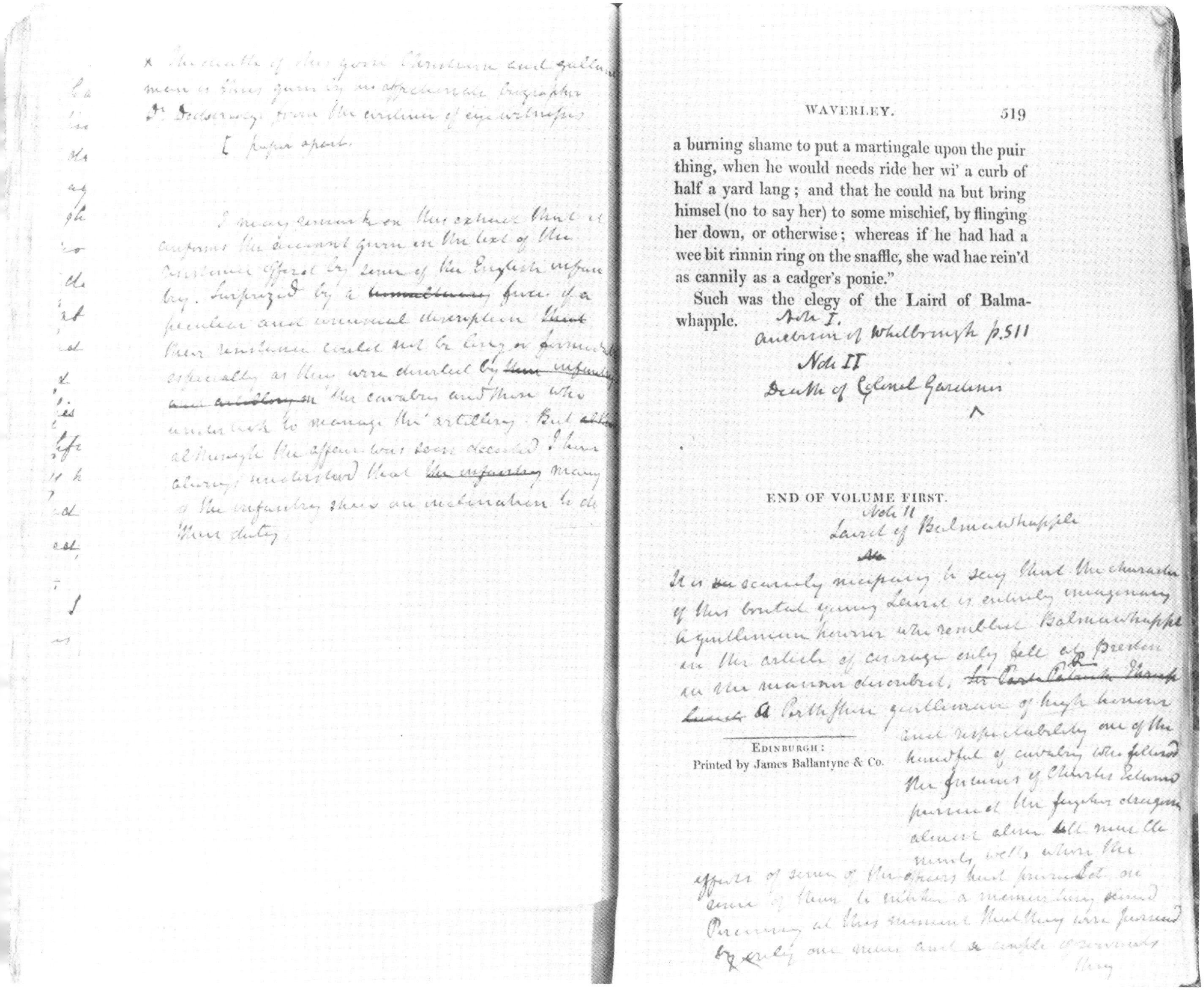
* The death of this good Christian and gallant man is thus given by his affectionate biographer Dr Doddridge from the evidence of eyewitnesses

[paper apart.

I may remark on this extract that it confirms the account given in the text of the resistance offered by some of the English infantry. Surprized by a force of a peculiar and unusual description their resistance could not be long or formidable especially as they were deserted by the cavalry and those who undertook to manage the artillery. But although the affair was soon decided I have always understood that many of the infantry shewd an inclination to do their duty.

WAVERLEY. 519

a burning shame to put a martingale upon the puir thing, when he would needs ride her wi' a curb of half a yard lang; and that he could na but bring himsel (no to say her) to some mischief, by flinging her down, or otherwise; whereas if he had had a wee bit rinnin ring on the snaffle, she wad hae rein'd as cannily as a cadger's ponie."

Such was the elegy of the Laird of Balmawhapple.

Note I. Anderson of Whitbrough p.511

Note II Death of Colonel Gardiner ^

END OF VOLUME FIRST.

Note II Laird of Balmawhapple

It is scarcely necessary to say that the character of this brutal young Laird is entirely imaginary. A gentleman however who resembled Balmawhapple in the article of courage only fell at Preston in the manner described. A Perthshire gentleman of high honour and respectability one of the handful of cavalry who followed the fortunes of Charles Edward pursued the fugitive dragoons almost alone till near the town of [illegible] when the efforts of some of the officers had prevailed on some of them to make a momentary stand. Perceiving at this moment that they were pursued by only one man and a couple of servants they

EDINBURGH:
Printed by James Ballantyne & Co.

PLATE 6 Vol. I *WAVERLEY*

In the Magnum edition three notes were supplied to illustrate the chapter describing the battle of Prestonpans. At the chapter end Scott indicates the order in which these notes should be arranged. Copy for the first note was written on an interleaf a few pages before. A long quotation (set out on a paper apart) was to link the beginning and end of the second note on the death of Colonel Gardiner, which passages are set out on the interleaf opposite p. 519. The beginning of the third note occupies the white space below the text and round the colophon at the end of the volume. (2. 173–75: notes ii–iii)

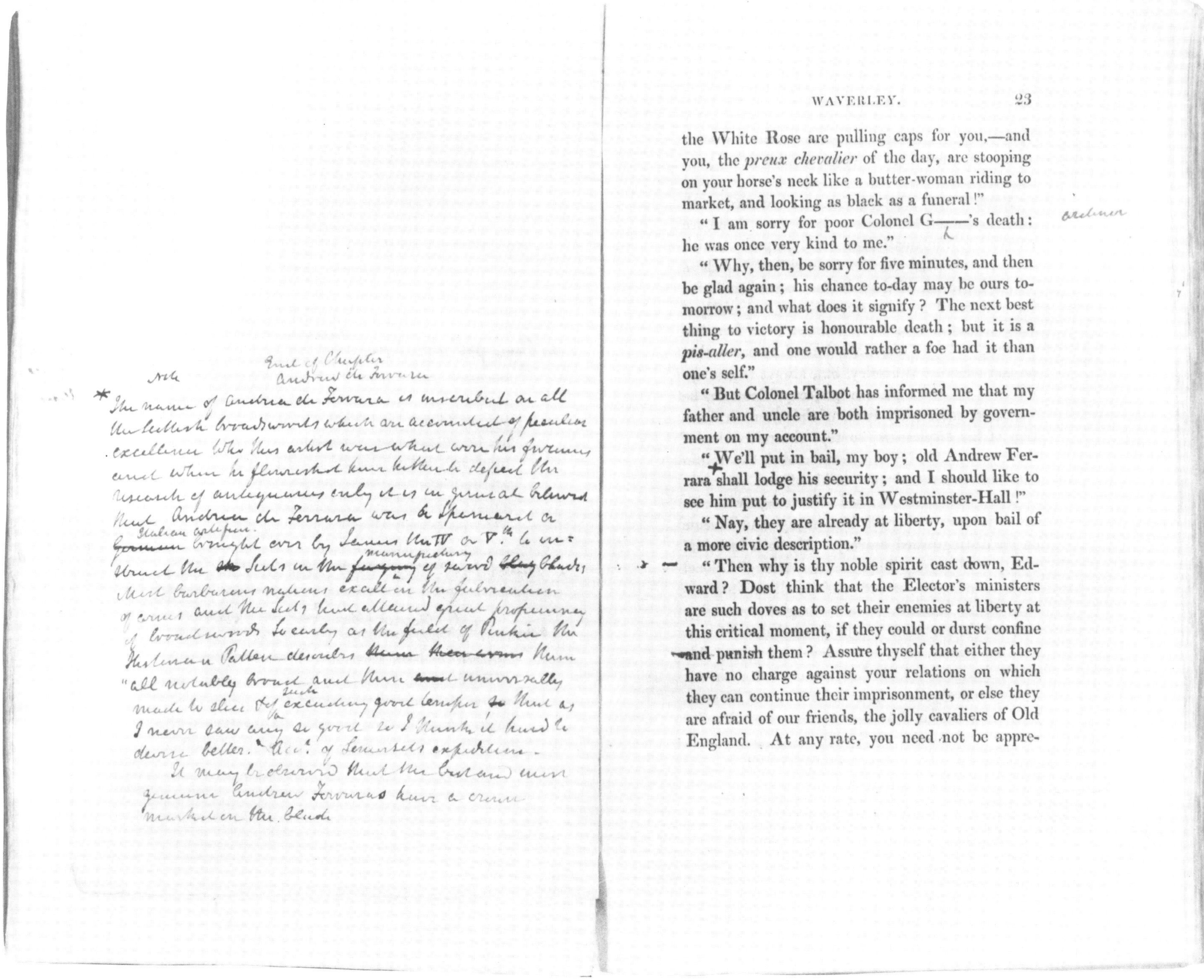

Note
End of Chapter
Andrew de Ferrara
* The name of Andrea de Ferrara is inscribed on all the Scottish broadswords which are accounted of peculiar excellence. Who this artist was what were his fortunes and when he flourished have hitherto defied the research of antiquaries only it is in general believed that Andrea de Ferrara was a Spaniard or Italian artificer brought over by James IV or Vth to instruct the Scots in the manufacturing of sword blades; Most barbarous nations excell in the fabrication of arms and the Scots had attained great proficiency in broadswords so early as the field of Pinkie the historian Patten describes them "all notably broad and thin universally made to slice & of such exceeding good temper that as I never saw any so good so I think it hard to devise better." Acct. of Somersets expedition.
It may be observed that the best and most genuine Andrew Ferraras have a crown marked on the blade
WAVERLEY. 23
the White Rose are pulling caps for you,—and you, the *preux chevalier* of the day, are stooping on your horse's neck like a butter-woman riding to market, and looking as black as a funeral!"
"I am sorry for poor Colonel G——'s death: he was once very kind to me."
Gardiner
"Why, then, be sorry for five minutes, and then be glad again; his chance to-day may be ours to-morrow; and what does it signify? The next best thing to victory is honourable death; but it is a *pis-aller*, and one would rather a foe had it than one's self."
"But Colonel Talbot has informed me that my father and uncle are both imprisoned by government on my account."
"We'll put in bail, my boy; old Andrew Ferrara* shall lodge his security; and I should like to see him put to justify it in Westminster-Hall!"
"Nay, they are already at liberty, upon bail of a more civic description."
"Then why is thy noble spirit cast down, Edward? Dost think that the Elector's ministers are such doves as to set their enemies at liberty at this critical moment, if they could or durst confine and punish them? Assure thyself that either they have no charge against your relations on which they can continue their imprisonment, or else they are afraid of our friends, the jolly cavaliers of Old England. At any rate, you need not be appre-

PLATE 7 Vol. II *WAVERLEY*
What Scott called 'the research of antiquaries' furnished a good deal of material for the annotation of the Magnum edition. Here a note on Scottish broadswords is added to explain an allusion to 'old Andrew Ferrara'. (2. 201)

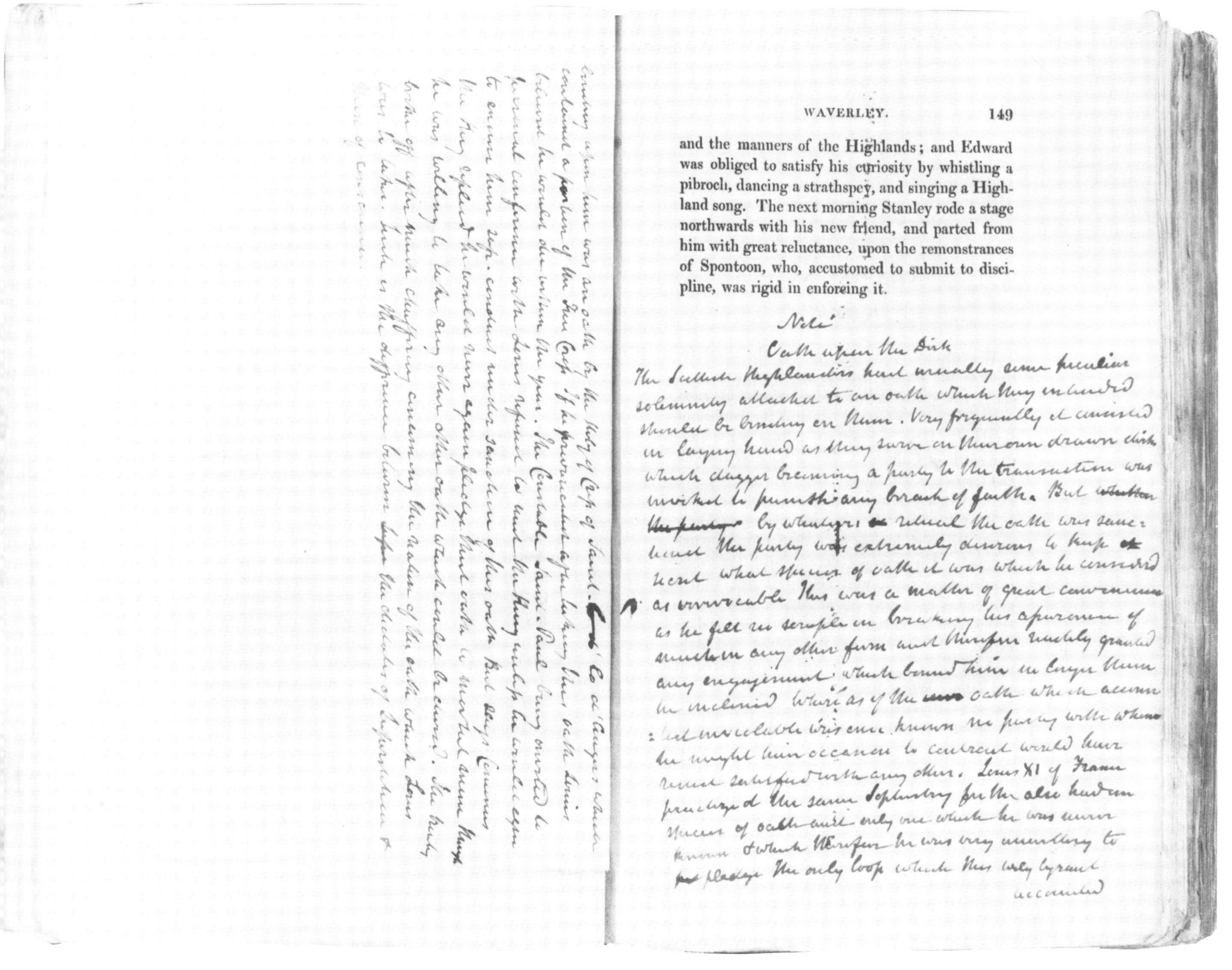

WAVERLEY. 149

and the manners of the Highlands; and Edward was obliged to satisfy his curiosity by whistling a pibroch, dancing a strathspey, and singing a Highland song. The next morning Stanley rode a stage northwards with his new friend, and parted from him with great reluctance, upon the remonstrances of Spontoon, who, accustomed to submit to discipline, was rigid in enforcing it.

Note

Oath upon the Dirk

The Scottish Highlanders had usually some peculiar solemnity attached to an oath which they intended should be binding on them. Very frequently it consisted in laying hand as they swore on their own drawn dirk which dagger becoming a party to the transaction was invoked to punish any breach of faith. But ~~whatever~~ ~~the form~~ by whatever ritual the oath was sanctioned the party was extremely desirous to keep secret what species of oath it was which he considered as inviolable. This was a matter of great convenience as he felt no scruple in breaking his assurance of another in any other form and therefore readily granted any engagement which bound him no longer than he inclined. Whereas if the oath which he accounted inviolable was once known the party with whom he might have occasion to contract would have rested satisfied with any other. Louis XI of France practised the same sophistry for he also had one species of oath and only one which he was never known & which therefore he was very unwilling to pledge. The only loop which this wily tyrant accounted binding upon him was an oath by the Holy Cross of Saint Lo d'Angers which contained a portion of the True Cross. If he prevaricated after taking this oath he would die within the year. The Constable Saint Paul being invited to personal conference with Louis refused to trust the King unless he would ensure him safe conduct under sanction of this oath. But the King replied that he would never again pledge it to any man but was willing to take any other oath which could be devised. The treaty broke off after much chaffering concerning the nature of the oath which Louis was to take. Such is the difference between the dictates of superstition & those of conscience.

PLATE 8 Vol. II *WAVERLEY*

As with broadswords, so with dirks; though in this case mention of another traditional Highland weapon is made the excuse for a note not on the history and use of the dirk itself, but rather for a discussion of the taking, keeping and breaking of oaths in Highland and other societies. (2. 318)

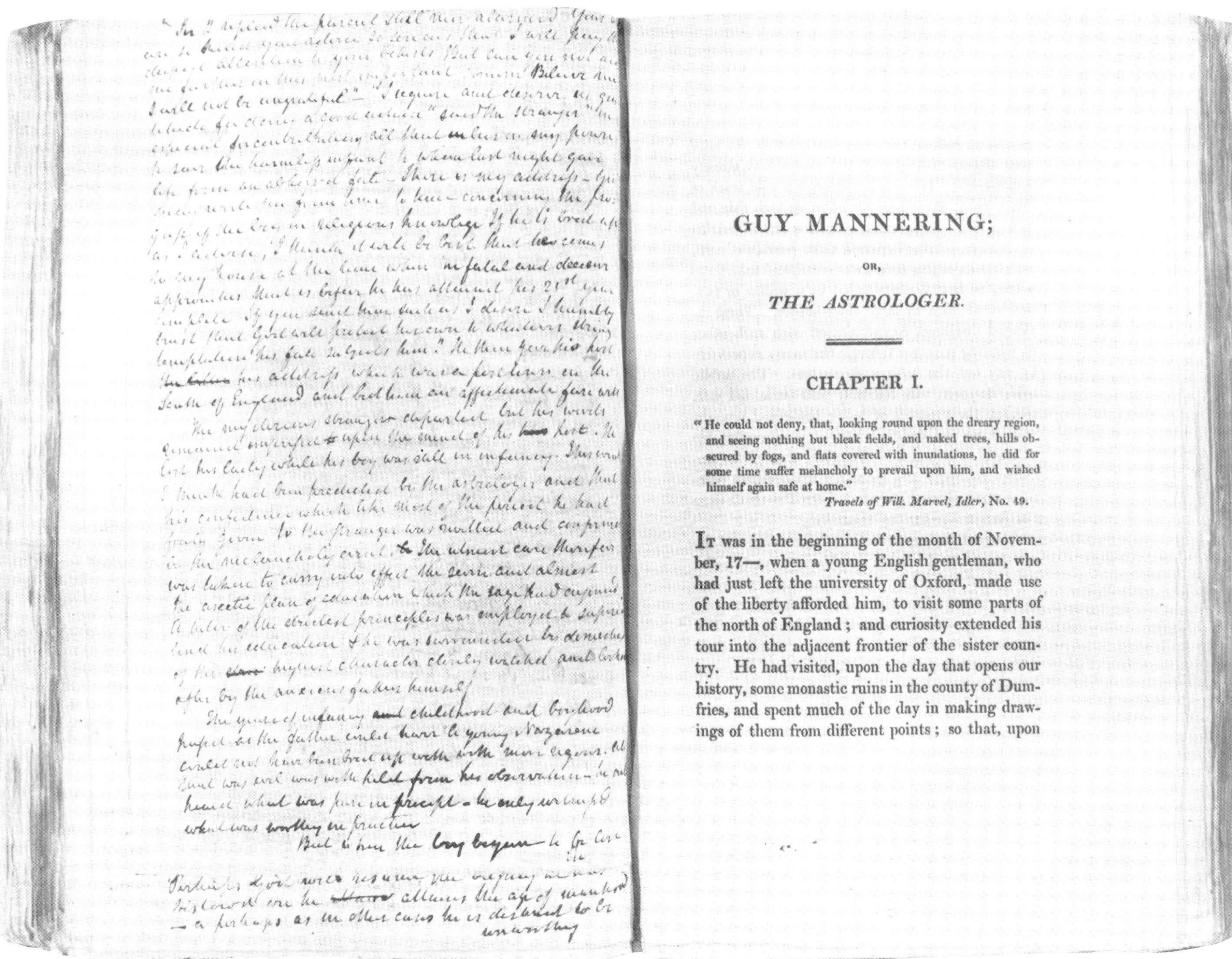

GUY MANNERING;

OR,

THE ASTROLOGER.

CHAPTER I.

"He could not deny, that, looking round upon the dreary region, and seeing nothing but bleak fields, and naked trees, hills obscured by fogs, and flats covered with inundations, he did for some time suffer melancholy to prevail upon him, and wished himself again safe at home."

Travels of Will. Marvel, Idler, No. 49.

It was in the beginning of the month of November, 17—, when a young English gentleman, who had just left the university of Oxford, made use of the liberty afforded him, to visit some parts of the north of England; and curiosity extended his tour into the adjacent frontier of the sister country. He had visited, upon the day that opens our history, some monastic ruins in the county of Dumfries, and spent much of the day in making drawings of them from different points; so that, upon

PLATE 9 Vol. II *GUY MANNERING*

A portion of the Introduction to the Magnum edition of *Guy Mannering*. This is written on interleaves and on blank pages in a volume of the 1822 *Novels and Tales* series. The section reproduced is part of the story of the astrologer and the 'doomed individual' whose horoscope the former has cast, which tale had been told to Scott by an old servant of his father's, and which was the germ of the present novel. (3. vi–vii)

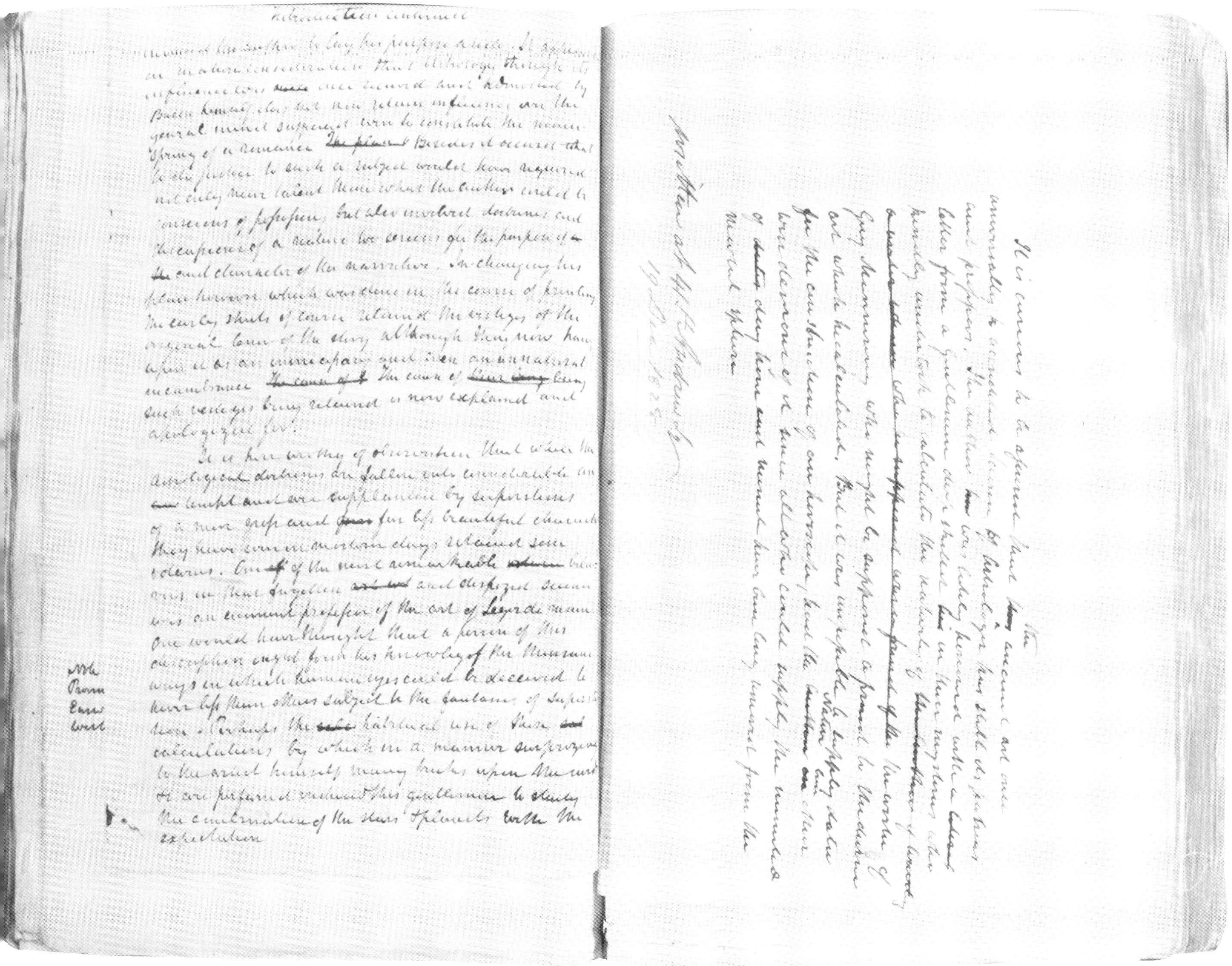

PLATE 10 Vol. II *GUY MANNERING*

An astrologer of the 1820s had offered to cast the horoscope of Scott as author of *Guy Mannering; or, The Astrologer*. On 19 December 1828 in Robert Cadell's shop at 41 St Andrew Square, Edinburgh, Scott wrote a brief account of this example of contemporary astrological practice. The paper bearing these observations, docketed by Cadell with the time and place of composition, was in due course incorporated in the Introduction to the novel in the Magnum edition. The actual document was carefully preserved, and ultimately bound into the Interleaved Set with the other materials accumulated for the new edition. (3. xviii–xix)

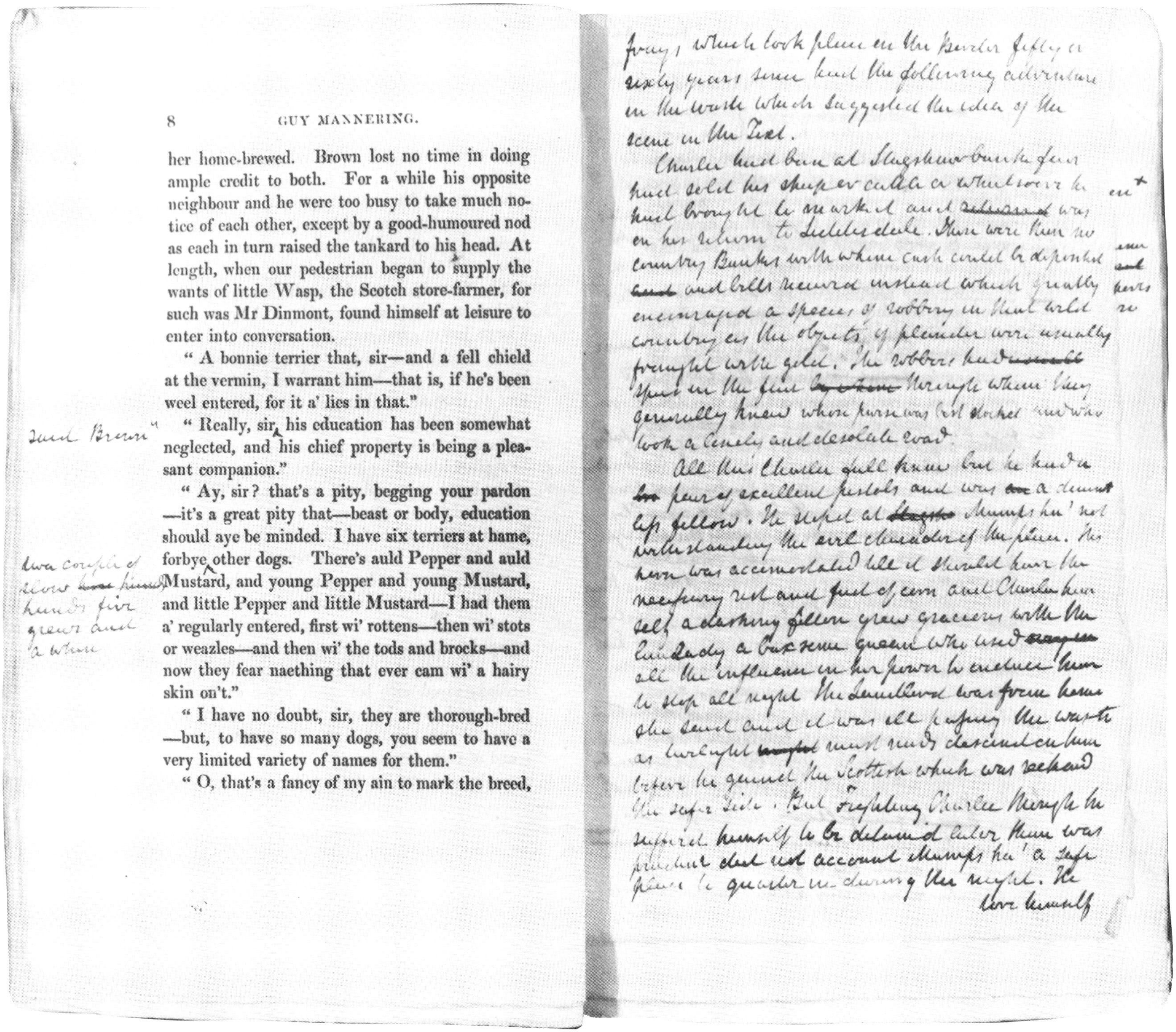
8 GUY MANNERING.

her home-brewed. Brown lost no time in doing ample credit to both. For a while his opposite neighbour and he were too busy to take much notice of each other, except by a good-humoured nod as each in turn raised the tankard to his head. At length, when our pedestrian began to supply the wants of little Wasp, the Scotch store-farmer, for such was Mr Dinmont, found himself at leisure to enter into conversation.

"A bonnie terrier that, sir—and a fell chield at the vermin, I warrant him—that is, if he's been weel entered, for it a' lies in that."

"Really, sir, his education has been somewhat neglected, and his chief property is being a pleasant companion."

"Ay, sir? that's a pity, begging your pardon—it's a great pity that—beast or body, education should aye be minded. I have six terriers at hame, forbye other dogs. There's auld Pepper and auld Mustard, and young Pepper and young Mustard, and little Pepper and little Mustard—I had them a' regularly entered, first wi' rottens—then wi' stots or weazles—and then wi' the tods and brocks—and now they fear naething that ever cam wi' a hairy skin on't."

"I have no doubt, sir, they are thorough-bred—but, to have so many dogs, you seem to have a very limited variety of names for them."

"O, that's a fancy of my ain to mark the breed,

said Brown"

twa couple of slow ~~hou~~ hunds hunds five grews and a whin

fray which took place on the Border fifty or sixty years since had the following adventure in the waste which suggested the idea of the scene in the text.

Charlie had been at Stagshaw Bank fair had sold his sheep or cattle or whatever he had brought to market and ~~released~~ was on his return to Liddesdale. There were then no country Banks where cash could be deposited ~~and~~ and bills received instead which greatly encouraged a species of robbery in that wild country as the objects of plunder were usually fraught with gold. The robbers had ~~[illegible]~~ spies in the fair ~~[illegible]~~ through whom they generally knew whose purse was best stocked and who took a lonely and desolate road.

All this Charlie full knew but he had a ~~[illegible]~~ pair of excellent pistols and was ~~[illegible]~~ a dumb-up fellow. He stopt at ~~Stag~~ Mumps ha' notwithstanding the evil character of the place. His horse was accomodated where it should have the necessary rest and feed of corn and Charlie himself a dashing fellow grew gracious with the landlady a buxom quean who used ~~[illegible]~~ all the influence in her power to induce him to stop all night. The landlord was from home she said and it was ill passing the waste as twilight ~~[illegible]~~ must needs descend on him before he gained the Scottish which was reckond the safer side. But Fighting Charlie though he suffered himself to be detained later than was prudent did not account Mumps ha' a safe place to quarter in during the night. He tore himself

in* and bars so

PLATE 11 Vol. III *GUY MANNERING*

The interchange on canine matters between Brown [Harry Bertram] and Dandie Dinmont as they eat at Mumps's Ha' inn is made more lively by the introduction of colourful Scots dialect words into the latter's speech.

The interleaf opposite bears part of a long note on Mumps's Ha' and its denizens, which was taken in at the end of the chapter. (3. 221: text; 228–29: note)

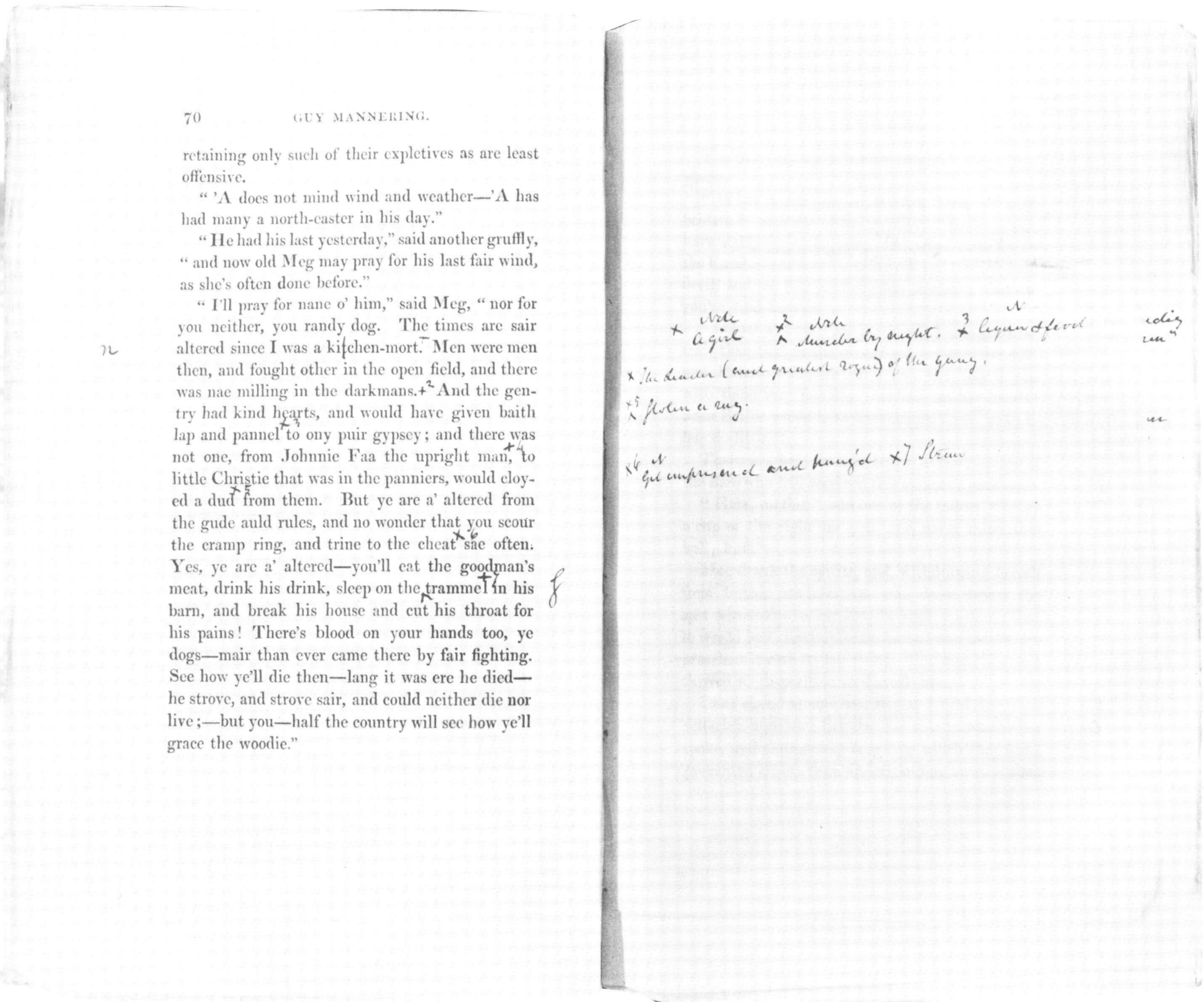

70 GUY MANNERING.

retaining only such of their expletives as are least offensive.

" 'A does not mind wind and weather—'A has had many a north-easter in his day."

" He had his last yesterday," said another gruffly, " and now old Meg may pray for his last fair wind, as she's often done before."

" I'll pray for nane o' him," said Meg, " nor for you neither, you randy dog. The times are sair altered since I was a kitchen-mort. Men were men then, and fought other in the open field, and there was nae milling in the darkmans. And the gentry had kind hearts, and would have given baith lap and pannel to ony puir gypsey; and there was not one, from Johnnie Faa the upright man, to little Christie that was in the panniers, would cloyed a dud from them. But ye are a' altered from the gude auld rules, and no wonder that you scour the cramp ring, and trine to the cheat sae often. Yes, ye are a' altered—you'll eat the goodman's meat, drink his drink, sleep on the strammel in his barn, and break his house and cut his throat for his pains! There's blood on your hands too, ye dogs—mair than ever came there by fair fighting. See how ye'll die then—lang it was ere he died—he strove, and strove sair, and could neither die nor live;—but you—half the country will see how ye'll grace the woodie."

× Note a girl ×2 Note Murder by night. ×3 ...

× The Leader (and greatest rogue) of the gang.

×5 Stolen a rag.

×6 N Get imprisoned and hang'd ×7 Straw

PLATE 12 Vol. III *GUY MANNERING*

An example of Scott helping the reader of the new edition by glossing difficult Scots words in a speech of Meg Merrilies. In the interleaved copy these words are numbered, but in the Magnum edition volume they appear grouped at the foot of the page and keyed to the text by symbols. (3. 286)

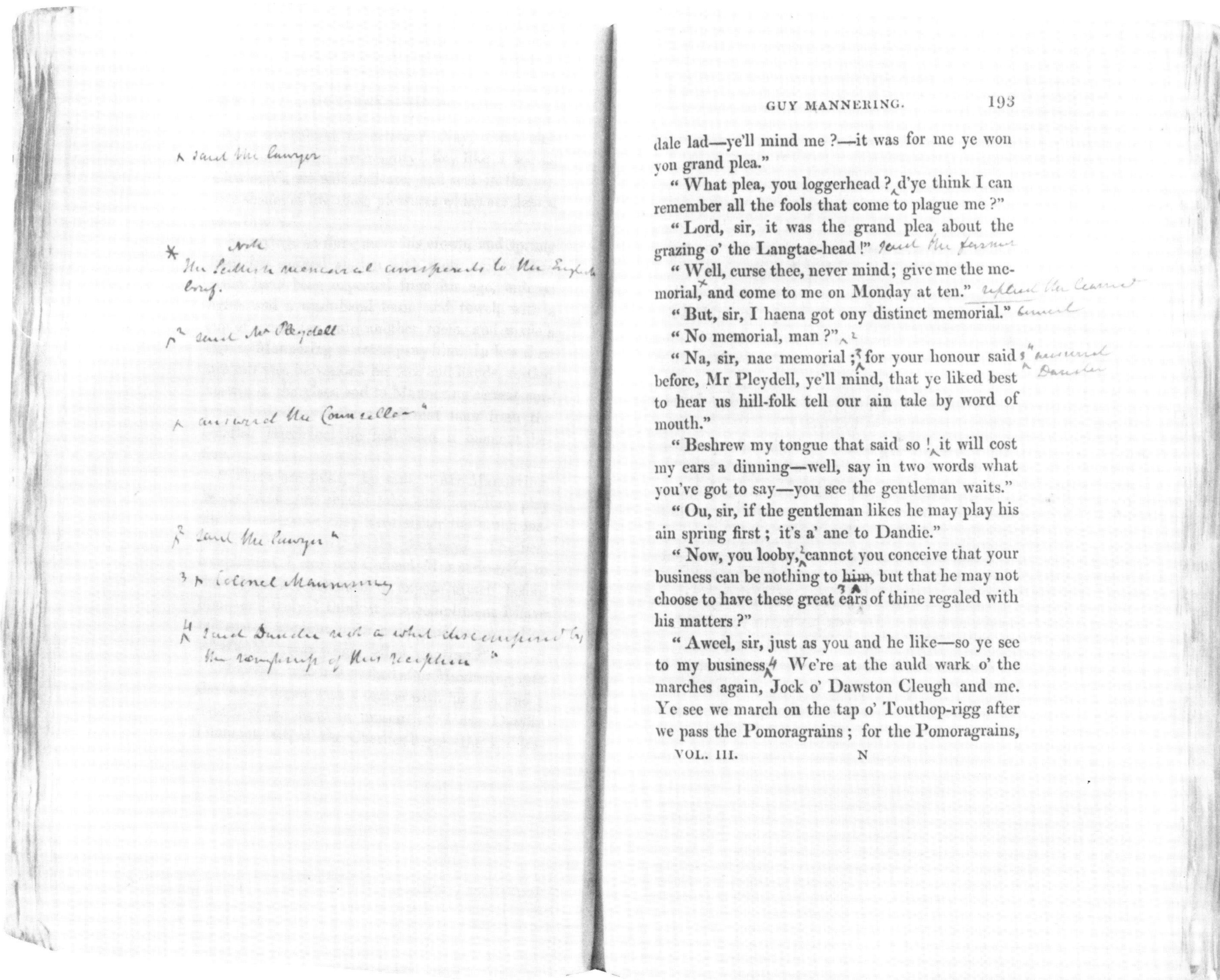

GUY MANNERING. 193

dale lad—ye'll mind me ?—it was for me ye won yon grand plea."

"What plea, you loggerhead ? d'ye think I can remember all the fools that come to plague me ?"

"Lord, sir, it was the grand plea about the grazing o' the Langtae-head !"

"Well, curse thee, never mind; give me the memorial, and come to me on Monday at ten."

"But, sir, I haena got ony distinct memorial."

"No memorial, man ?"

"Na, sir, nae memorial ; for your honour said before, Mr Pleydell, ye'll mind, that ye liked best to hear us hill-folk tell our ain tale by word of mouth."

"Beshrew my tongue that said so ! it will cost my ears a dinning—well, say in two words what you've got to say—you see the gentleman waits."

"Ou, sir, if the gentleman likes he may play his ain spring first ; it's a' ane to Dandie."

"Now, you looby, cannot you conceive that your business can be nothing to him, but that he may not choose to have these great ears of thine regaled with his matters ?"

"Aweel, sir, just as you and he like—so ye see to my business. We're at the auld wark o' the marches again, Jock o' Dawston Cleugh and me. Ye see we march on the tap o' Touthop-rigg after we pass the Pomoragrains ; for the Pomoragrains,

VOL. III. N

PLATE 13 Vol. III *GUY MANNERING*

An instance of Scott filling in the text in a passage where there is a great deal of dialogue by the addition of formulae of the 'said so-and-so' type to speeches. The intention, of course, was to clarify the text; but the effect is to slow the pace of the dialogue and to weary the reader. (4. 88–89)

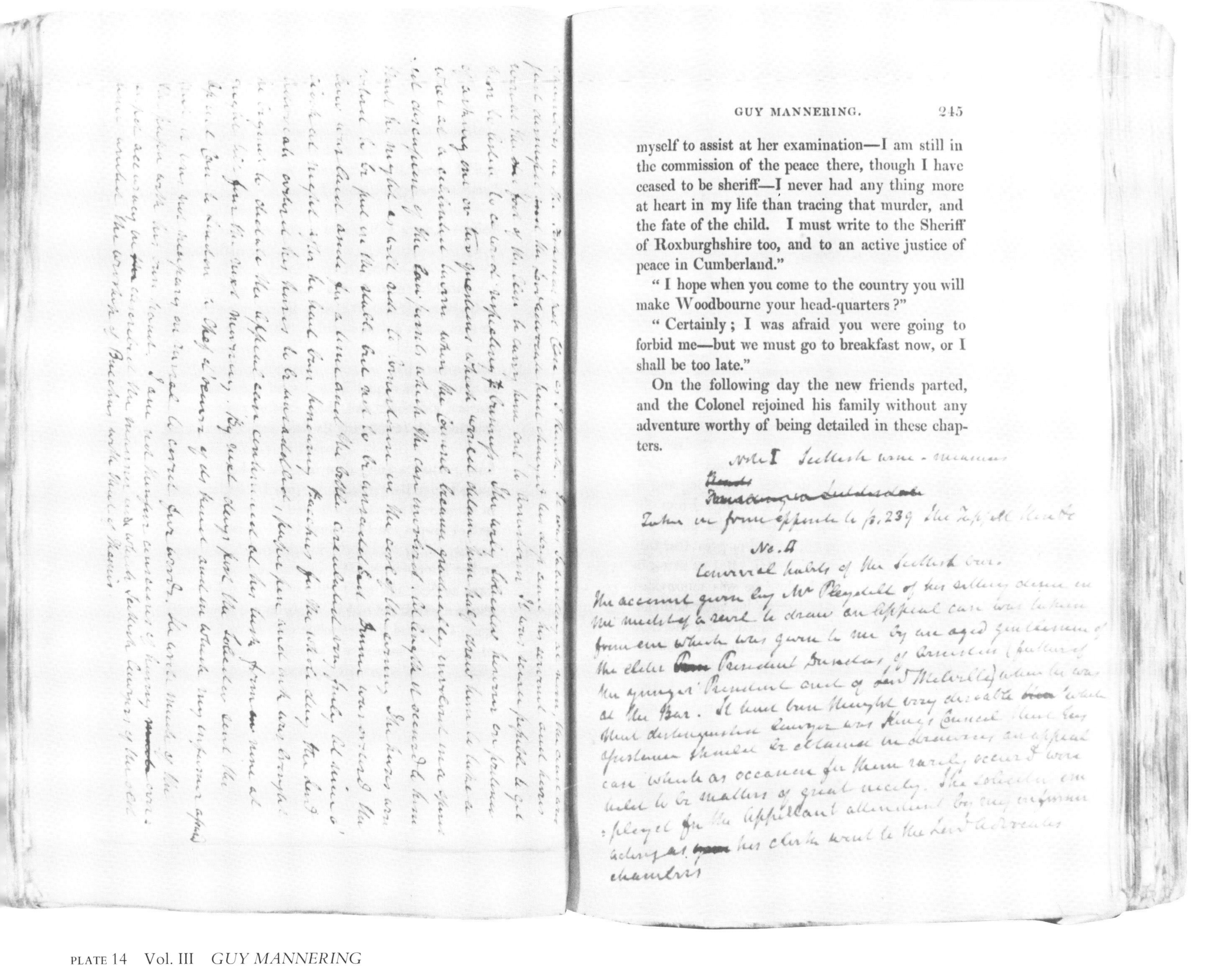

GUY MANNERING. 245

myself to assist at her examination—I am still in the commission of the peace there, though I have ceased to be sheriff—I never had any thing more at heart in my life than tracing that murder, and the fate of the child. I must write to the Sheriff of Roxburghshire too, and to an active justice of peace in Cumberland."

"I hope when you come to the country you will make Woodbourne your head-quarters?"

"Certainly; I was afraid you were going to forbid me—but we must go to breakfast now, or I shall be too late."

On the following day the new friends parted, and the Colonel rejoined his family without any adventure worthy of being detailed in these chapters.

PLATE 14 Vol. III *GUY MANNERING*

The white space at the end of a chapter is used to begin a note which is continued and concluded on the facing interleaf. Immediately below the print on p.245 is Scott's direction to the printer to take in material for another note already added on an earlier interleaf. This note was to be headed 'Scottish wine-measures', but the Magnum text has the title as 'Tappit Hen', i.e. the pewter measure itself. Both notes were occasioned by the splendid description of Pleydell's clerk, and the man's ability to draw up complicated legal documents even when far gone in drink. The second note on 'Convivial Habits of the Scottish Bar', with its delightful anecdote of a late Lord President of the Court of Session, was designed to show how Scots lawyers 'of the old time'—though the author himself had some personal knowledge of the matter—could unite 'the worship of Bacchus with that of Themis'. (4. 137–38: notes i–ii)

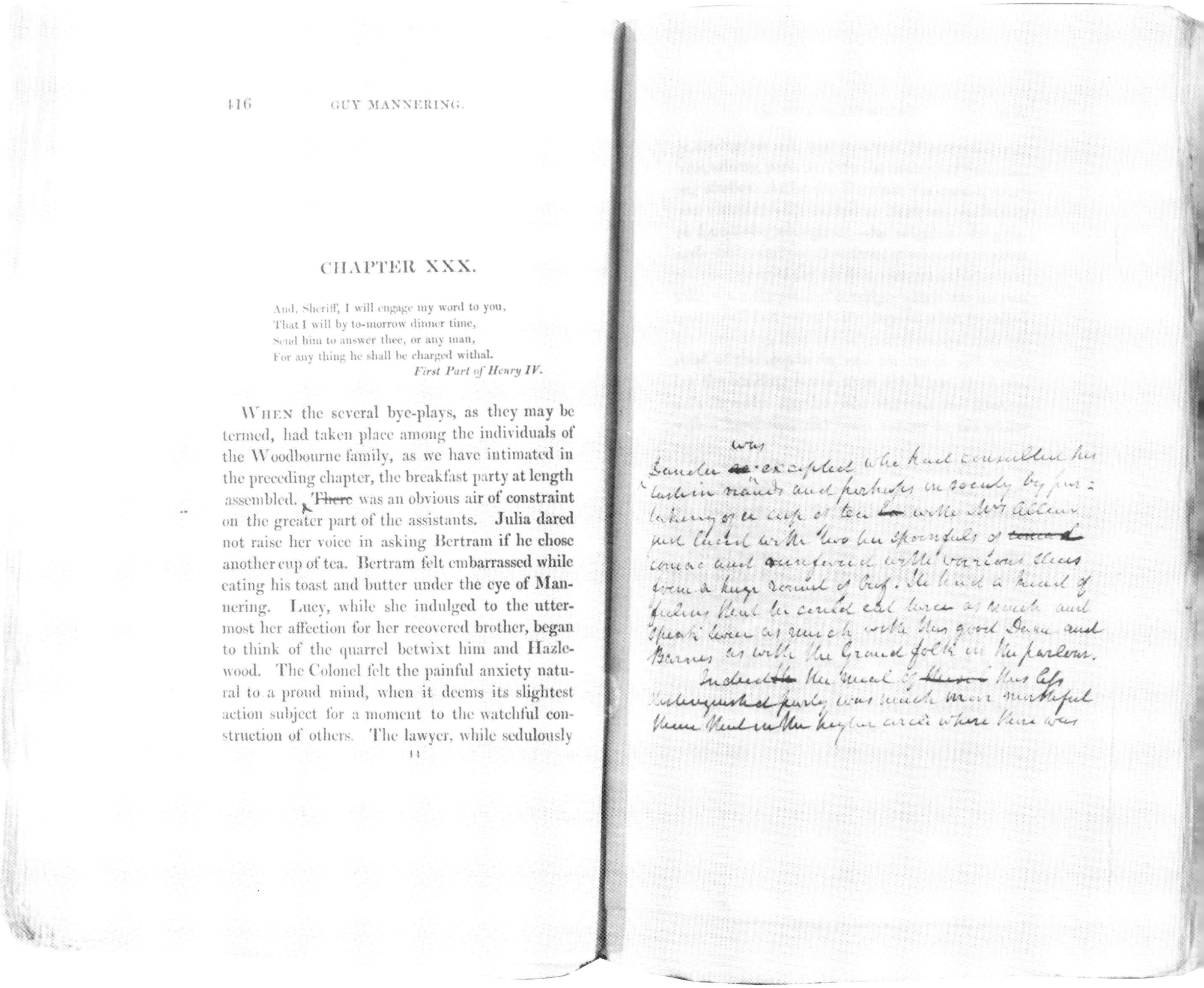

416 GUY MANNERING.

CHAPTER XXX.

And, Sheriff, I will engage my word to you,
That I will by to-morrow dinner time,
Send him to answer thee, or any man,
For any thing he shall be charged withal.
First Part of Henry IV.

When the several bye-plays, as they may be termed, had taken place among the individuals of the Woodbourne family, as we have intimated in the preceding chapter, the breakfast party at length assembled. ~~There~~ was an obvious air of constraint on the greater part of the assistants. Julia dared not raise her voice in asking Bertram if he chose another cup of tea. Bertram felt embarrassed while eating his toast and butter under the eye of Mannering. Lucy, while she indulged to the uttermost her affection for her recovered brother, began to think of the quarrel betwixt him and Hazlewood. The Colonel felt the painful anxiety natural to a proud mind, when it deems its slightest action subject for a moment to the watchful construction of others. The lawyer, while sedulously

Dandie was excepted who had consulted his
tastes in viands and perhaps in society by partaking of a cup of tea with Mrs Allan
just laced with two tea spoonfuls of
coniac and reinforced with various slices
from a huge round of beef. He had a kind of
feeling that he could eat twice as much and
speak twice as much with this good Dame and
Barnes as with the Grand folk in the parlour.
Indeed the meal of this less
distinguished party was much more mirthful
than that in the higher circle where there was

PLATE 15 Vol. III *GUY MANNERING*
Social truths are emphasised by the insertion in the text of a passage describing breakfasting arrangements more comfortable to humbler characters than had been the case implied in earlier editions of the novel. (4. 299)

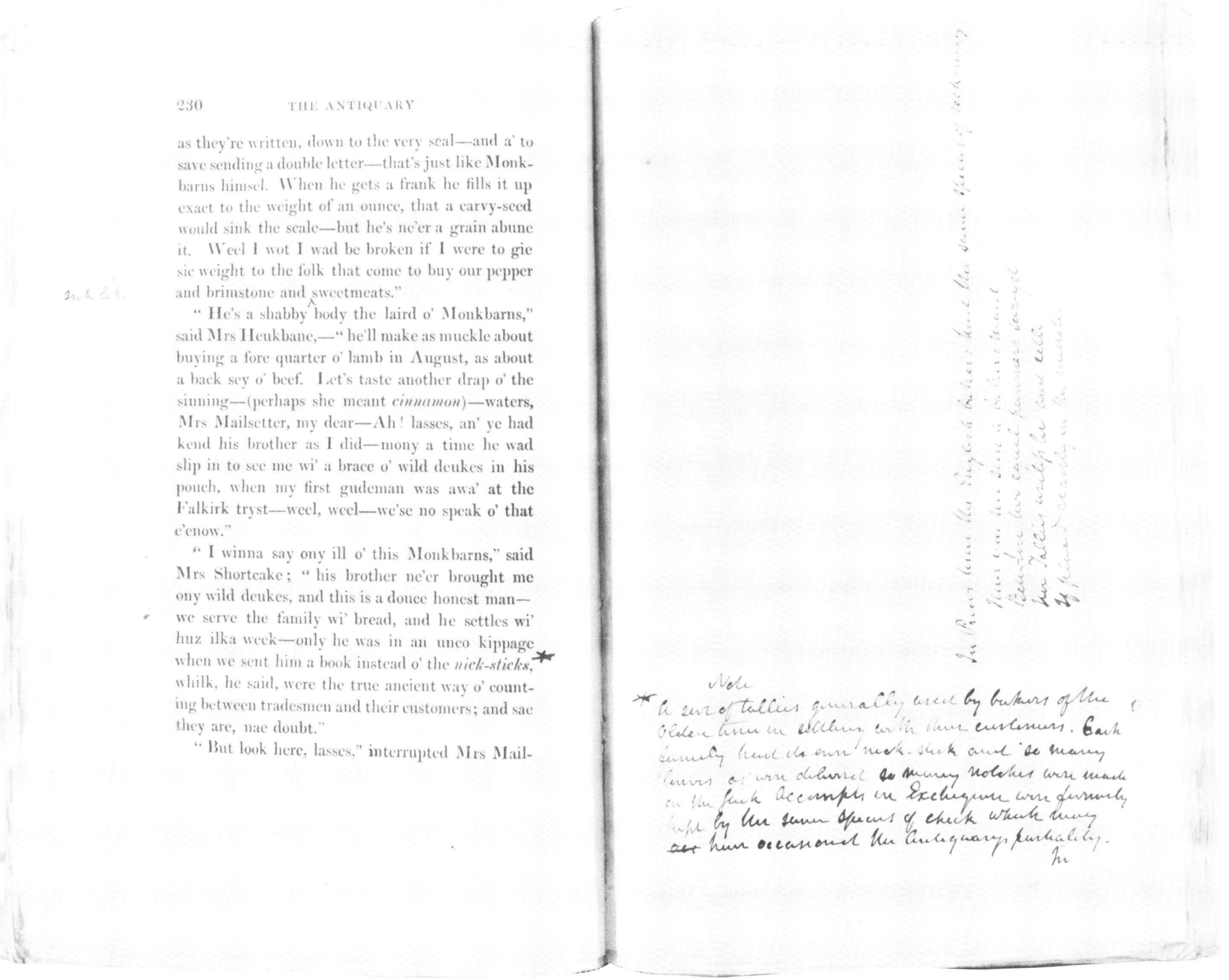

as they're written, down to the very seal—and a' to save sending a double letter—that's just like Monkbarns himsel. When he gets a frank he fills it up exact to the weight of an ounce, that a carvy-seed would sink the scale—but he's ne'er a grain abune it. Weel I wot I wad be broken if I were to gie sic weight to the folk that come to buy our pepper and brimstone and sweetmeats."

"He's a shabby body the laird o' Monkbarns," said Mrs Heukbane,—"he'll make as muckle about buying a fore quarter o' lamb in August, as about a back sey o' beef. Let's taste another drap o' the sinning—(perhaps she meant *cinnamon*)—waters, Mrs Mailsetter, my dear—Ah! lasses, an' ye had kend his brother as I did—mony a time he wad slip in to see me wi' a brace o' wild deukes in his pouch, when my first gudeman was awa' at the Falkirk tryst—weel, weel—we'se no speak o' that e'enow."

"I winna say ony ill o' this Monkbarns," said Mrs Shortcake; "his brother ne'er brought me ony wild deukes, and this is a douce honest man—we serve the family wi' bread, and he settles wi' huz ilka week—only he was in an unco kippage when we sent him a book instead o' the *nick-sticks*,* whilk, he said, were the true ancient way o' counting between tradesmen and their customers; and sae they are, nae doubt."

"But look here, lasses," interrupted Mrs Mail-

Note

* A sort of tallies generally used by bakers of the olden time in settling with their customers. Each family had its own nick-stick and so many loaves as were delivered so many notches were made on the stick. Accompts in Exchequer were formerly kept by the same species of check which may have occasioned the Antiquary's partiality.

PLATE 16 Vol. IV *THE ANTIQUARY*

The laird of Monkbarns liked to have things done in the old time-honoured way, and that included having his baker's bill calculated on 'nick-sticks' or tallies, rather than in an account-book. Here Scott adds a note on tallies and old-fashioned accounting methods. This he renders more interesting by appending a literary allusion in the form of a quotation from Matthew Prior. (5. 205)

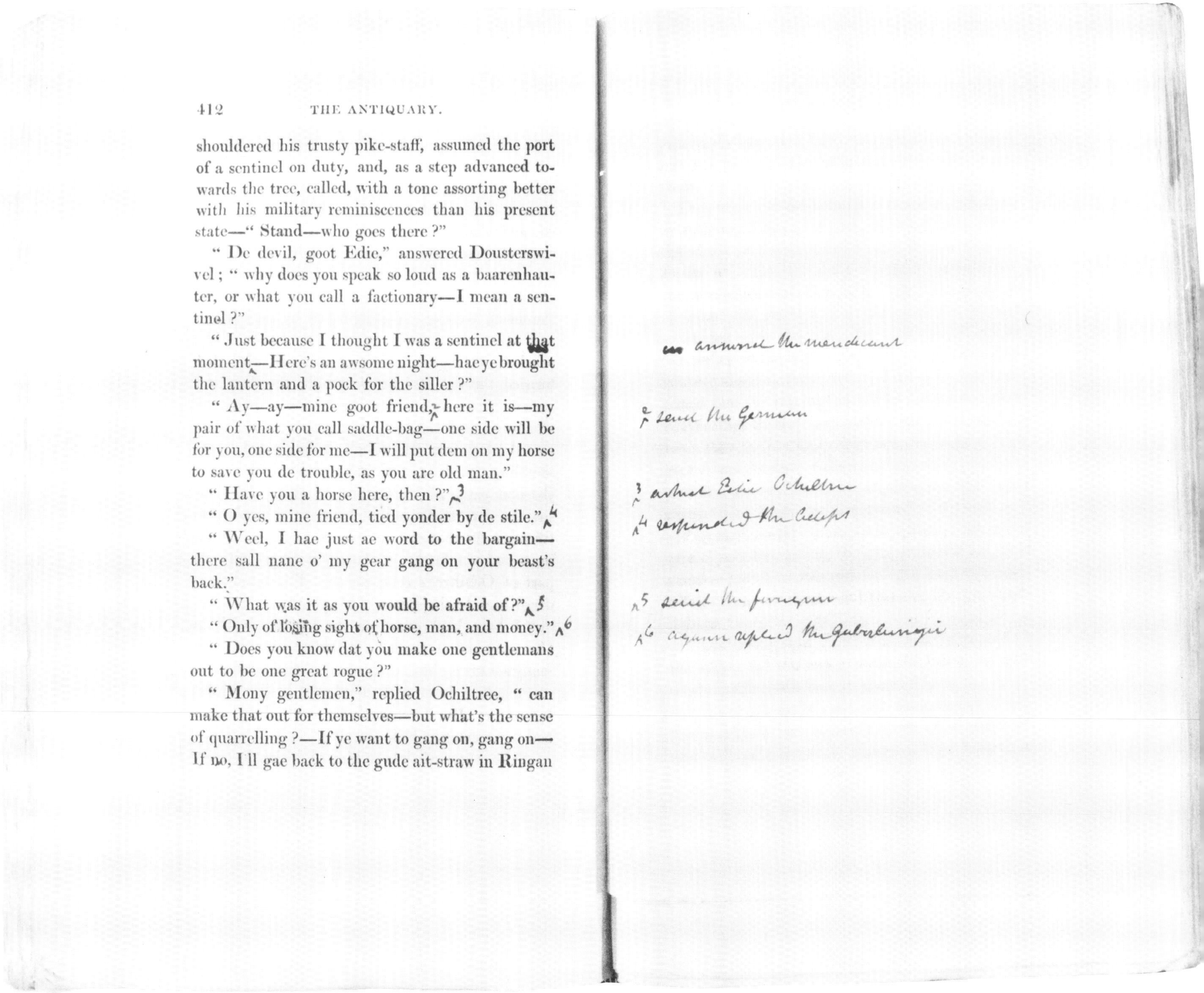

412 THE ANTIQUARY.

shouldered his trusty pike-staff, assumed the port of a sentinel on duty, and, as a step advanced towards the tree, called, with a tone assorting better with his military reminiscences than his present state—"Stand—who goes there?"

"De devil, goot Edie," answered Dousterswivel; "why does you speak so loud as a baarenhauter, or what you call a factionary—I mean a sentinel?"

"Just because I thought I was a sentinel at that moment—Here's an awsome night—hae ye brought the lantern and a pock for the siller?"

"Ay—ay—mine goot friend,—here it is—my pair of what you call saddle-bag—one side will be for you, one side for me—I will put dem on my horse to save you de trouble, as you are old man."

"Have you a horse here, then?"[3]

"O yes, mine friend, tied yonder by de stile."[4]

"Weel, I hae just ae word to the bargain—there sall nane o' my gear gang on your beast's back."

"What was it as you would be afraid of?"[5]

"Only of losing sight of horse, man, and money."[6]

"Does you know dat you make one gentlemans out to be one great rogue?"

"Mony gentlemen," replied Ochiltree, "can make that out for themselves—but what's the sense of quarrelling?—If ye want to gang on, gang on—If no, I'll gae back to the gude ait-straw in Ringan

answered the mendicant

2 said the German

3 asked Edie Ochiltree

4 responded the Adept

5 said the foreigner

6 again replied the Gaberlunzie

PLATE 17 Vol. IV *THE ANTIQUARY*
An example of Scott's efforts to clarify a page of dialogue by means of formulas which to help the printer he keys to the text by numbers. (6. 50)

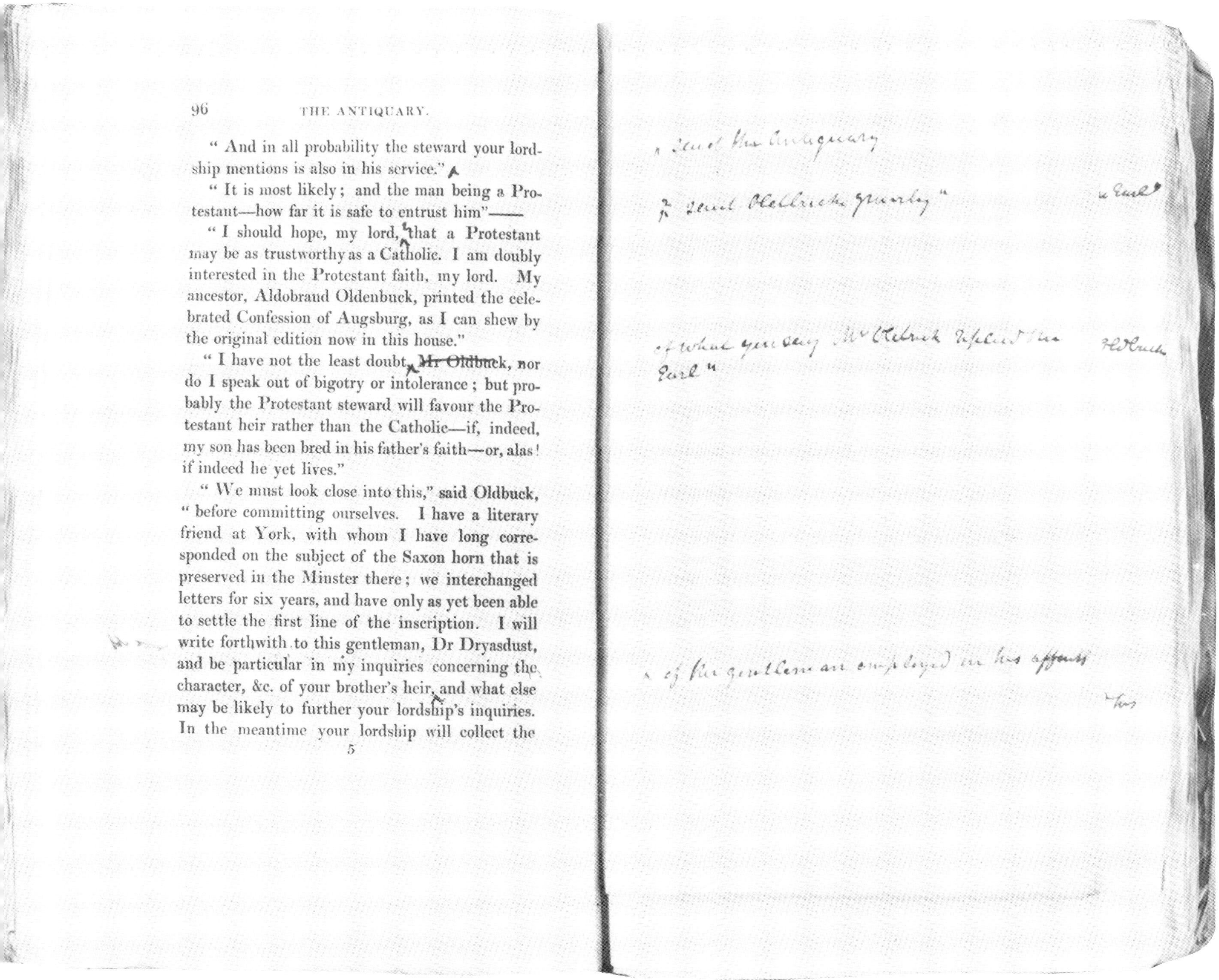

96 THE ANTIQUARY.

"And in all probability the steward your lordship mentions is also in his service."

"It is most likely; and the man being a Protestant—how far it is safe to entrust him"——

"I should hope, my lord, that a Protestant may be as trustworthy as a Catholic. I am doubly interested in the Protestant faith, my lord. My ancestor, Aldobrand Oldenbuck, printed the celebrated Confession of Augsburg, as I can shew by the original edition now in this house."

"I have not the least doubt, ~~Mr Oldbuck~~, nor do I speak out of bigotry or intolerance; but probably the Protestant steward will favour the Protestant heir rather than the Catholic—if, indeed, my son has been bred in his father's faith—or, alas! if indeed he yet lives."

"We must look close into this," said Oldbuck, "before committing ourselves. I have a literary friend at York, with whom I have long corresponded on the subject of the Saxon horn that is preserved in the Minster there; we interchanged letters for six years, and have only as yet been able to settle the first line of the inscription. I will write forthwith to this gentleman, Dr Dryasdust, and be particular in my inquiries concerning the character, &c. of your brother's heir, and what else may be likely to further your lordship's inquiries. In the meantime your lordship will collect the

5

PLATE 18 Vol. V *THE ANTIQUARY*
A further instance of tidying up the dialogue, and of making slight additions to the text in the interests of clarity and completeness. (6. 193–94)

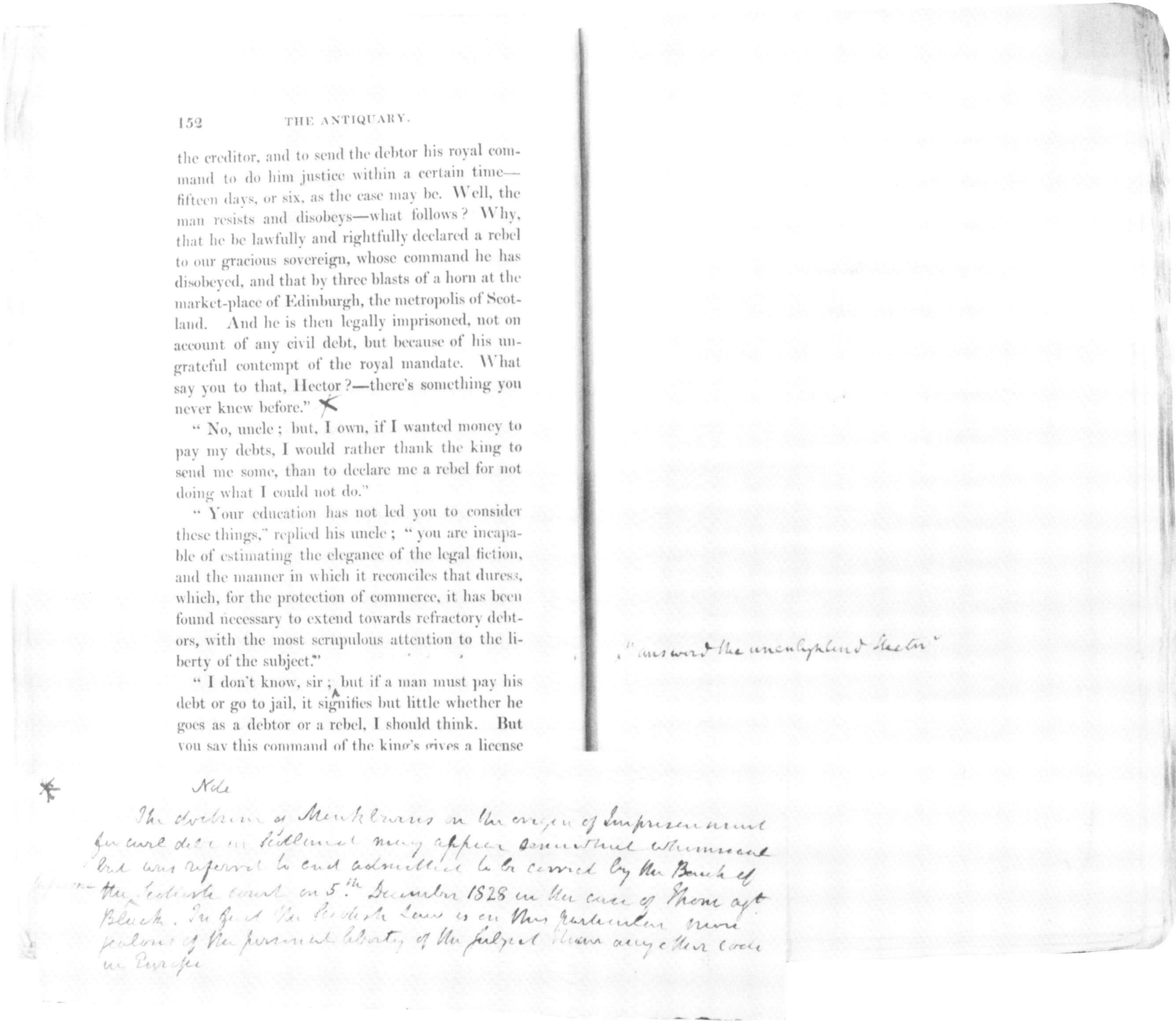
152 THE ANTIQUARY.

the creditor, and to send the debtor his royal command to do him justice within a certain time—fifteen days, or six, as the case may be. Well, the man resists and disobeys—what follows? Why, that he be lawfully and rightfully declared a rebel to our gracious sovereign, whose command he has disobeyed, and that by three blasts of a horn at the market-place of Edinburgh, the metropolis of Scotland. And he is then legally imprisoned, not on account of any civil debt, but because of his ungrateful contempt of the royal mandate. What say you to that, Hector?—there's something you never knew before." ✱

"No, uncle; but, I own, if I wanted money to pay my debts, I would rather thank the king to send me some, than to declare me a rebel for not doing what I could not do."

"Your education has not led you to consider these things," replied his uncle; "you are incapable of estimating the elegance of the legal fiction, and the manner in which it reconciles that duress, which, for the protection of commerce, it has been found necessary to extend towards refractory debtors, with the most scrupulous attention to the liberty of the subject."

"answered the unenlightened Hector"

"I don't know, sir; ^ but if a man must pay his debt or go to jail, it signifies but little whether he goes as a debtor or a rebel, I should think. But you say this command of the king's gives a license

✱ Note

The doctrine of Monkbarns on the origin of Imprisonment for civil debt in Scotland may appear somewhat whimsical but was referred to and admitted to be correct by the Bench of the Scottish court on 5th December 1828 in the case of Thome agt Black. In fact the Scottish Law is on this particular more jealous of the personal liberty of the subject than any other code in Europe

PLATE 19 Vol. V *THE ANTIQUARY*

This is an interesting case of Scott displaying his own legal learning in a fictional character's speech. Oldbuck is made to expound the Scots legal position on imprisonment for civil debt. Hector M'Intyre's attention wandered during his uncle's discourse—just as Scott's own concentration was wont to do as he sat in court as Clerk of Session. Nevertheless Scott was able to add to the veracity of Oldbuck's legal argument by citing (on the small slip of paper attached to p.152) a reference to a Court of Session judgement of December 1828 which supported what Scott had already made the Antiquary tell his audience when the novel was first published in 1816. (6. 243–44)

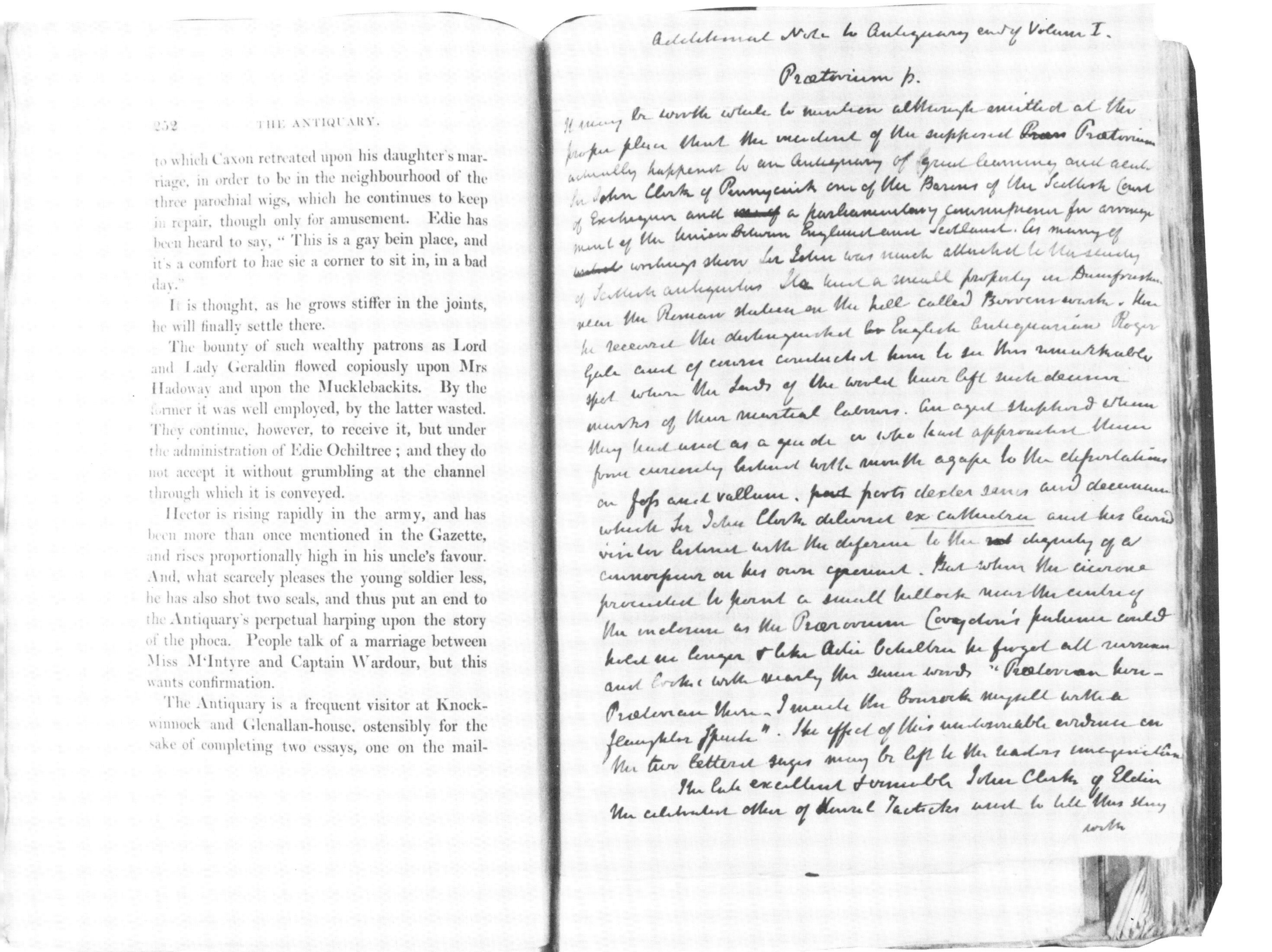

252 THE ANTIQUARY.

to which Caxon retreated upon his daughter's marriage, in order to be in the neighbourhood of the three parochial wigs, which he continues to keep in repair, though only for amusement. Edie has been heard to say, " This is a gay bein place, and it's a comfort to hae sic a corner to sit in, in a bad day."

It is thought, as he grows stiffer in the joints, he will finally settle there.

The bounty of such wealthy patrons as Lord and Lady Geraldin flowed copiously upon Mrs Hadoway and upon the Mucklebackits. By the former it was well employed, by the latter wasted. They continue, however, to receive it, but under the administration of Edie Ochiltree ; and they do not accept it without grumbling at the channel through which it is conveyed.

Hector is rising rapidly in the army, and has been more than once mentioned in the Gazette, and rises proportionally high in his uncle's favour. And, what scarcely pleases the young soldier less, he has also shot two seals, and thus put an end to the Antiquary's perpetual harping upon the story of the phoca. People talk of a marriage between Miss M'Intyre and Captain Wardour, but this wants confirmation.

The Antiquary is a frequent visitor at Knockwinnock and Glenallan-house, ostensibly for the sake of completing two essays, one on the mail-

Additional Note to Antiquary end of Volume I.

Praetorium p.

It may be worth while to mention although omitted at the proper place that the incident of the supposed Praetorium actually happened to an Antiquary of great learning and acuteness Sir John Clerk of Pennycuik one of the Barons of the Scottish Court of Exchequer and a parliamentary commissioner for arrangement of the Union between England and Scotland. As many of [his] writings show Sir John was much attached to the study of Scottish antiquities. He had a small property in Dumfriesshire near the Roman station on the hill called Burrenswark. Here he received the distinguished English antiquarian Roger Gale and of course conducted him to see this remarkable spot where the lords of the world have left such decisive marks of their martial labours. An aged shepherd whom they had used as a guide or who had approached them from curiosity listened with mouth agape to the dissertations on fosse and vallum, porta dextra sinistra and decumana which Sir John Clerk delivered ex cathedra and his learned visitor listened with the deference to the dignity of a connoisseur on his own ground. But when the cicerone proceeded to point a small hillock near the centre of the enclosure as the Praetorium Corydon's patience could hold no longer & like Edie Ochiltree he forgot all reverence and broke with nearly the same words "Praetorian here—Praetorian there—I made the bourock myself with a flaughter spade". The effect of this undeniable evidence on the two lettered sages may be left to the readers imagination.

The late excellent & amiable John Clerk of Eldin the celebrated author of Naval Tactics used to tell this story with

PLATE 20 Vol. V *THE ANTIQUARY*

An additional note to *The Antiquary* (on a paper apart, bound into the interleaved volume) which describes the origin of the celebrated episode of Oldbuck at the Kaim of Kinprunes. The hilarious incident when the fictional antiquary maintained that a piece of ground was not only a Roman *praetorium* but moreover Agricola's very camp before the battle of Mons Graupius—though only to be deflated by Edie Ochiltree's declaration that he had made the earthwork or 'bourock' in question some years before—was based on a real-life antiquary's undoing in similar circumstances. This was the famous Sir John Clerk of Penicuik, the leading antiquary in Scotland in the second quarter of the eighteenth century, of whom Scott had heard this and other stories from his son John Clerk of Eldin, himself the father of Scott's intimate friend William Clerk. As Scott relates the story here, the *praetorium* incident occurred in Dumfriesshire when the English antiquary Roger Gale was Clerk's guest. Gale indeed visited Clerk in 1739, and the two antiquaries inspected Roman (or, in this case, imagined Roman) sites in that part of Scotland where the Clerk family owned property at Dumcrieff and Middlebie.

This note was not in fact printed in the Magnum edition, but it was included, in a slightly altered form, in the Centenary Edition. (3. 421–22)

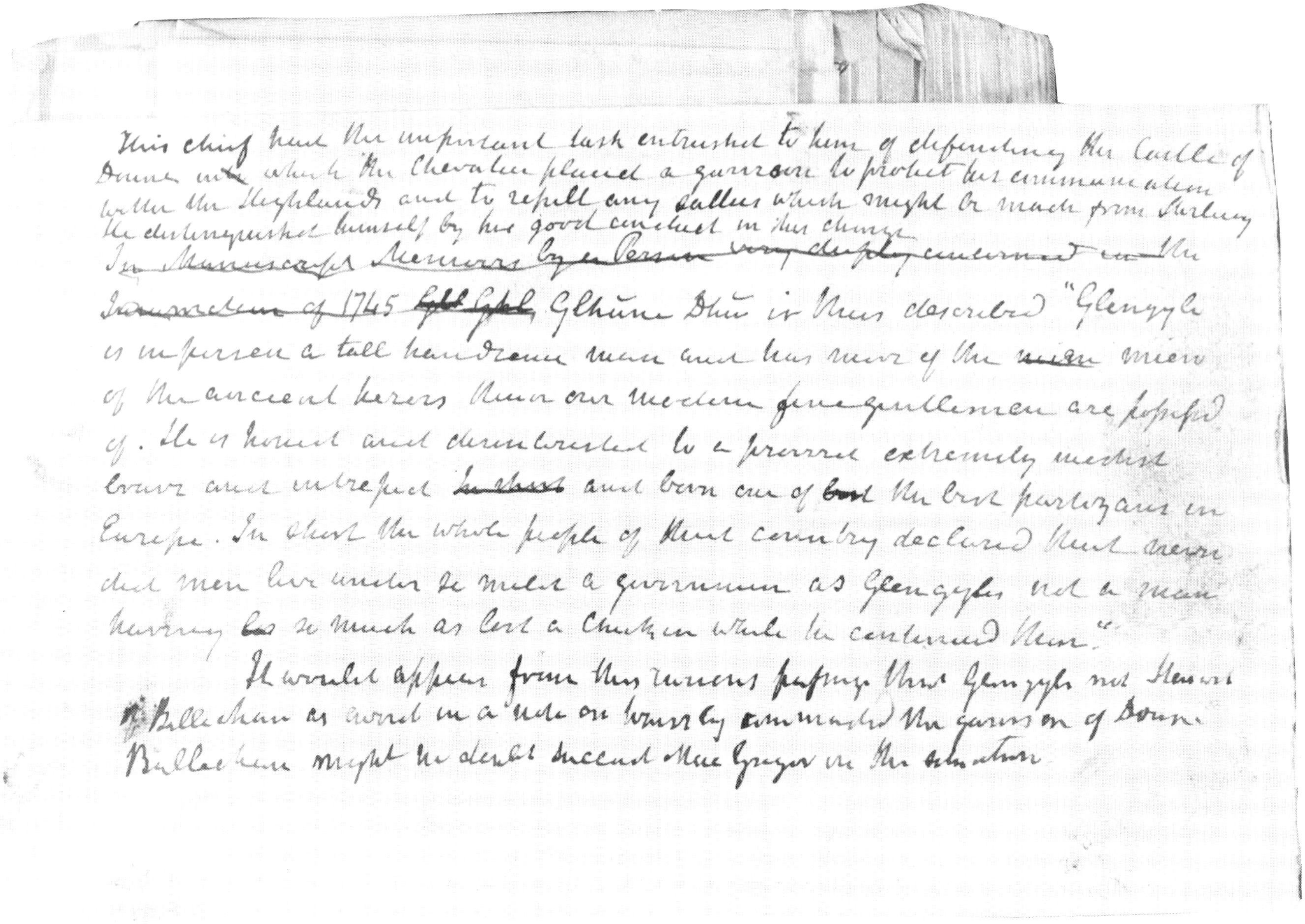
This chief had the important task entrusted to him of defending the Castle of Doune into which the Chevalier placed a garrison to protect his communication betwixt the Highlands and to repell any sallies which might be made from Stirling. He distinguished himself by his good conduct in this charge.
In Manuscript Memoirs by a ~~Person very deeply concerned in the Insurrection of 1745~~ ~~Glgl~~ Glhune Dhu is thus described "Glengyle is in person a tall handsome man and has more of the ~~mien~~ mien of the ancient heroes than our modern fine gentlemen are possessed of. He is honest and disinterested to a proverb extremely modest brave and intrepid ~~in short~~ and born one of ~~best~~ the best partizans in Europe. In short the whole people of that country declared that never did men live under so mild a government as Glengyles not a man having ~~lost~~ so much as lost a chicken while he continued there."
It would appear from this curious passage that Glengyle not Stewart of Ballechan as averred in a note on Waverley commanded the garrison of Doune. Ballechan might no doubt succeed MacGregor in the situation.

PLATES 21–22 Vol. V *ROB ROY*
The final Appendix (VI) to the Introduction to *Rob Roy* is composed of material which came to Scott's notice—the phrase he uses is 'fell under the author's eye'—while the sheets of the Magnum edition were passing through the press. The slip on which this Appendix is written (thus endorsed by Cadell) is covered with the printer's fingerprints. Scott has used a fragment of an unfinished letter for this note. Both sides of the paper are here reproduced. (7. cxxxiv–cxxxv)

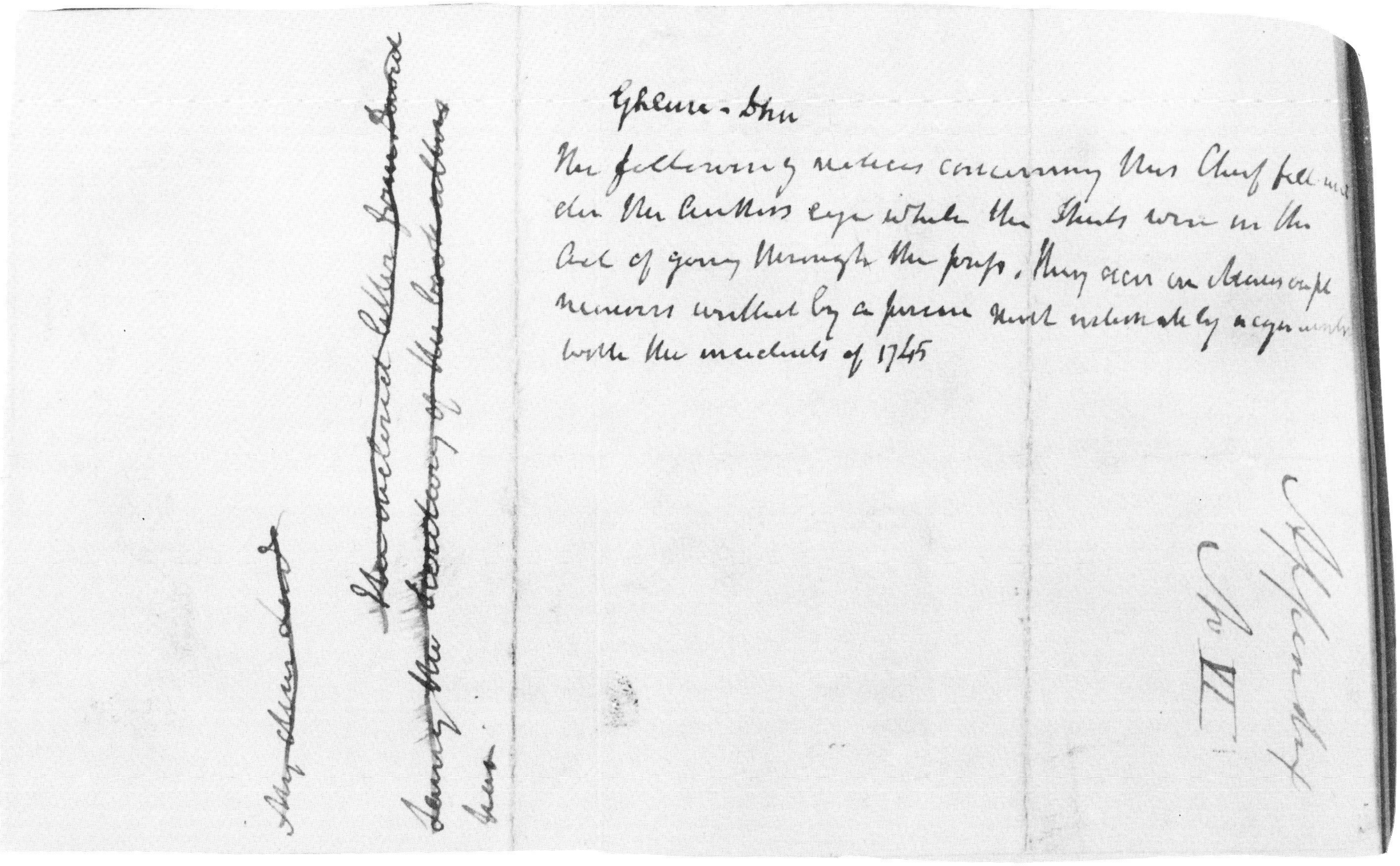
Ghlune-Dhu
The following notices concerning this Chief fell under the Author's eye while the sheets were in the act of going through the press. They occur in Manuscript memoirs written by a person most intimately acquainted with the incidents of 1745
Appendix No. II

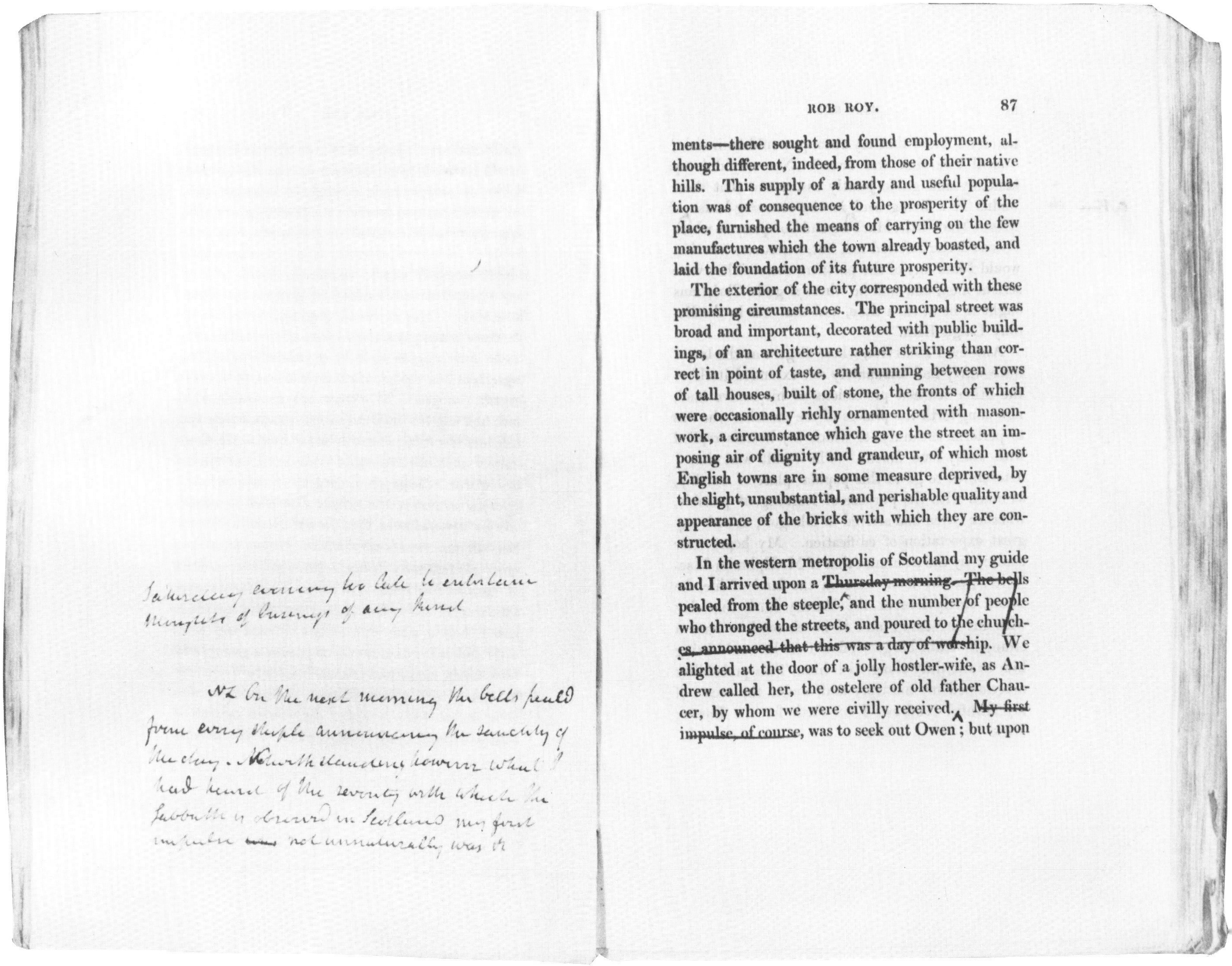
ROB ROY. 87

ments—there sought and found employment, although different, indeed, from those of their native hills. This supply of a hardy and useful population was of consequence to the prosperity of the place, furnished the means of carrying on the few manufactures which the town already boasted, and laid the foundation of its future prosperity.

The exterior of the city corresponded with these promising circumstances. The principal street was broad and important, decorated with public buildings, of an architecture rather striking than correct in point of taste, and running between rows of tall houses, built of stone, the fronts of which were occasionally richly ornamented with mason-work, a circumstance which gave the street an imposing air of dignity and grandeur, of which most English towns are in some measure deprived, by the slight, unsubstantial, and perishable quality and appearance of the bricks with which they are constructed.

In the western metropolis of Scotland my guide and I arrived upon a ~~Thursday morning. The bells~~ ~~pealed from the steeple, and the number of people who thronged the streets, and poured to the churches, announced that this was a day of worship.~~ We alighted at the door of a jolly hostler-wife, as Andrew called her, the ostelere of old father Chaucer, by whom we were civilly received. ~~My first impulse, of course~~, was to seek out Owen; but upon

Saturday evening too late to entertain thoughts of business of any kind

NP On the next morning the bells pealed from every steeple announcing the sanctity of the day. Notwithstanding however what I had heard of the severity with which the Sabbath is observed in Scotland my first impulse not unnaturally was to

PLATE 23 Vol. VI *ROB ROY*

In his description of the arrival in Glasgow of Francis Osbaldistone and Andrew Fairservice, Scott had made his characters enter the city on a Thursday morning. The pre-Magnum text states: 'The bells pealed from the steeple, and the number of people who thronged the streets, and poured to the churches, announced that this was a day of worship.' Here Scott had not actually made a very obvious error over the days of the week: rather had he been alluding to the Presbyterian custom of the fast-Thursday which preceded a communion Sunday. Clearly this apparent oddity had to be explained, for many readers will have thought that here was a glaring solecism of the type so much remarked upon in *The Antiquary*, where on one celebrated occasion the sun was observed to set in the east. But now for once Scott blenched in the face of this problem, or for some other reason preferred not to go into the fairly complicated annotation necessary to clarify the point and justify his original text. The solution which he can be seen here to have adopted was to make the travellers arrive on a Saturday evening; to indicate clearly that the Sabbath did indeed follow on the morrow; and to introduce—in a newly-created paragraph—a telling allusion to the Scottish Sunday. (8. 26)

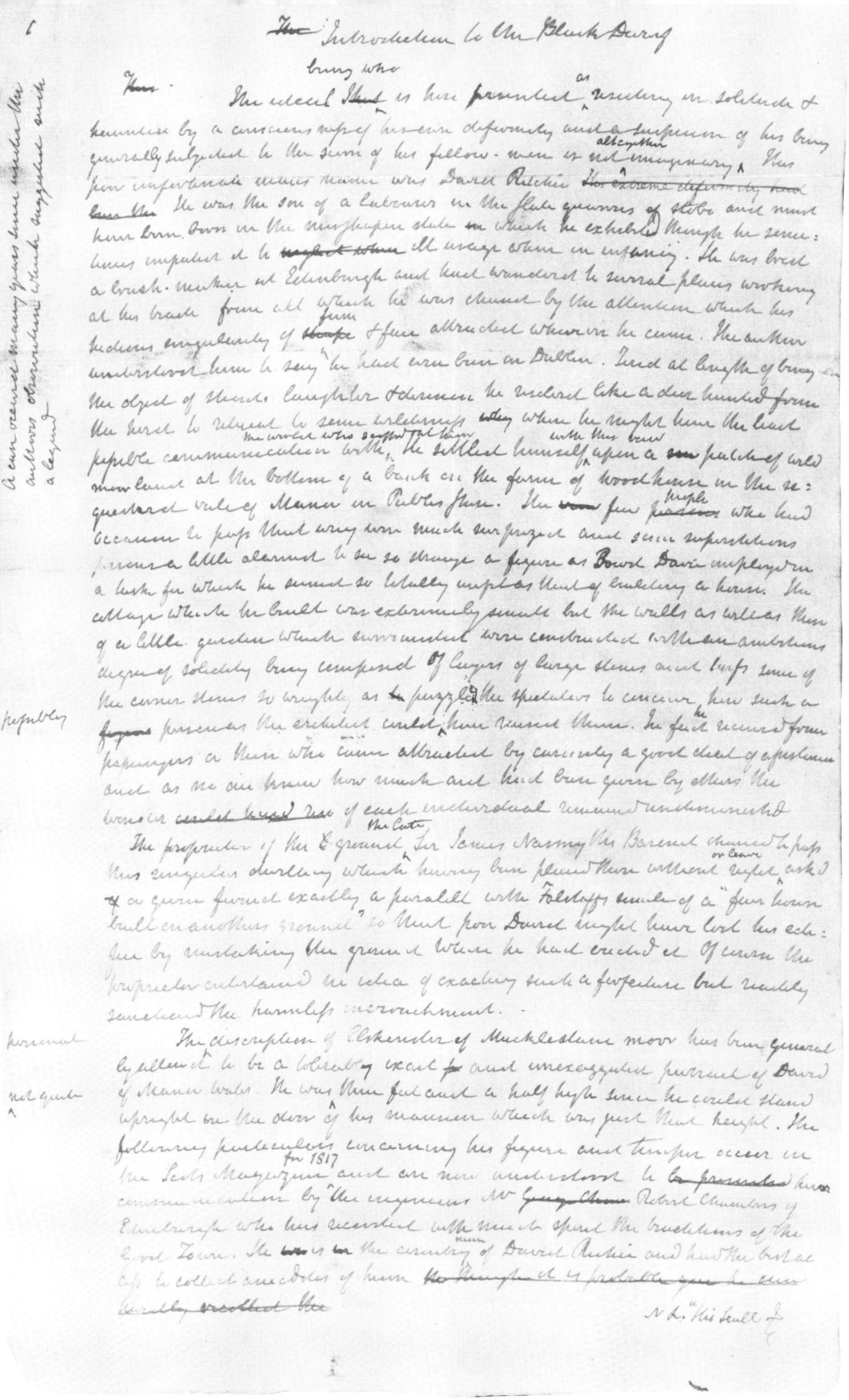

~~The~~ Introduction to the Black Dwarf

~~Thus~~. The ideal ~~that~~ [being who] is here presented as residing in solitude & harmless by a conscious sense of his own deformity and a suspicion of his being generally subjected to the scorn of his fellow-men is not ~~imaginary~~ [altogether]. This poor unfortunate whose name was David Ritchie ~~whose extreme deformity had been the~~ He was the son of a labourer in the slate quarries of Stobo and must have been born in the misshapen state in which he exhibited though he sometimes imputed it to ~~neglect when~~ ill usage when in infancy. He was bred a brush-maker at Edinburgh and had wandered to several places working at his trade from all which he was chased by the attention which his hideous singularity of ~~shape~~ [form] & face attracted wherever he came. The author understood him to say he had even been in Dublin. Tired at length of being the object of shouts, laughter & derision he resolved like a deer hunted from the herd to retreat to some wilderness ~~where~~ where he might have the least possible communication with [the world who scoffed at him]. He settled himself [with his bees] upon a ~~sm~~ patch of wild moorland at the bottom of a bank on the farm of Woodhouse in the sequestered vale of Manor in Peebles shire. The ~~won~~ few ~~persons~~ [people] who had occasion to pass that way were much surprised and some superstitious persons a little alarmed to see so strange a figure as Bow'd Davie employed in a task for which he seemed so totally unfit as that of building a house. The cottage which he built was extremely small but the walls as well as those of a little garden which surrounded were constructed with an ambitious degree of solidity being composed of layers of large stones and turf some of the corner stones so weighty as ~~to~~ puzzled the spectators to conceive how such a ~~figure~~ person as the architect could have raised them. In fact he received from passengers or those who came attracted by curiosity a good deal of assistance and as no one knew how much aid had been given by others the wonder ~~could keep~~ was of each individual remained undiminished.

The proprietor of the ground [the late] Sir James Nasmyth the Baronet chanced to pass this singular dwelling which having been placed there without right [or leave] asked ~~of~~ a given formed exactly a parallel with Falstaff's simile of a "fair house built on another's ground" so that poor David might have lost his edifice by mistaking the ground where he had erected it. Of course the proprietor entertained no idea of exacting such a forfeiture but readily sanctioned the harmless encroachment.

The description of Elshender of Mucklestane moor has been generally allowed to be a tolerably exact ~~&~~ and unexaggerated portrait of David of Manor water. He was then feet and a half high since he could stand upright in the door of his mansion which was just that height. The following particulars concerning his figure and temper occur in the Scots Magazine [for 1817] and are now understood to ~~be furnished~~ have been communicated by the ingenious Mr ~~George Cham~~ Robert Chambers of Edinburgh who has recorded with much spirit the traditions of the Good Town. He ~~was in~~ the country [near] of David Ritchie and had the best access to collect anecdotes of him ~~He thought it probable ....~~

N.L. "His skull &c"

[Margin:] A circumstance many years since under the authors observation which suggested such a legend

[Margin:] possibly

[Margin:] personal

[Margin:] not quite

PLATE 24 Vol. VII *THE BLACK DWARF*
In the Introduction to the novel, of which the initial folio is here reproduced, Scott describes the original of Elshender, the Dwarf. This fictional character was, like so many in the Waverley Novels, based upon a real person known to Scott, or of whom he had been made aware through the stories or writings of others, in this case Robert Chambers's memoir of Bow'd Davie Ritchie of Peeblesshire. (9. xvii–xx)

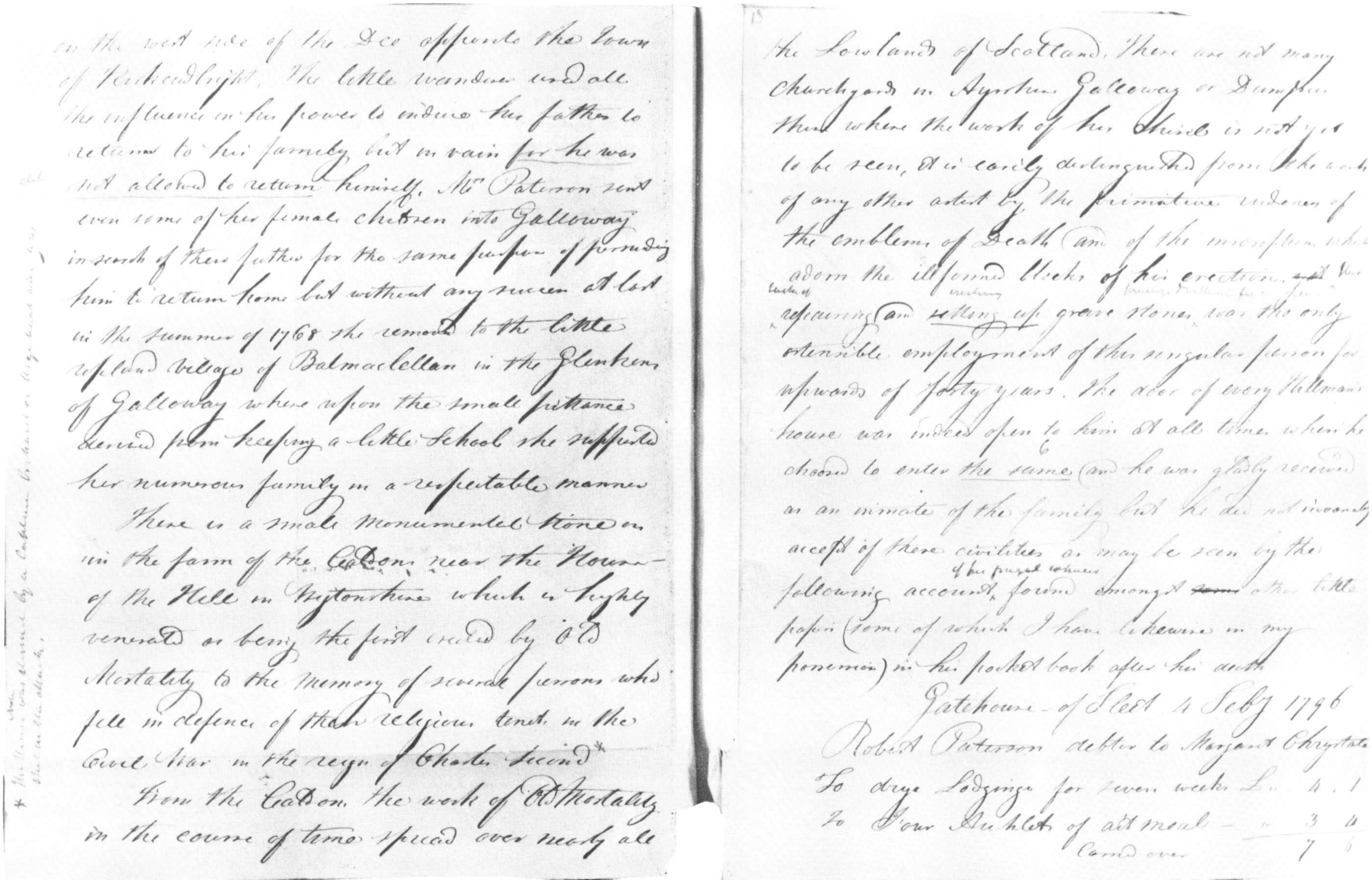

on the west side of the Dee opposite the town of Kirkcudbright. The little wanderer used all the influence in her power to induce her father to return to his family but in vain for he was not allowed to return himself. Mrs Paterson sent even some of her female children into Galloway in search of their father for the same purpose of persuading him to return home but without any success. At last in the summer of 1768 she removed to the little upland village of Balmaclellan in the Glenkens of Galloway where upon the small pittance derived from keeping a little School she supported her numerous family in a respectable manner

There is a small monumental stone on in the farm of the Caldons near the House of the Hill in Wigtonshire which is highly venerated as being the first erected by Old Mortality to the memory of several persons who fell in defence of their religious tenets in the Civil War in the reign of Charles Second*

From the Caldons the work of Old Mortality in the course of time spread over nearly all

* The stone was erected by a Captain [illegible]

the Lowlands of Scotland. There are not many Churchyards in Ayrshire Galloway or Dumfries shire where the work of his chisel is not yet to be seen, It is easily distinguished from the work of any other artist by the primitive rudeness of the emblems of Death (and of the inscriptions which adorn the ill formed blocks of his erection. [illegible] repairing (and setting up grave stones was the only ostensible employment of this singular person for upwards of forty years. The door of every Hillman's house was indeed open to him at all times when he choosed to enter the same (and he was gladly received as an inmate of the family but he did not invariably accept of these civilities as may be seen by the following account found amongst other little papers (some of which I have likewise in my possession) in his pocket book after his death

Gatehouse of Fleet 4 Feby 1796

Robert Paterson debtor to Margaret Chrystale

To drye Lodgings for seven weeks £ 4 1
To Four Auchlets of aet meal — 3 4
Carried over 7 5

PLATE 25 Vol. VII *OLD MORTALITY*

Part of Joseph Train's letter to Scott of 31 March 1829, which contains an account of Robert Paterson, the original of Old Mortality. This is an interesting example of the way Scott used information supplied to him by his correspondents. Their letters became quarries for material to use in introductions or notes. Scott has edited and annotated this particular letter in red ink for incorporation in the Introduction to the Magnum edition of the novel. (9. 231–33)

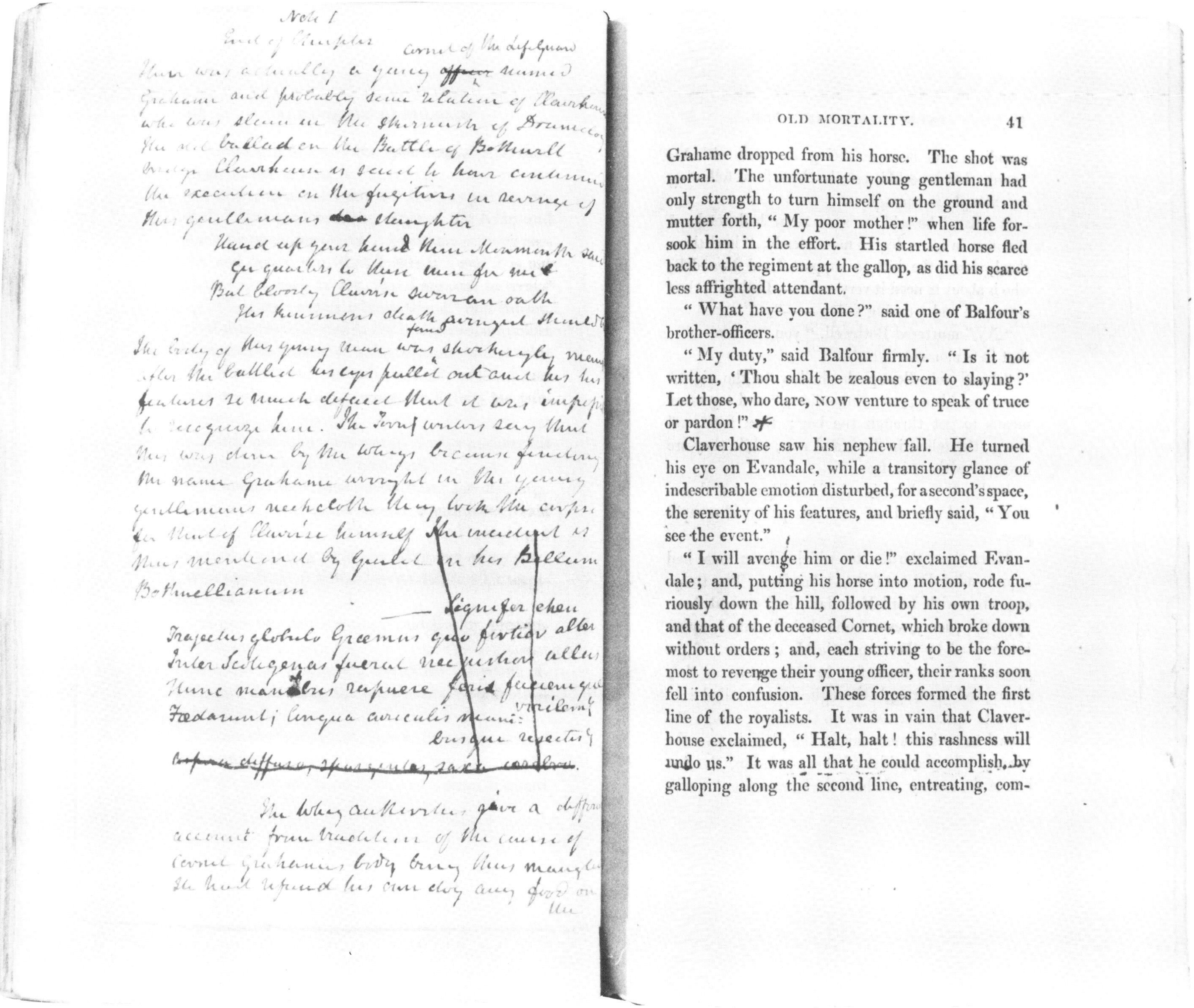
Note I
End of Chapter
Cornet of the Lifeguards
There was actually a young ~~officer~~ named Grahame and probably some relation of Claverhouse who was slain in the skirmish of Drumclog. The old ballad on the Battle of Bothwell Bridge Claverhouse is said to have continued the execution on the fugitives in revenge of this gentleman's slaughter

Haud up your hand then Monmouth said
Gie quarters to these men for me
But bloody Claver swore an oath
His kinsman's death avenged should be

The body of this young man was shockingly mangled after the battle his eyes pulled out and his features so much defaced that it was impossible to recognize him. The Tory writers say that this was done by the Whigs because finding the name Grahame wrought in the young gentleman's neckcloth they took the corpse for that of Claverse himself. The incident is thus mentioned by Guild in his Bellum Bothuellianum

— Signifer eheu
Trajectus globulo Graemus quo fortior alter
Inter Scotigenas fuerat nec justior ullus
Hunc manibus rapuere feri faciemque virilem
Foedarunt; lingua auriculis manuque resectis
~~Aspera diffuso spargunt saxa cerebro~~

The Whig authorities give a different account from tradition of the cause of Cornet Grahame's body being thus mangled. He had refused his own dog any food on the

Grahame dropped from his horse. The shot was mortal. The unfortunate young gentleman had only strength to turn himself on the ground and mutter forth, "My poor mother!" when life forsook him in the effort. His startled horse fled back to the regiment at the gallop, as did his scarce less affrighted attendant.

"What have you done?" said one of Balfour's brother-officers.

"My duty," said Balfour firmly. "Is it not written, 'Thou shalt be zealous even to slaying?' Let those, who dare, NOW venture to speak of truce or pardon!" *

Claverhouse saw his nephew fall. He turned his eye on Evandale, while a transitory glance of indescribable emotion disturbed, for a second's space, the serenity of his features, and briefly said, "You see the event."

"I will avenge him or die!" exclaimed Evandale; and, putting his horse into motion, rode furiously down the hill, followed by his own troop, and that of the deceased Cornet, which broke down without orders; and, each striving to be the foremost to revenge their young officer, their ranks soon fell into confusion. These forces formed the first line of the royalists. It was in vain that Claverhouse exclaimed, "Halt, halt! this rashness will undo us." It was all that he could accomplish, by galloping along the second line, entreating, com-

PLATE 26 Vol. VIII *OLD MORTALITY*
The dramatic death of Cornet Grahame, and the subsequent story of Claverhouse's defeat at Drumclog, provided Scott with ample scope for annotation in the Magnum edition. The notes to two existing chapters were grouped together at the end of the second. The way in which the material for these notes is arranged—as additions written on interleaves, or as quotations set out on bound-in papers apart—is particularly confusing for readers of the Interleaved Set. Note i was to have included a quotation from a seventeenth-century Latin poem by Andrew Guild. In the end this extract from 'Bellum Bothuellianum' was appended to Note iii. This plate shows part of Note i, with the deleted portion of the poem clearly visible. (10. 139)

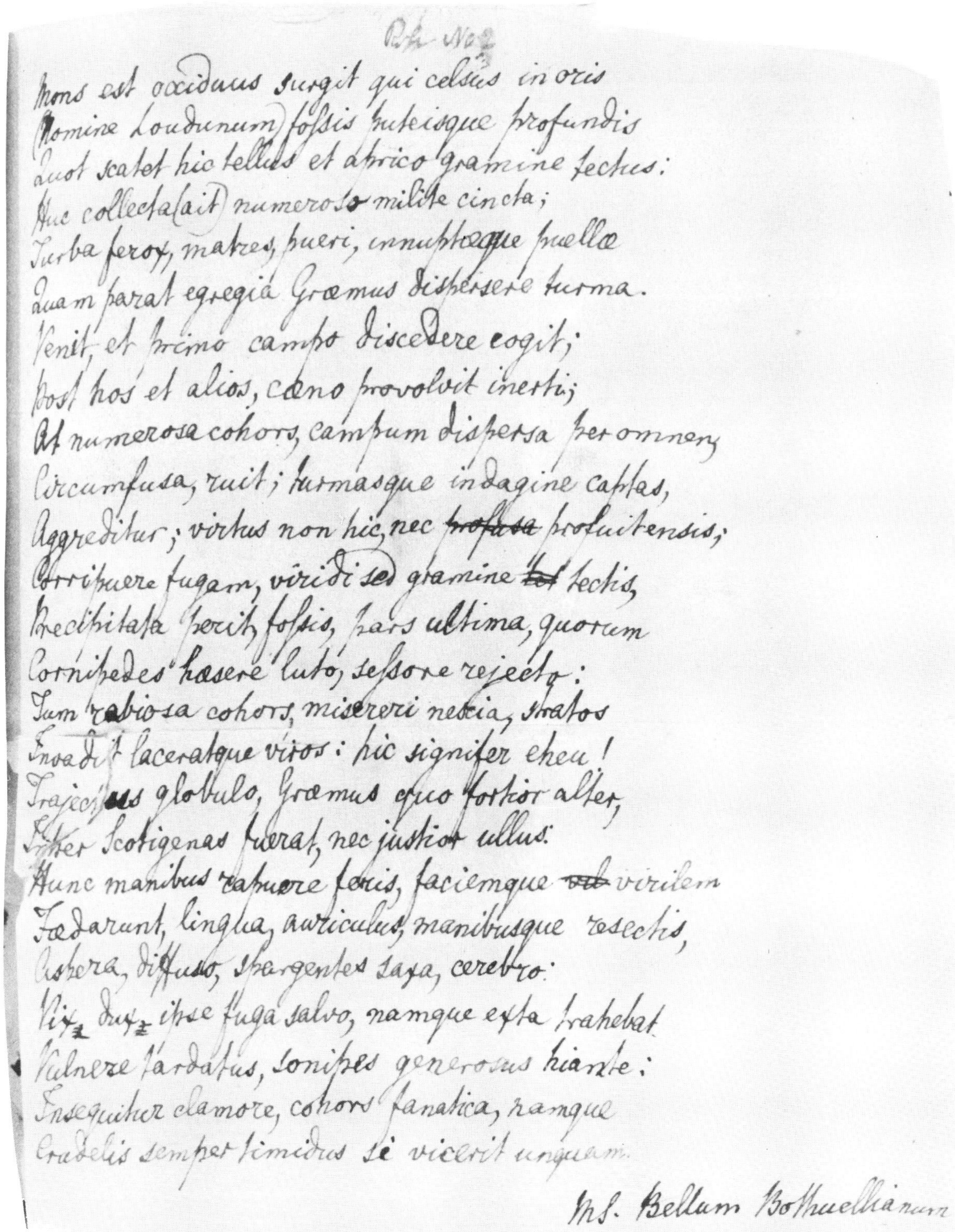

Mons est occiduus surgit qui celsus in oris
Nomine Loudunum, fossis puteisque profundis
Quot scatet hic tellus et aprico gramine tectus:
Huc collecta (ait) numeroso milite cincta;
Turba ferox, matres, pueri, innuptaeque puellae
Quam parat egregia Graemus dispersere turma.
Venit, et primo campo discedere cogit;
Post hos et alios, coeno provolvit inerti;
At numerosa cohors, campum dispersa per omnem
Circumfusa, ruit; turmasque indagine captas,
Aggreditur; virtus non hic, nec ~~profusa~~ profuit ensis;
Corripuere fugam, viridi sed gramine ~~tot~~ tectis,
Praecipitata perit, fossis, pars ultima, quorum
Cornipedes haesere luto, sessore rejecto:
Tum rabiosa cohors, misereri nescia, stratos
Invadit laceratque viros: hic signifer eheu!
Trajectus globulo, Graemus quo fortior alter,
Inter Scotigenas fuerat, nec justior ullus:
Hunc manibus rapuere feris, faciemque ~~vi~~ virilem
Foedarunt, lingua, auriculis, manibusque resectis,
Aspera, diffuso, spargentes saxa, cerebro:
Vix dux ipse fuga salvo, namque exta trahebat
Vulnere tardatus, sonipes generosus hiante:
Insequitur clamore, cohors fanatica, namque
Crudelis semper timidus si vicerit unquam.

MS. Bellum Bothuellianum

PLATE 27 Vol. VIII *OLD MORTALITY*
Andrew Guild's manuscript of 'Bellum Bothuellianum' was presented to the Advocates' Library [now the National Library of Scotland] in 1769 (Adv. MS. 19.3.26). As a young man Scott had transcribed the portion referring to Cornet Grahame (f.42v): the young officer's death, and the fate of his body at the hands of the Whigs, had evidently made an impression on him. This early transcript, written in his bold legal hand, Scott now used late in life in making up his notes on the novel. (10. 141–42: Note iii)

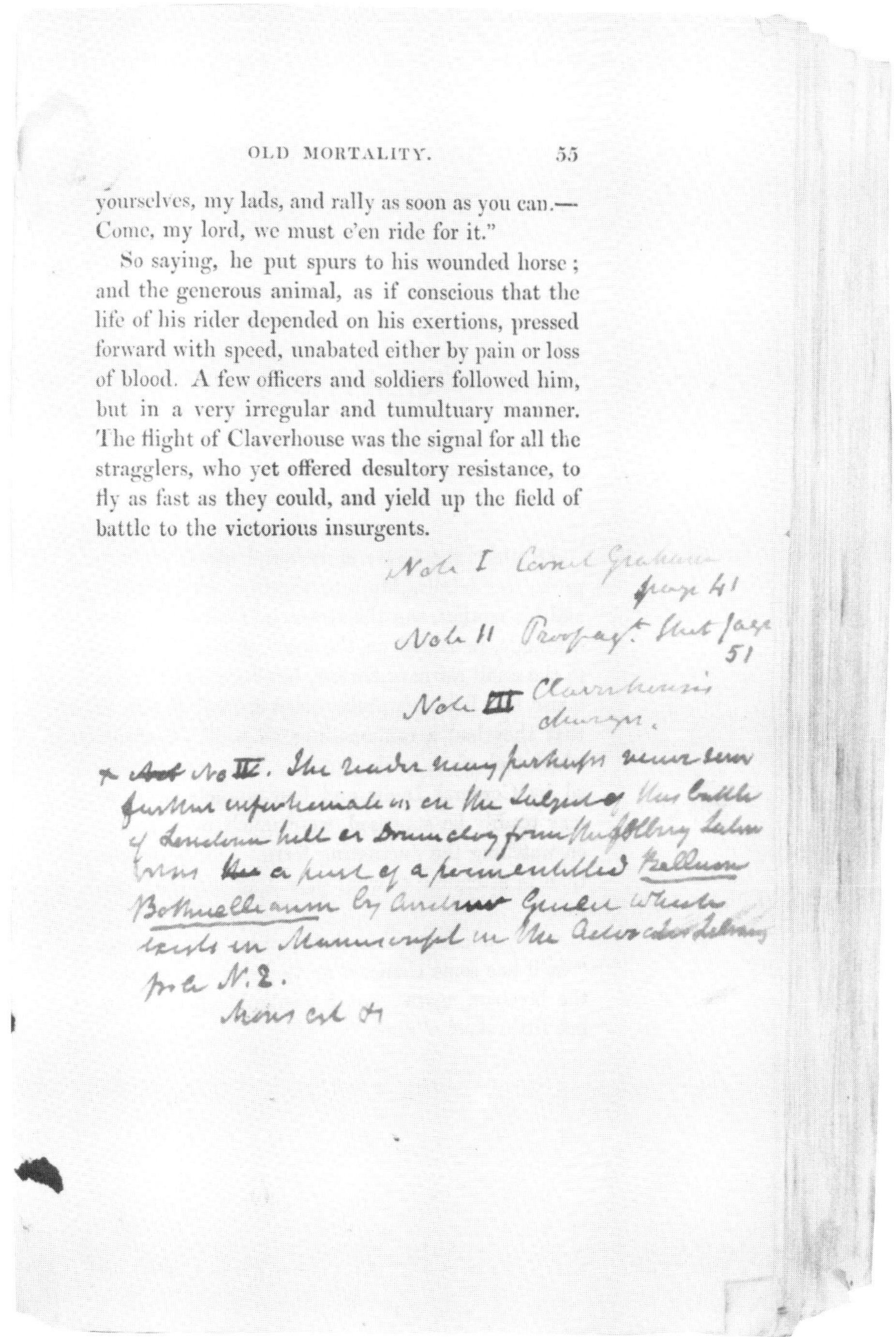

OLD MORTALITY. 55

yourselves, my lads, and rally as soon as you can.— Come, my lord, we must e'en ride for it."

So saying, he put spurs to his wounded horse; and the generous animal, as if conscious that the life of his rider depended on his exertions, pressed forward with speed, unabated either by pain or loss of blood. A few officers and soldiers followed him, but in a very irregular and tumultuary manner. The flight of Claverhouse was the signal for all the stragglers, who yet offered desultory resistance, to fly as fast as they could, and yield up the field of battle to the victorious insurgents.

Note I Cornet Grahame page 41

Note II Proof agt. Shot page 51

Note III Claverhouse's charger.

x ~~Art~~ No IV. The reader may perhaps receive some further information on the subject of this battle of Loudoun hill or Drumclog from [illegible] [illegible] a part of a poem entitled Bellum Bothuellianum by Andrew Guild which exists in Manuscript in the Advocates Library [illegible] N. 2.

[illegible]

PLATE 28 Vol. VIII *OLD MORTALITY*

The arrangement of notes for the chapter on the battle of Drumclog. The subjects are: i: 'Cornet Grahame'; ii: 'Proof Against Shot Given By Satan'; iii: 'Claverhouse's Charger'. The fourth note detailed here (with the reference to the source material in the Advocates' Library, i.e. that early transcription by Scott seen in Plate 27) was in fact incorporated in Note iii in the Magnum edition. (10. 139–42)

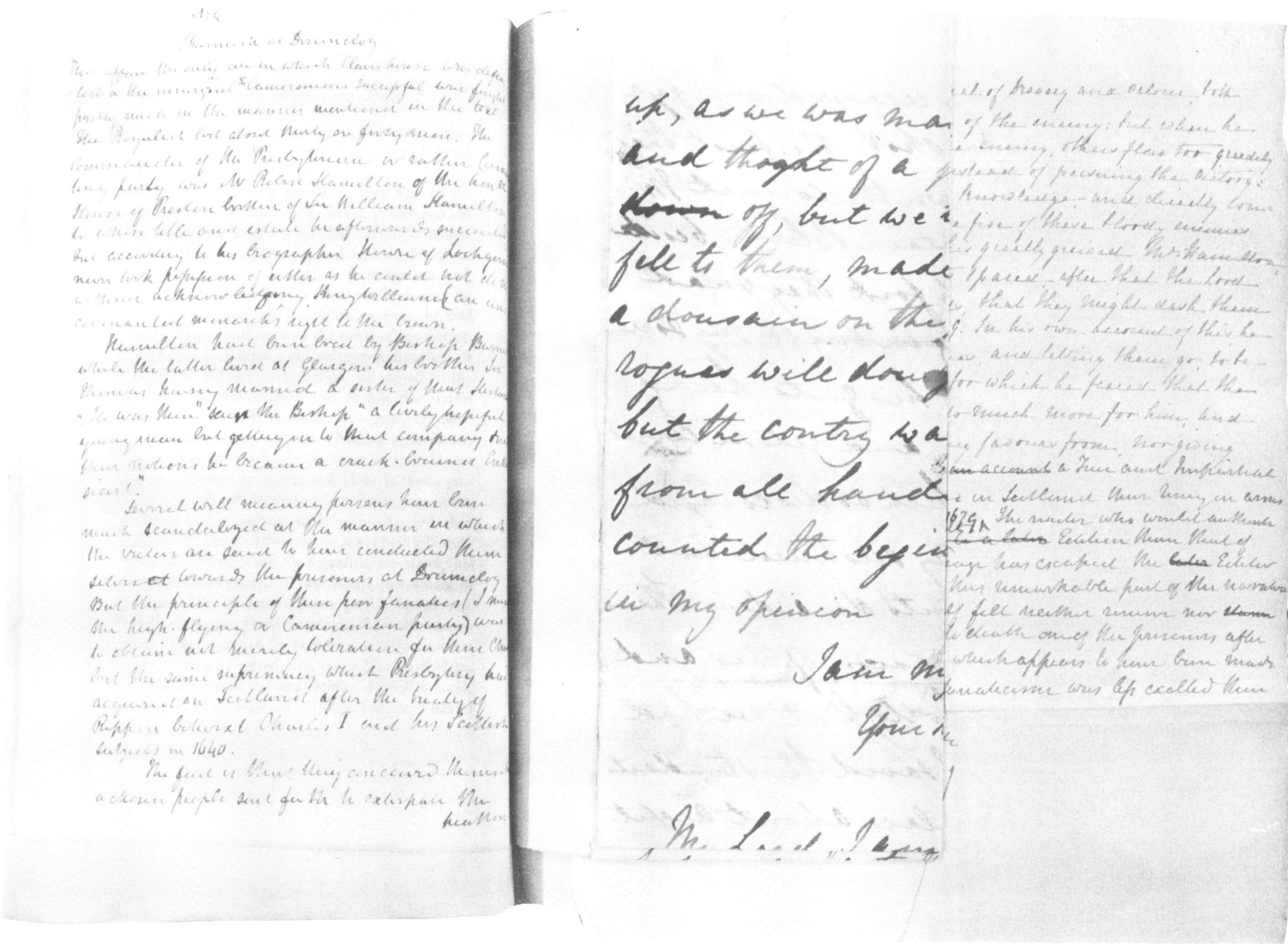

PLATE 29 Vol. VIII *OLD MORTALITY*

The complicated annotation relating to the battle of Drumclog comprises (reading from left to right in the photograph) interleaves bearing Scott's notes; a paper apart containing a transcript of a letter of Claverhouse to the Earl of Linlithgow (this displaying printer's fingerprints); and a further paper apart with a quotation in the hand of Anne Rutherford Scott, with linking material in Scott's own hand. (10. 155–58)

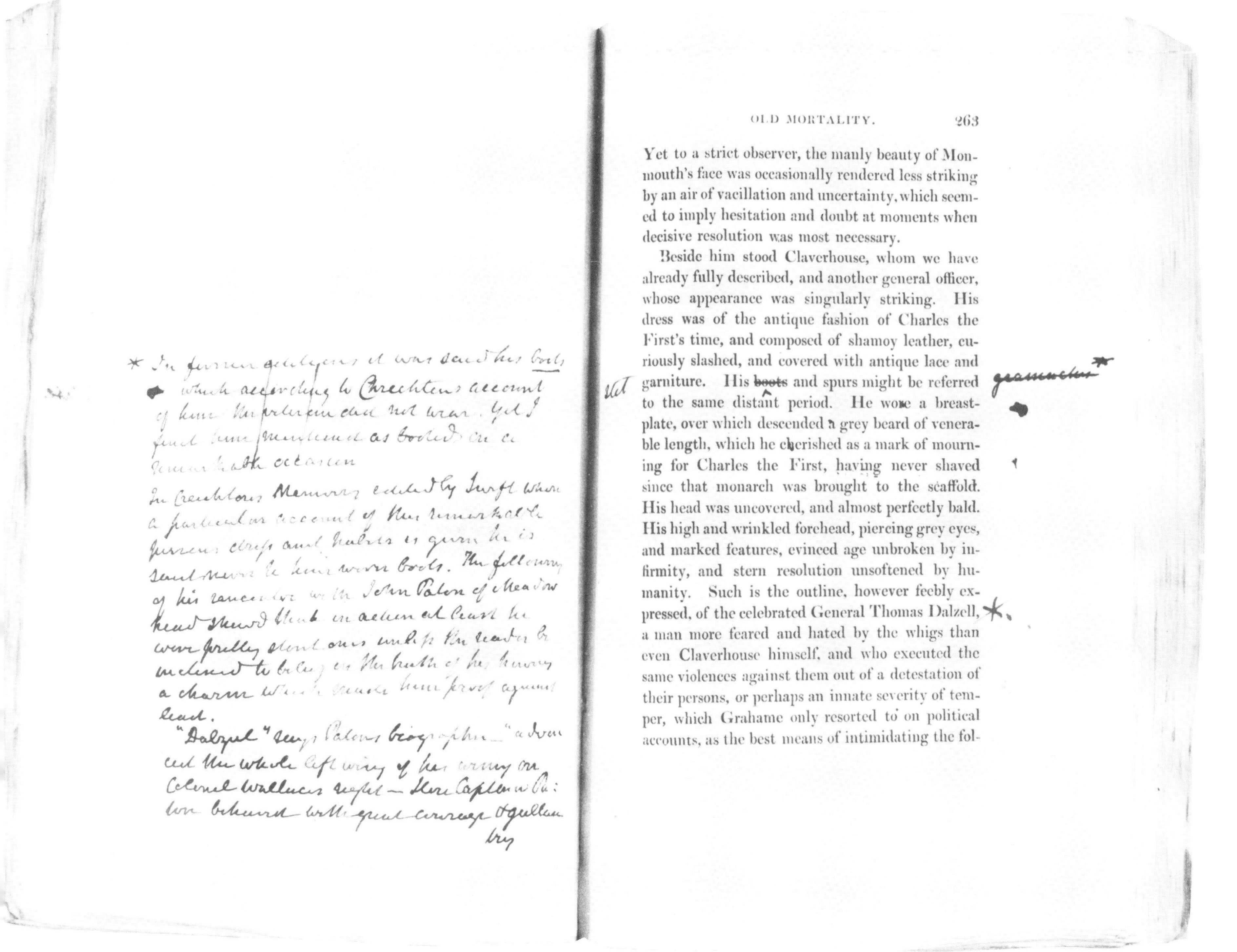

OLD MORTALITY. 263

Yet to a strict observer, the manly beauty of Monmouth's face was occasionally rendered less striking by an air of vacillation and uncertainty, which seemed to imply hesitation and doubt at moments when decisive resolution was most necessary.

Beside him stood Claverhouse, whom we have already fully described, and another general officer, whose appearance was singularly striking. His dress was of the antique fashion of Charles the First's time, and composed of shamoy leather, curiously slashed, and covered with antique lace and garniture. His ~~boots~~ and spurs might be referred to the same distant period. He wore a breastplate, over which descended a grey beard of venerable length, which he cherished as a mark of mourning for Charles the First, having never shaved since that monarch was brought to the scaffold. His head was uncovered, and almost perfectly bald. His high and wrinkled forehead, piercing grey eyes, and marked features, evinced age unbroken by infirmity, and stern resolution unsoftened by humanity. Such is the outline, however feebly expressed, of the celebrated General Thomas Dalzell,* a man more feared and hated by the whigs than even Claverhouse himself, and who executed the same violences against them out of a detestation of their persons, or perhaps an innate severity of temper, which Grahame only resorted to on political accounts, as the best means of intimidating the fol-

* In former editions it was said his boots which according to Creichton's account of him the general did not wear. Yet I find him mentioned as booted on a remarkable occasion
In Creichtons Memoirs edited by Swift where a particular account of this remarkable persons dress and habits is given he is said never to have worn boots. The following of his rencontre with John Paton of Meadowhead shows that in action at least he wore jack boots unless the reader be inclined to believe in the truth of his having a charm which made him proof against lead.
"Dalzell" says Patons biographer "advanced the whole left wing of his army on Colonel Wallace's right — Here Captain Paton behaved with great courage & gallantry

PLATE 30 Vol. VIII *OLD MORTALITY*

In the text on p.263 Scott suggests that the outline of the dress and appearance of General Tam Dalyell might be only 'feebly expressed'. Doubt of the effectiveness of the description caused Scott to attempt a strengthening exercise in his note, where the reader is alerted to the existence of a more complete description, and is also given further information about the General's most famous item of apparel, his enormous boots which still survive at the House of the Binns, West Lothian. (10. 342)

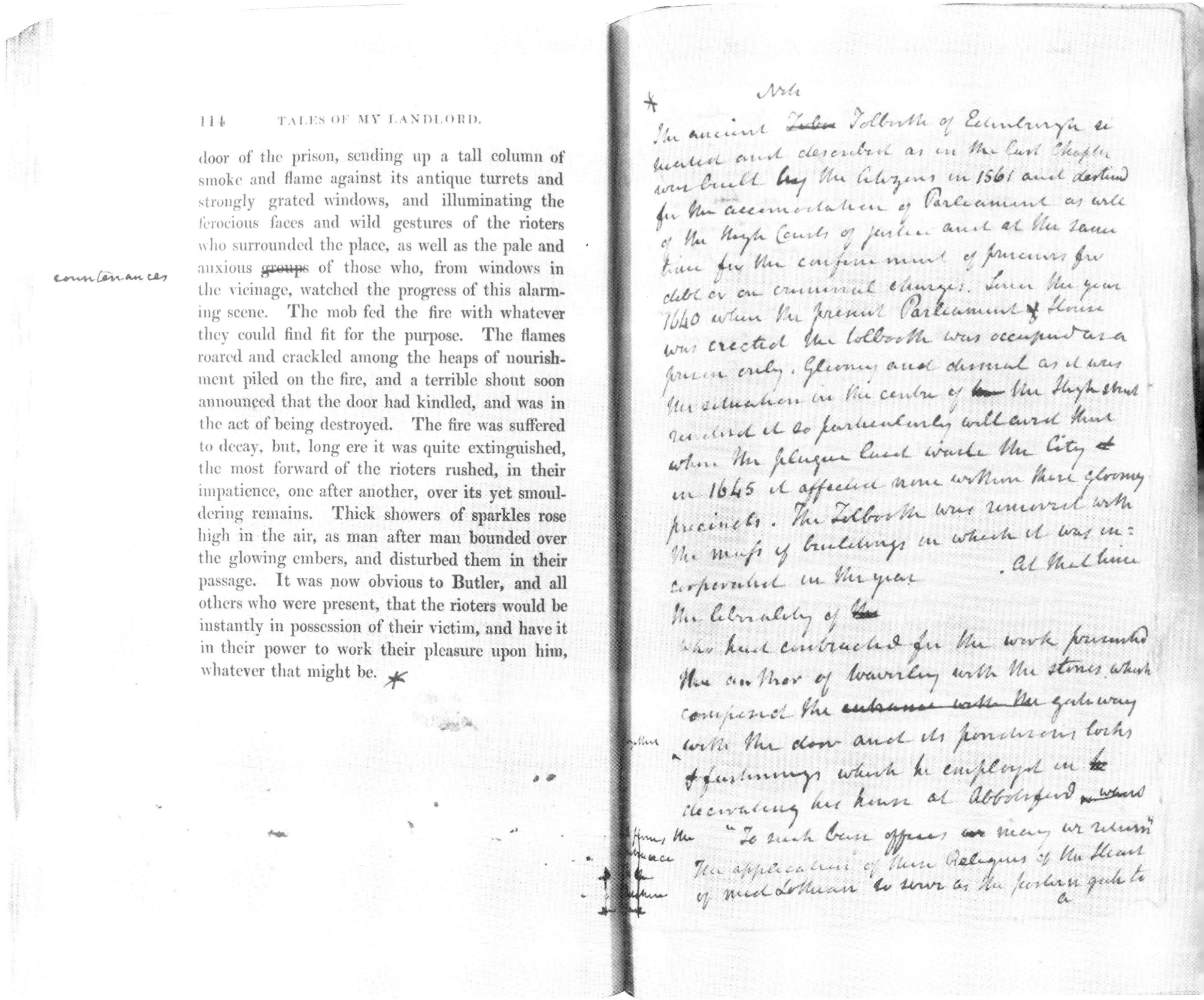

114 TALES OF MY LANDLORD.

door of the prison, sending up a tall column of smoke and flame against its antique turrets and strongly grated windows, and illuminating the ferocious faces and wild gestures of the rioters who surrounded the place, as well as the pale and anxious ~~groups~~ countenances of those who, from windows in the vicinage, watched the progress of this alarming scene. The mob fed the fire with whatever they could find fit for the purpose. The flames roared and crackled among the heaps of nourishment piled on the fire, and a terrible shout soon announced that the door had kindled, and was in the act of being destroyed. The fire was suffered to decay, but, long ere it was quite extinguished, the most forward of the rioters rushed, in their impatience, one after another, over its yet smouldering remains. Thick showers of sparkles rose high in the air, as man after man bounded over the glowing embers, and disturbed them in their passage. It was now obvious to Butler, and all others who were present, that the rioters would be instantly in possession of their victim, and have it in their power to work their pleasure upon him, whatever that might be. *

Note

* The ancient ~~Tolbo~~ Tolbooth of Edinburgh situated and described as in the last Chapter was built by the Citizens in 1561 and destined for the accomodation of Parliament as well of the High Courts of Justice and at the same time for the confinement of prisoners for debt or on criminal charges. Since the year 1640 when the present Parliament House was erected the Tolbooth was occupied as a prison only. Gloomy and dismal as it was the situation in the centre of ~~the~~ the High street rendered it so particularly well aired that when the plague laid waste the City & in 1645 it affected none within these gloomy precincts. The Tolbooth was removed with the mass of buildings in which it was incorporated in the year . At that time the liberality of ~~the~~ who had contracted for the work presented the author of Waverley with the stones which composed the ~~entrance with the~~ gateway together with the door and its ponderous locks & fastenings which he employed in ~~the~~ decorating his house at Abbotsford ~~where~~

"To such base offices we may return"

The application of these Reliques of the Heart of Mid Lothian to serve as the postern gate to a

PLATE 31 Vol. IX *THE HEART OF MID-LOTHIAN*

A personal anecdote is introduced into a note on the Tolbooth of Edinburgh (i.e. the Heart of Mid-Lothian). Scott tells the reader how the Author of Waverley was presented with the stones of the gateway of the old building, together with its door, when the structure was finally demolished in 1817, and how these relics had been employed in decorating the entrance to the kitchen-court at Abbotsford. (11. 256)

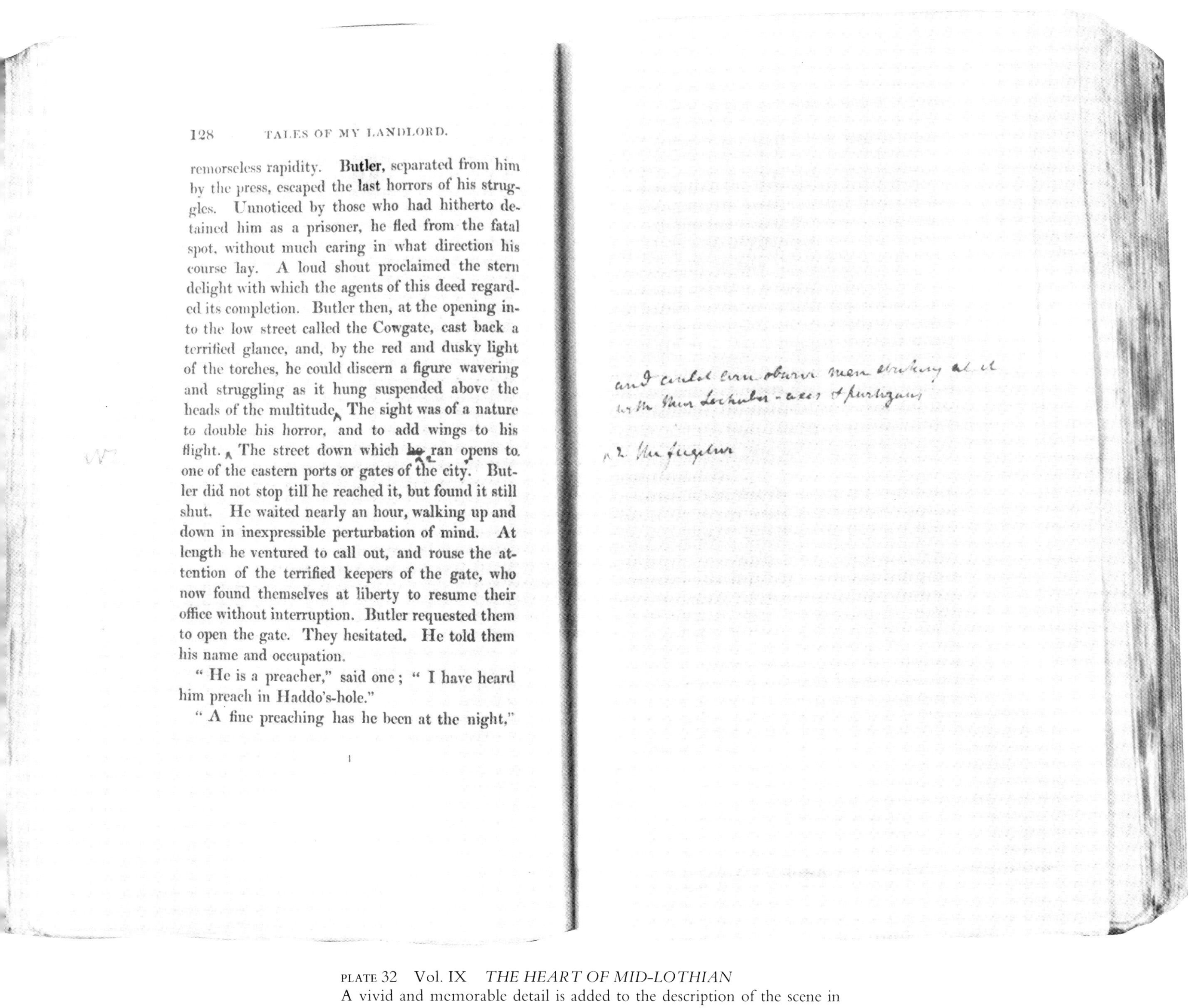

remorseless rapidity. Butler, separated from him by the press, escaped the last horrors of his struggles. Unnoticed by those who had hitherto detained him as a prisoner, he fled from the fatal spot, without much caring in what direction his course lay. A loud shout proclaimed the stern delight with which the agents of this deed regarded its completion. Butler then, at the opening into the low street called the Cowgate, cast back a terrified glance, and, by the red and dusky light of the torches, he could discern a figure wavering and struggling as it hung suspended above the heads of the multitude. The sight was of a nature to double his horror, and to add wings to his flight. The street down which he ran opens to one of the eastern ports or gates of the city. Butler did not stop till he reached it, but found it still shut. He waited nearly an hour, walking up and down in inexpressible perturbation of mind. At length he ventured to call out, and rouse the attention of the terrified keepers of the gate, who now found themselves at liberty to resume their office without interruption. Butler requested them to open the gate. They hesitated. He told them his name and occupation.

"He is a preacher," said one; "I have heard him preach in Haddo's-hole."

"A fine preaching has he been at the night,"

I

and could even observe men striking at it with their Lochaber-axes & partizans

2. the fugitive

PLATE 32 Vol. IX *THE HEART OF MID-LOTHIAN*
A vivid and memorable detail is added to the description of the scene in Edinburgh on the night of the murder of Captain Porteous. (11. 270)

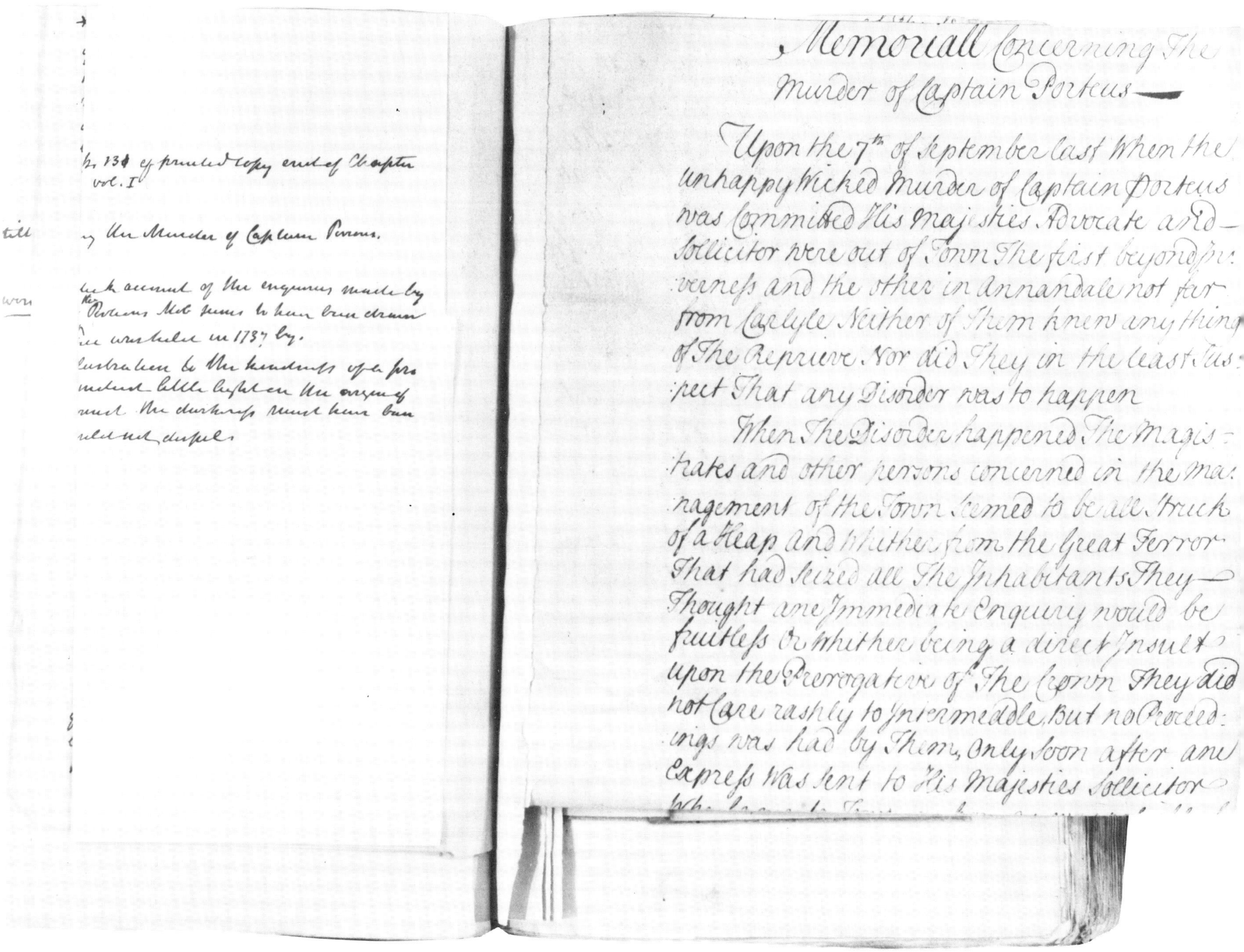

Memoriall Concerning The
Murder of Captain Porteus —

Upon the 7th of September last When the
unhappy Wicked Murder of Captain Porteus
was Committed His Majesties Advocate and
Sollicitor were out of Town The first beyond In-
verness and the other in Annandale not far
from Carlyle Neither of Them knew any thing
of The Reprieve Nor did They in the least Suspect That any Disorder was to happen

When The Disorder happened The Magis-
trates and other persons concerned in the Ma-
nagement of the Town Seemed to be all Struck
of a Heap And Whither from the Great Terror
That had Seized all The Inhabitants They
Thought an Immediate Enquiry would be
fruitless Or Whither being a direct Insult
upon the Prerogative of The Crown They did
not Care rashly to Intermeddle, But no Proceedings was had by Them, Only Soon after an
Express Was Sent to His Majesties Sollicitor

PLATE 33 Vol. IX *THE HEART OF MID-LOTHIAN*

Scott's use of historical documents as source materials for his novels, and for his later notes upon them, is nicely illustrated by this Memorial Concerning the Murder of Captain Porteous, dated 1737. This inconclusive document had been drawn up by the Solicitor General of the day, and Scott owed the authentic illustration 'to the kindness of a professional friend'—itself an instance of the pride and interest which Scott's fellow lawyers took in the literary work of their colleague. The Memorial furnished material for a Magnum edition note some eight full pages in length. (11. 274ff.)

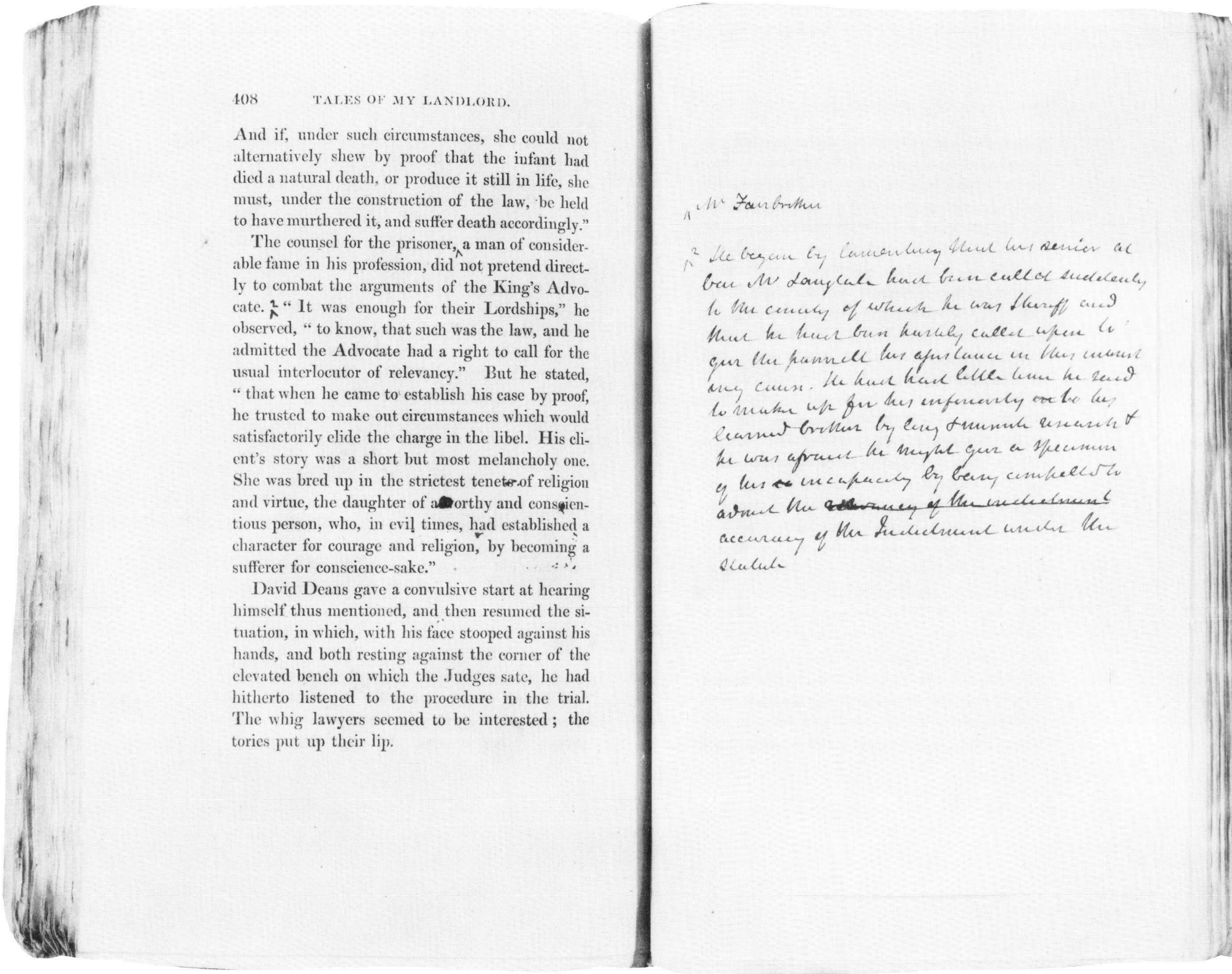

408 TALES OF MY LANDLORD.

And if, under such circumstances, she could not alternatively shew by proof that the infant had died a natural death, or produce it still in life, she must, under the construction of the law, be held to have murthered it, and suffer death accordingly."

The counsel for the prisoner, a man of considerable fame in his profession, did not pretend directly to combat the arguments of the King's Advocate. "It was enough for their Lordships," he observed, "to know, that such was the law, and he admitted the Advocate had a right to call for the usual interlocutor of relevancy." But he stated, "that when he came to establish his case by proof, he trusted to make out circumstances which would satisfactorily elide the charge in the libel. His client's story was a short but most melancholy one. She was bred up in the strictest tenets of religion and virtue, the daughter of a worthy and conscientious person, who, in evil times, had established a character for courage and religion, by becoming a sufferer for conscience-sake."

David Deans gave a convulsive start at hearing himself thus mentioned, and then resumed the situation, in which, with his face stooped against his hands, and both resting against the corner of the elevated bench on which the Judges sate, he had hitherto listened to the procedure in the trial. The whig lawyers seemed to be interested; the tories put up their lip.

Mr Fairbrother

He began by lamenting that his senior at bar Mr Langtale had been called suddenly to the county of which he was Sheriff and that he had been hastily called upon to give the pannell his assistance in this interesting cause. He had had little time he said to make up for his inferiority to his learned brother by long & minute research & he was afraid he might give a specimen of his incapacity by being compelled to admit the ~~relevancy of the indictment~~ accuracy of the Indictment under the statute

PLATE 34 Vol. IX *THE HEART OF MID-LOTHIAN*
The reported speech of the advocate defending Effie Deans is considerably expanded to add authenticity and colour to the narrative of her trial.
(12. 128–29)

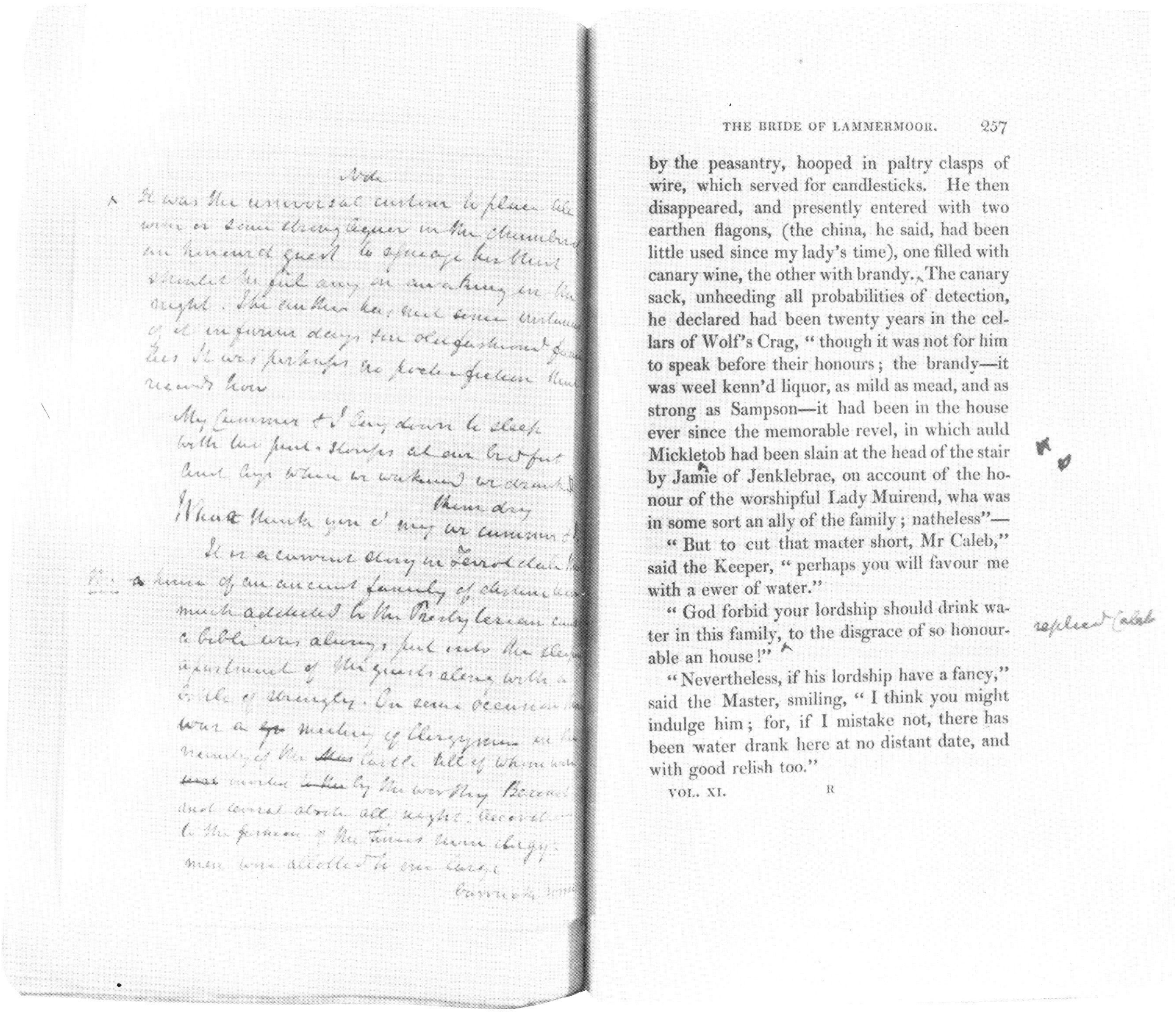

Note

It was the universal custom to place ale wine or some strong liquor in the chamber of an honoured guest to assuage his thirst should he feel any on awaking in the night. The custom has led some instances of it in former days [illegible] old fashioned families. It was perhaps the [illegible] record how

My Cummer & I lay down to sleep
With two pint-stoups at our bed feet
And aye when we wakened we drank them dry
What think you o' my wee cummer & I.

It is a current story in Teviotdale that in the house of an ancient family of distinction much addicted to the Presbyterian cause a bible was always put into the sleeping apartment of the guests along with a bottle of strong ale. On some occasion there was a meeting of clergymen in the vicinity of the castle all of whom were invited to dinner by the worthy Baronet and several abode all night. According to the fashion of the times seven clergymen were allotted to one large

barrack room

THE BRIDE OF LAMMERMOOR. 257

by the peasantry, hooped in paltry clasps of wire, which served for candlesticks. He then disappeared, and presently entered with two earthen flagons, (the china, he said, had been little used since my lady's time), one filled with canary wine, the other with brandy. The canary sack, unheeding all probabilities of detection, he declared had been twenty years in the cellars of Wolf's Crag, " though it was not for him to speak before their honours; the brandy—it was weel kenn'd liquor, as mild as mead, and as strong as Sampson—it had been in the house ever since the memorable revel, in which auld Mickletob had been slain at the head of the stair by Jamie of Jenklebrae, on account of the honour of the worshipful Lady Muirend, wha was in some sort an ally of the family; natheless"—

" But to cut that matter short, Mr Caleb," said the Keeper, " perhaps you will favour me with a ewer of water."

" God forbid your lordship should drink water in this family, to the disgrace of so honourable an house!" replied Caleb

"Nevertheless, if his lordship have a fancy," said the Master, smiling, " I think you might indulge him; for, if I mistake not, there has been water drank here at no distant date, and with good relish too."

VOL. XI. R

PLATE 35 Vol. XI *THE BRIDE OF LAMMERMOOR*
An allusion to the old custom of placing flagons of alcoholic refreshment in the bedchambers of guests gives Scott the opportunity to digress further on 'Ancient Hospitality' in a note for the Magnum edition. The chance is also taken to retail a good story about Scottish clergymen who, when sharing a room, preferred to have but one Bible among them and a further bottle of ale each, rather than a Bible each and only one bottle of ale per head. (14. 91)

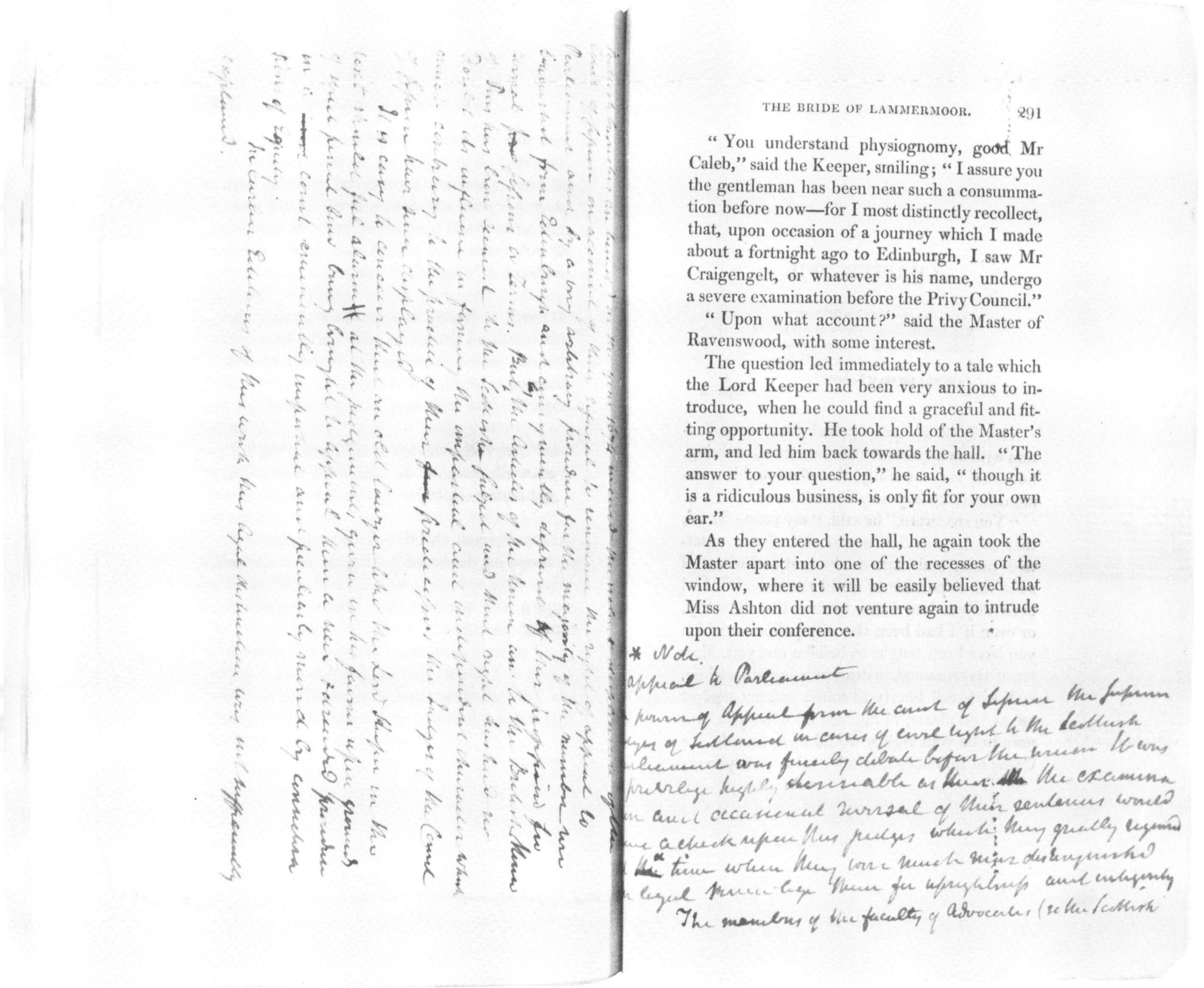
THE BRIDE OF LAMMERMOOR. 291

"You understand physiognomy, good Mr Caleb," said the Keeper, smiling; "I assure you the gentleman has been near such a consummation before now—for I most distinctly recollect, that, upon occasion of a journey which I made about a fortnight ago to Edinburgh, I saw Mr Craigengelt, or whatever is his name, undergo a severe examination before the Privy Council."

"Upon what account?" said the Master of Ravenswood, with some interest.

The question led immediately to a tale which the Lord Keeper had been very anxious to introduce, when he could find a graceful and fitting opportunity. He took hold of the Master's arm, and led him back towards the hall. "The answer to your question," he said, "though it is a ridiculous business, is only fit for your own ear."

As they entered the hall, he again took the Master apart into one of the recesses of the window, where it will be easily believed that Miss Ashton did not venture again to intrude upon their conference.

PLATE 36 Vol. XI *THE BRIDE OF LAMMERMOOR*

Scott ends this note, entitled 'Appeal to Parliament', with the sentence (written on the interleaf): 'In earlier editions of this Work, this legal distinction was not sufficiently explained.' It had evidently troubled the Clerk of Session—possibly in idle moments in court, as when Mark Napier sketched him—that he had not been clear in his own lawyer's mind as to the real position in matters of appeals to Parliament in the period between 1689 and the Union of 1707. The solution was to move the whole setting of this novel from before to after the Union; and to this end he tried systematically to make all references throughout the novel to the Scottish courts and to Parliament conform to a time when there was only the one Parliament of Great Britain, and the House of Lords, to which appeals from the Court of Session in Edinburgh could be referred. (14. 116)

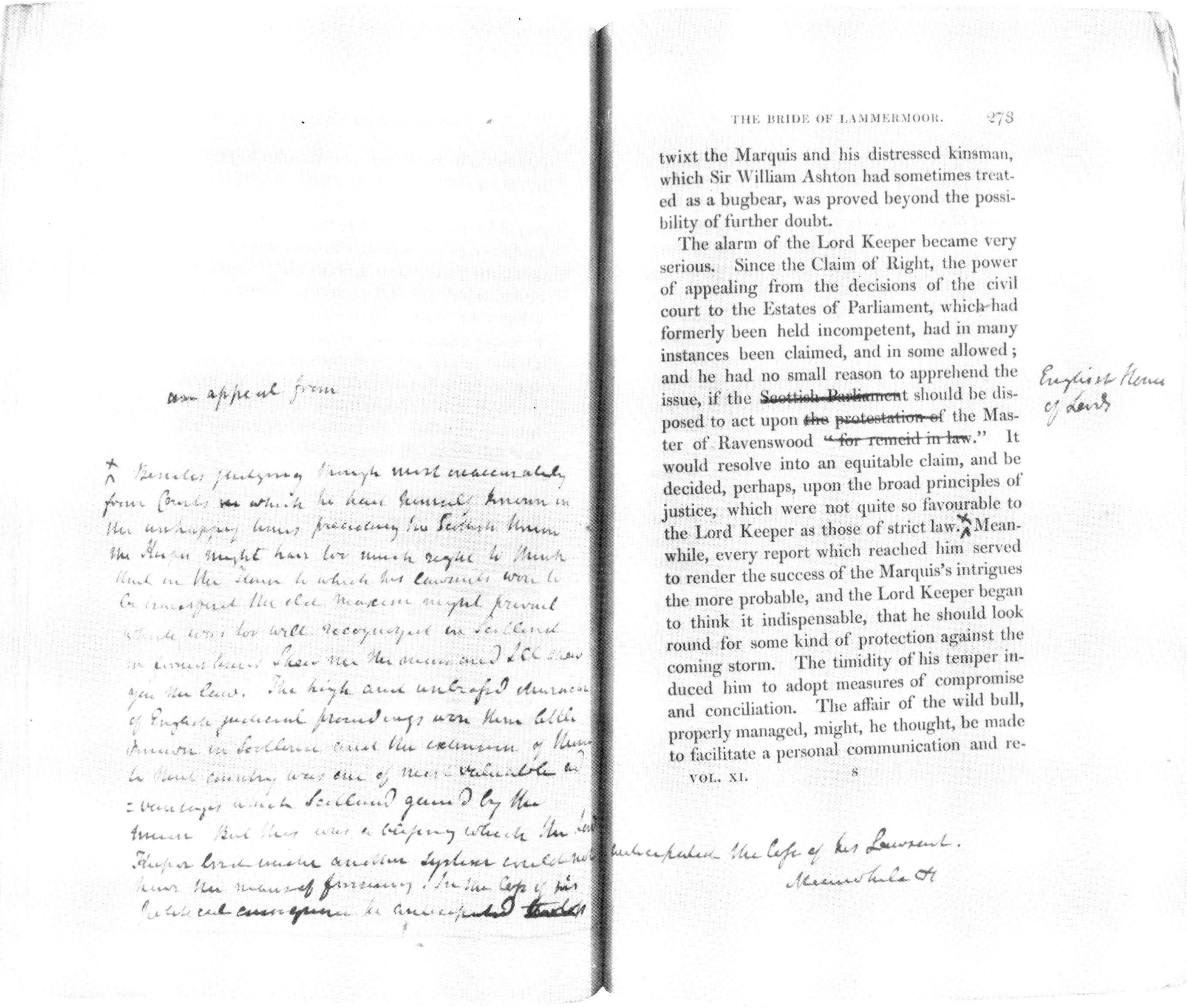

twixt the Marquis and his distressed kinsman, which Sir William Ashton had sometimes treated as a bugbear, was proved beyond the possibility of further doubt.

The alarm of the Lord Keeper became very serious. Since the Claim of Right, the power of appealing from the decisions of the civil court to the Estates of Parliament, which had formerly been held incompetent, had in many instances been claimed, and in some allowed; and he had no small reason to apprehend the issue, if the ~~Scottish Parliament~~ should be disposed to act upon ~~the protestation of~~ the Master of Ravenswood ~~"for remeid in law."~~ It would resolve into an equitable claim, and be decided, perhaps, upon the broad principles of justice, which were not quite so favourable to the Lord Keeper as those of strict law.^ Meanwhile, every report which reached him served to render the success of the Marquis's intrigues the more probable, and the Lord Keeper began to think it indispensable, that he should look round for some kind of protection against the coming storm. The timidity of his temper induced him to adopt measures of compromise and conciliation. The affair of the wild bull, properly managed, might, he thought, be made to facilitate a personal communication and re-

English House of Lords

an appeal from

^ Besides judging though most inaccurately from Courts which he had formerly known in the unhappy times preceding the Scottish Union the Keeper might have too much right to think that in the House to which his lawsuits were to be transferred the old maxim might prevail which was too well recognized in Scotland in former times Shew me the man and I'll shew you the law. The high and unbiassed character of English judicial proceedings were then little known in Scotland and the extension of them to that country was one of most valuable advantages which Scotland gained by the Union. But this was a blessing which the Lord Keeper lived under another system could not know the means of foreseeing. In the loss of his political consequence he anticipated ~~the loss~~ anticipated the loss of his Lawsuit. Meanwhile &c

PLATE 37 Vol. XI *THE BRIDE OF LAMMERMOOR*
The time-change of the novel (see Plate 36) is here well illustrated. The question of appeal is altered from one of appeal to the old Scottish Parliament, to appeal to the post-Union (British) House of Lords; and to the actual text of the novel—rather than simply being relegated to the place of a note—is added a didactic and expository section in which Scott attempts to clarify for the reader a complex legal position. Here is Scott the editor at his most conscientious. (14. 100)

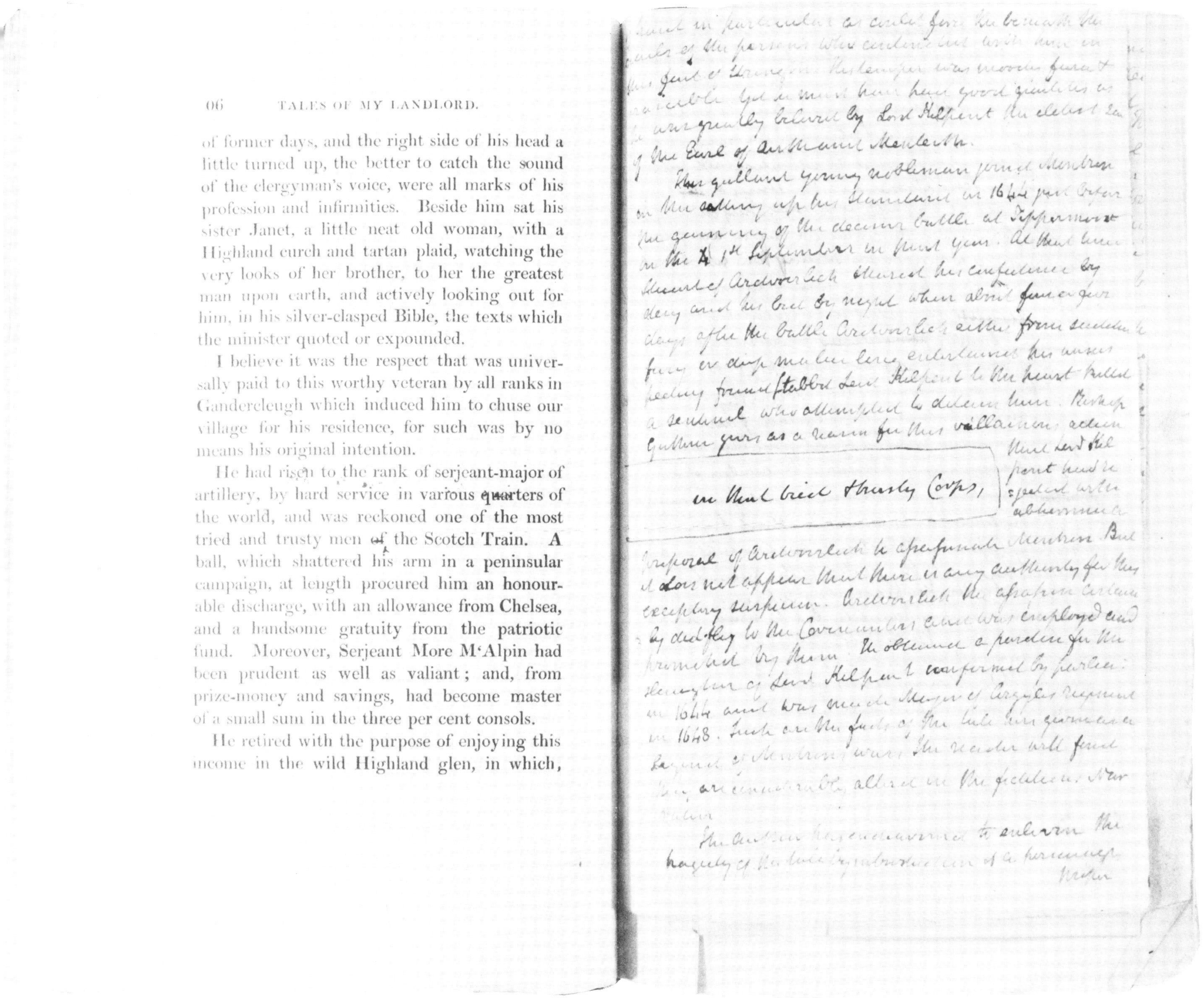
06 TALES OF MY LANDLORD.

of former days, and the right side of his head a little turned up, the better to catch the sound of the clergyman's voice, were all marks of his profession and infirmities. Beside him sat his sister Janet, a little neat old woman, with a Highland curch and tartan plaid, watching the very looks of her brother, to her the greatest man upon earth, and actively looking out for him, in his silver-clasped Bible, the texts which the minister quoted or expounded.

I believe it was the respect that was universally paid to this worthy veteran by all ranks in Gandercleugh which induced him to chuse our village for his residence, for such was by no means his original intention.

He had risen to the rank of serjeant-major of artillery, by hard service in various quarters of the world, and was reckoned one of the most tried and trusty men of the Scotch Train. A ball, which shattered his arm in a peninsular campaign, at length procured him an honourable discharge, with an allowance from Chelsea, and a handsome gratuity from the patriotic fund. Moreover, Serjeant More M'Alpin had been prudent as well as valiant; and, from prize-money and savings, had become master of a small sum in the three per cent consols.

He retired with the purpose of enjoying this income in the wild Highland glen, in which,

PLATE 38 Vol. XII *A LEGEND OF MONTROSE*
Part of the Introduction to the Magnum edition (this written on a fly-title of the 1822 *Novels and Tales* volume, on interleaves, and with long quotations on papers apart) laps round an alteration to the text already entered on an interleaf. (The alteration not printed in the Magnum edition: see 15. xxxiv.) (15. viii–ix)

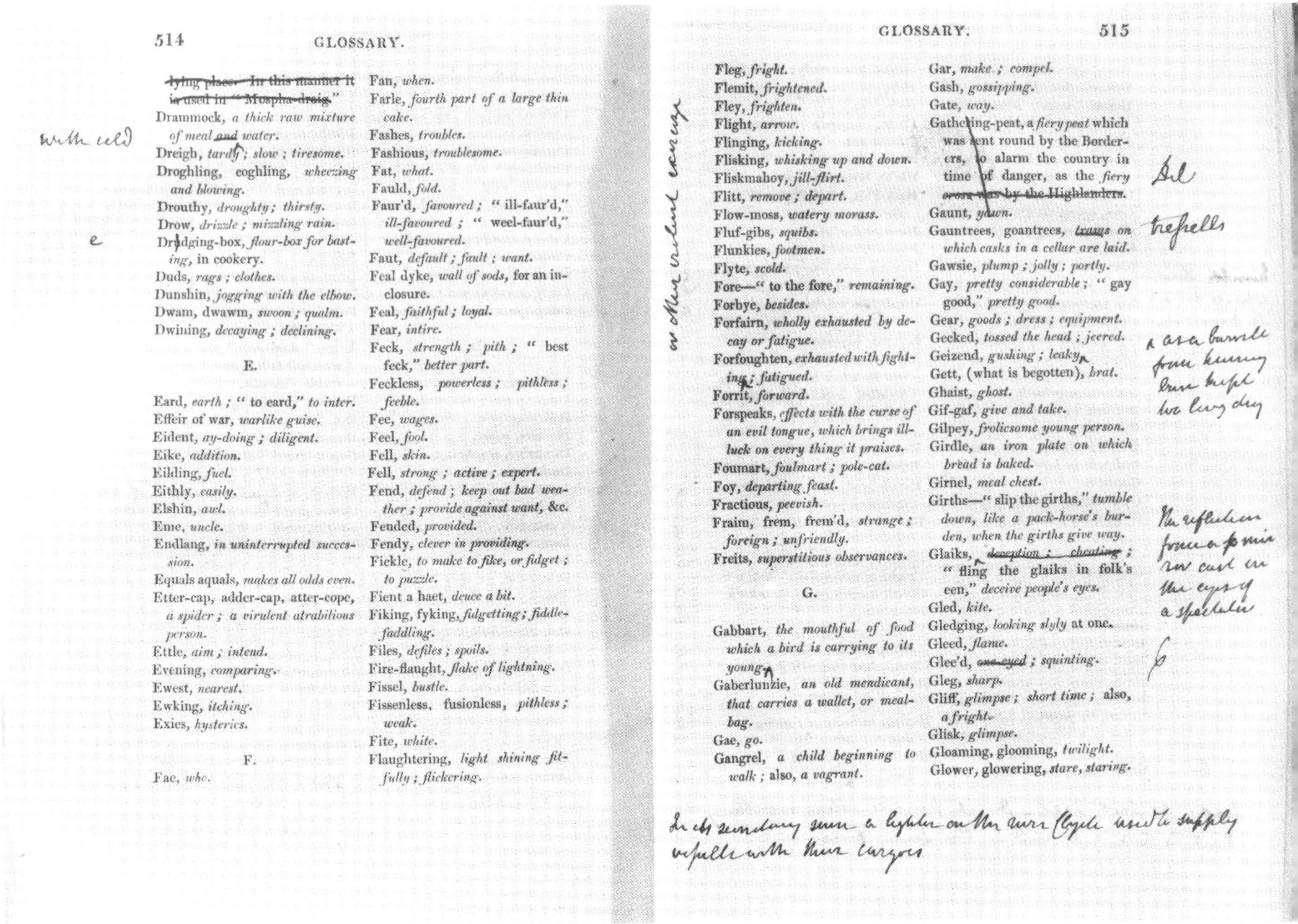
514 GLOSSARY.

~~lying place. In this manner it is used in "Mospha-draig."~~

Drammock, *a thick raw mixture of meal ~~and~~ water.*

Dreigh, *tardy; slow; tiresome.*

Droghling, coghling, *wheezing and blowing.*

Drouthy, *droughty; thirsty.*

Drow, *drizzle; mizzling rain.*

Dradging-box, *flour-box for basting,* in cookery.

Duds, *rags; clothes.*

Dunshin, *jogging with the elbow.*

Dwam, dwawm, *swoon; qualm.*

Dwining, *decaying; declining.*

E.

Eard, *earth;* "to eard," *to inter.*

Effeir of war, *warlike guise.*

Eident, *ay-doing; diligent.*

Eike, *addition.*

Eilding, *fuel.*

Eithly, *easily.*

Elshin, *awl.*

Eme, *uncle.*

Endlang, *in uninterrupted succession.*

Equals aquals, *makes all odds even.*

Etter-cap, adder-cap, atter-cope, *a spider; a virulent atrabilious person.*

Ettle, *aim; intend.*

Evening, *comparing.*

Ewest, *nearest.*

Ewking, *itching.*

Exies, *hysterics.*

F.

Fae, *who.*

Fan, *when.*

Farle, *fourth part of a large thin cake.*

Fashes, *troubles.*

Fashious, *troublesome.*

Fat, *what.*

Fauld, *fold.*

Faur'd, *favoured;* "ill-faur'd," *ill-favoured;* "weel-faur'd," *well-favoured.*

Faut, *default; fault; want.*

Feal dyke, *wall of sods,* for an inclosure.

Feal, *faithful; loyal.*

Fear, *intire.*

Feck, *strength; pith;* "best feck," *better part.*

Feckless, *powerless; pithless; feeble.*

Fee, *wages.*

Feel, *fool.*

Fell, *skin.*

Fell, *strong; active; expert.*

Fend, *defend; keep out bad weather; provide against want,* &c.

Fended, *provided.*

Fendy, *clever in providing.*

Fickle, *to make to fike, or fidget; to puzzle.*

Fient a haet, *deuce a bit.*

Fiking, fyking, *fidgetting; fiddle-faddling.*

Files, *defiles; spoils.*

Fire-flaught, *flake of lightning.*

Fissel, *bustle.*

Fissenless, fusionless, *pithless; weak.*

Fite, *white.*

Flaughtering, *light shining fitfully; flickering.*

GLOSSARY. 515

Fleg, *fright.*

Flemit, *frightened.*

Fley, *frighten.*

Flight, *arrow.*

Flinging, *kicking.*

Flisking, *whisking up and down.*

Fliskmahoy, *jill-flirt.*

Flitt, *remove; depart.*

Flow-moss, *watery morass.*

Fluf-gibs, *squibs.*

Flunkies, *footmen.*

Flyte, *scold.*

Fore—"to the fore," *remaining.*

Forbye, *besides.*

Forfairn, *wholly exhausted by decay or fatigue.*

Forfoughten, *exhausted with fighting; fatigued.*

Forrit, *forward.*

Forspeaks, *effects with the curse of an evil tongue, which brings ill-luck on every thing it praises.*

Foumart, *foulmart; pole-cat.*

Foy, *departing feast.*

Fractious, *peevish.*

Fraim, frem, frem'd, *strange; foreign; unfriendly.*

Freits, *superstitious observances.*

G.

Gabbart, *the mouthful of food which a bird is carrying to its young.*

Gaberlunzie, *an old mendicant, that carries a wallet, or meal-bag.*

Gae, *go.*

Gangrel, *a child beginning to walk; also, a vagrant.*

Gar, *make; compel.*

Gash, *gossipping.*

Gate, *way.*

Gathering-peat, *a fiery peat* which was sent round by the Borderers, to alarm the country in time of danger, as the *fiery* ~~cross was by the Highlanders.~~

Gaunt, *yawn.*

Gauntrees, goantrees, ~~*trams*~~ *on which casks in a cellar are laid.*

Gawsie, *plump; jolly; portly.*

Gay, *pretty considerable;* "gay good," *pretty good.*

Gear, *goods; dress; equipment.*

Gecked, *tossed the head; jeered.*

Geizend, *gushing; leaky.*

Gett, (what is begotten), *brat.*

Ghaist, *ghost.*

Gif-gaf, *give and take.*

Gilpey, *frolicsome young person.*

Girdle, *an iron plate on which bread is baked.*

Girnel, *meal chest.*

Girths—"slip the girths," *tumble down, like a pack-horse's burden, when the girths give way.*

Glaiks, ~~*deception; cheating*~~; "fling the glaiks in folk's een," *deceive people's eyes.*

Gled, *kite.*

Gledging, *looking slyly* at one.

Gleed, *flame.*

Glee'd, ~~*one-eyed*~~*; squinting.*

Gleg, *sharp.*

Gliff, *glimpse; short time;* also, *a fright.*

Glisk, *glimpse.*

Gloaming, glooming, *twilight.*

Glower, glowering, *stare, staring.*

PLATE 39 Vol. XII [*A LEGEND OF MONTROSE*]
Emendations to the Glossary at the end of the twelve-volume *Novels and Tales of the Author of Waverley* series which forms the first section of the Interleaved Set.

facing page

PLATE 40 Vol. XIII *IVANHOE*
The initial folio of the Introduction. This paper begins: 'The Author of the Waverley Novels had hitherto proceeded in an unabated course of popularity, and might, in his peculiar district of literature, have been termed *L'Enfant Gâté* of success. It was plain, however, that frequent publication must finally wear out the public favour, unless some mode could be devised to give an appearance of novelty to subsequent productions.' This novel, with its English medieval theme, was the result of Scott's realisation of the need for variety and change. The theory behind the production of the Magnum edition, too, was partly that a new generation of readers had to be captured, and the interest of an existing readership reawakened, by fitting out the novels in a new dress with annotation and lengthy semi-autobiographical introductions such as this. (16. iii–vi)

Introduction to Ivanhoe.

The Author of the ~~Scot~~ Waverley novels had hitherto proceeded in an unabated course of popularity and might in his peculiar district of literature have been termed L'Enfant Gaté of success It was plain however that this must finally wear out the publick favour unless some mode could be fallen upon to give an appearance of Novelty to fresh attempts to engage their attention. Scottish manners Scottish dialect and Scottish characters of note being those with which I was most intimately and familiarly acquainted were those upon which I had hitherto relied for giving efficacy to my narratives. It was however obvious that the species of interest must give ~~give~~ a species of sameness and repetition if exclusively resorted to and that the reader was likely to adopt the language of Edwin in Parnel's tale

—— "Reverse the spell" he cries
And let it fairly now suffice
The gambol has been shown

Nothing can be more dangerous for the fame of a professor of the fine arts than to permit (if he can possibly prevent it) that the character of a mannerist should be attached to him or that he should be supposed ~~capable~~ capable of ~~excellence~~ success only in a particular and limited style The publick are in general very ready to adopt the opinion that he who pleased them in one peculiar mode of composition is by means of that very talent rendered incapable of venturing upon other subjects. The effect of this disinclination on the part of the public towards the artificers of their pleasures when they attempt to enlarge their means of amusing may be seen in the censures usually passed by vulgar criticism upon actors or artists who venture to change the character that in so doing they may ~~to~~ enlarge the scale of their art.^A The restrictions indeed are not always originating in prejudice. It may often happen on the stage that an actor by possessing in a preeminent degree the external qualities necessary to give effect to comedy may be deprived of the right to aspire to tragic excellence And in painting or literary composition a poet artist ~~may~~ may be master exclusively of those ~~or~~ modes of thought & powers of expression which confine him to a single course of subjects. But much more frequently the same capacity which carries a man to popularity in one department will obtain for him success in another ~~and~~ that must be more particularly the case in composition than either in acting or painting because the adventurer in that department is not is not ~~impeded in~~ impeded in his exertions by any peculiarity of features or conformation of person proper for particular parts or by any ~~habits of using~~ using the pencil limited to a particular class of subjects

Whether this reasoning be correct or otherwise the present author felt that in confining himself to subjects purely Scottish he was not only likely to weary out the indulgence of his readers but also greatly to limit his own power of affording them pleasure In a highly polished country where so much genius is monthly employed in catering for publick amusement a fresh topic such as he had himself the happiness to chance upon is the untasted spring of the ~~des~~ desert

Men bless their stars and ~~call it~~ Luxury

But when ~~horses~~ men and horses steers camels and dromedaries have poached

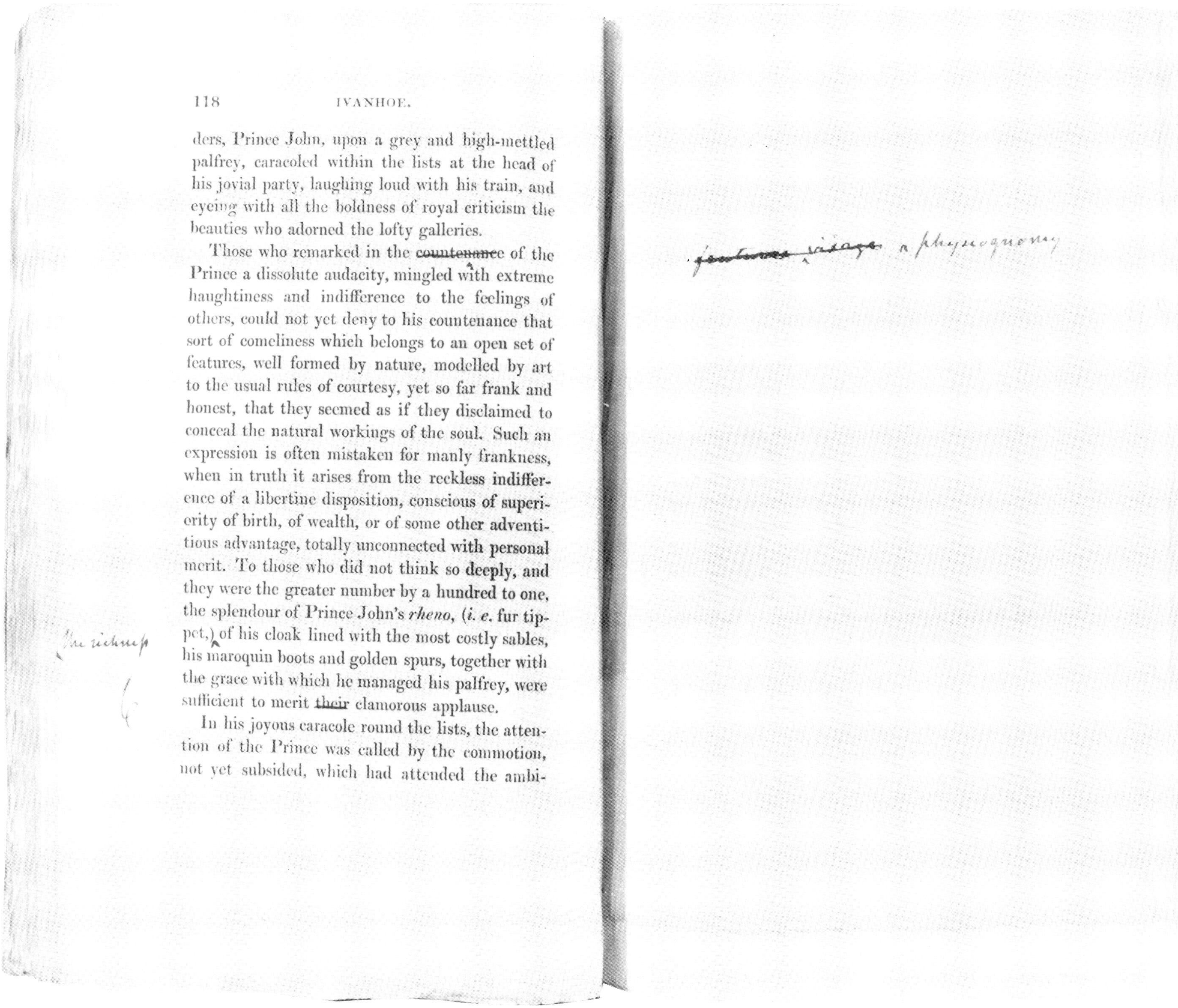

118 IVANHOE.

ders, Prince John, upon a grey and high-mettled palfrey, caracoled within the lists at the head of his jovial party, laughing loud with his train, and eyeing with all the boldness of royal criticism the beauties who adorned the lofty galleries.

Those who remarked in the ~~countenance~~ of the Prince a dissolute audacity, mingled with extreme haughtiness and indifference to the feelings of others, could not yet deny to his countenance that sort of comeliness which belongs to an open set of features, well formed by nature, modelled by art to the usual rules of courtesy, yet so far frank and honest, that they seemed as if they disclaimed to conceal the natural workings of the soul. Such an expression is often mistaken for manly frankness, when in truth it arises from the reckless indifference of a libertine disposition, conscious of superiority of birth, of wealth, or of some other adventitious advantage, totally unconnected with personal merit. To those who did not think so deeply, and they were the greater number by a hundred to one, the splendour of Prince John's *rheno*, (*i. e.* fur tippet,) of his cloak lined with the most costly sables, his maroquin boots and golden spurs, together with the grace with which he managed his palfrey, were sufficient to merit ~~their~~ clamorous applause.

In his joyous caracole round the lists, the attention of the Prince was called by the commotion, not yet subsided, which had attended the ambi-

PLATE 41 Vol. XIII *IVANHOE*
Scott's search for just the right word is evident from his alteration of 'countenance', to 'features', to 'visage', to 'physiognomy'. (16. 110)

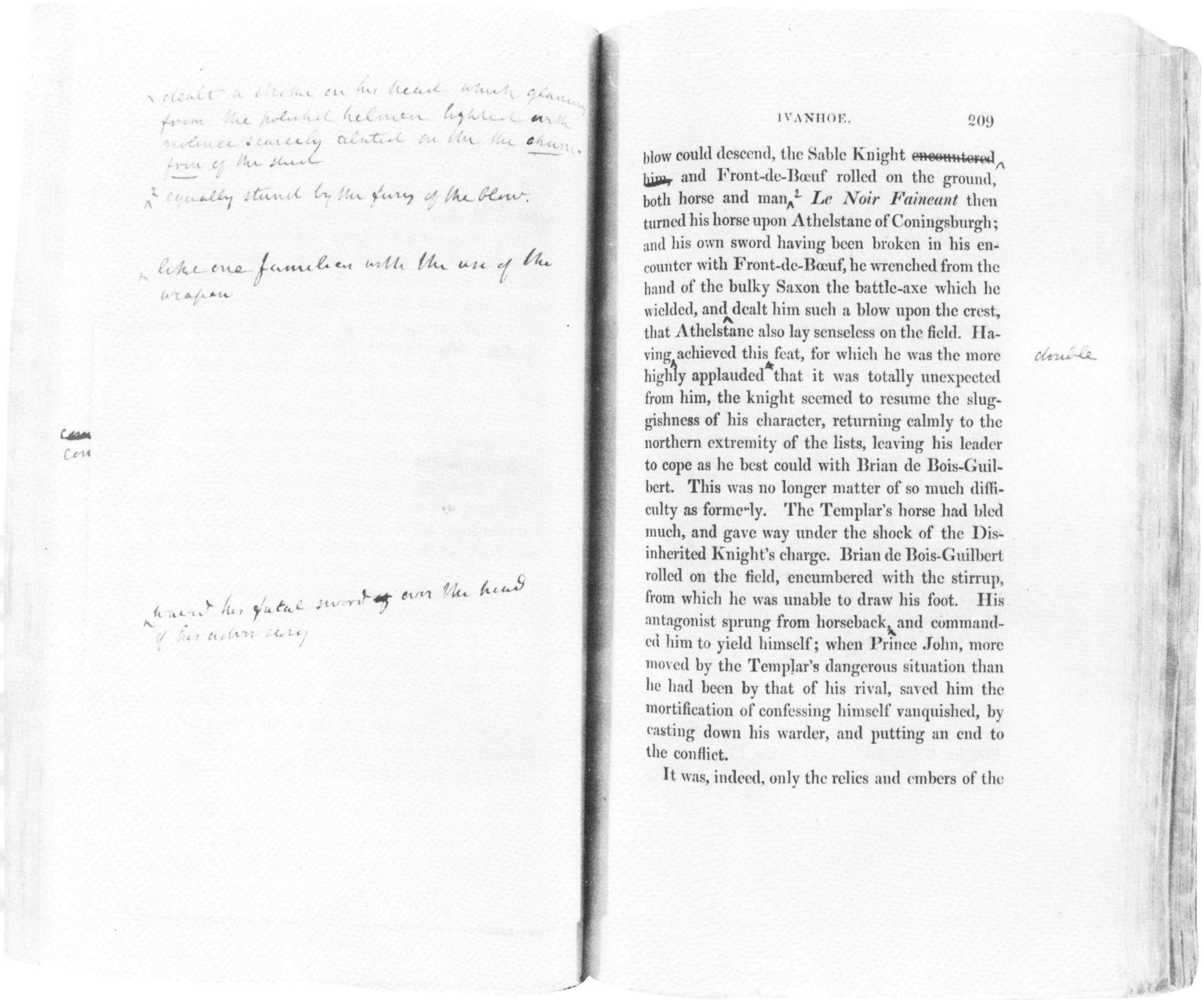
dealt a stroke on his head which glancing from the polished helmet lighted with violence scarcely abated on the the chamfron of the steed

equally stunned by the fury of the blow.

like one familiar with the use of the weapon

waved his fatal sword over the head of his adversary

IVANHOE. 209

blow could descend, the Sable Knight ~~encountered him,~~ and Front-de-Bœuf rolled on the ground, both horse and man. Le Noir Faineant then turned his horse upon Athelstane of Coningsburgh; and his own sword having been broken in his encounter with Front-de-Bœuf, he wrenched from the hand of the bulky Saxon the battle-axe which he wielded, and dealt him such a blow upon the crest, that Athelstane also lay senseless on the field. Having achieved this feat, for which he was the more highly applauded that it was totally unexpected from him, the knight seemed to resume the sluggishness of his character, returning calmly to the northern extremity of the lists, leaving his leader to cope as he best could with Brian de Bois-Guilbert. This was no longer matter of so much difficulty as formerly. The Templar's horse had bled much, and gave way under the shock of the Disinherited Knight's charge. Brian de Bois-Guilbert rolled on the field, encumbered with the stirrup, from which he was unable to draw his foot. His antagonist sprung from horseback, and commanded him to yield himself; when Prince John, more moved by the Templar's dangerous situation than he had been by that of his rival, saved him the mortification of confessing himself vanquished, by casting down his warder, and putting an end to the conflict.

It was, indeed, only the relics and embers of the

double

PLATE 42 Vol. XIII *IVANHOE*
Colourful and dramatic details added to the tournament scene reflect the enduring interest of Scott—the sometime Edinburgh Light Dragoon—in the romance of war and chivalry and the military life. (16. 192–93)

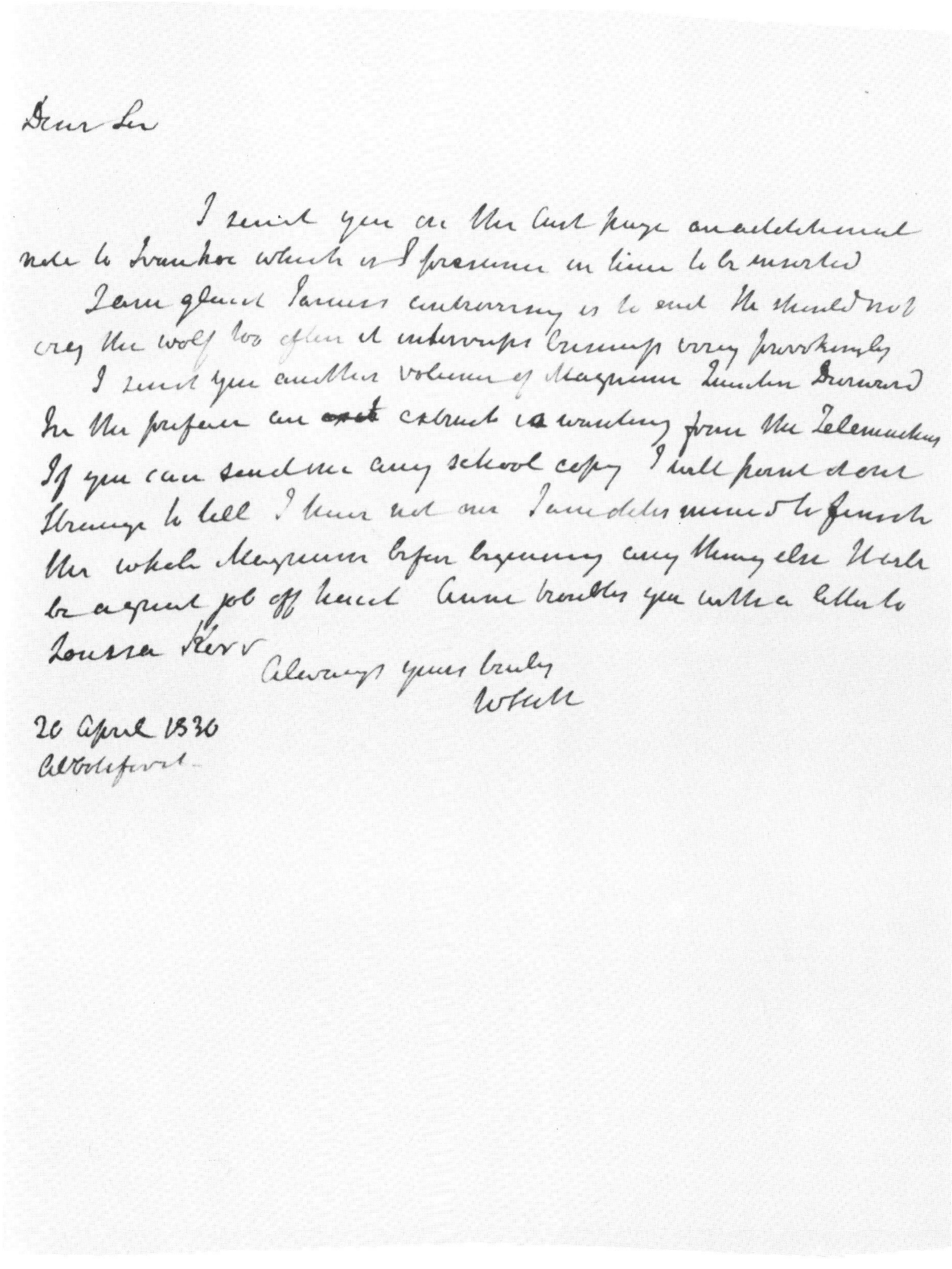

Dear Sir

I send you on the last page an additional note to Ivanhoe which is I presume in time to be inserted
I am glad James's controversy is at end He should not cry the wolf too often it interrupts business very provokingly
I send you another volume of Magnum Quentin Durward In the preface an ~~ext~~ extract is wanting from the Telemachus If you can send me any school copy I will point it out Strange to tell I have not one I am determined to finish the whole Magnum before beginning any thing else It will be a great job off hand Anne troubles you with a letter to Louisa Kerr

Always yours truly
W Scott

20 April 1830
Abbotsford

PLATE 43 Vol. XIII *IVANHOE*
Scott's letter to Cadell of 20 April 1830 (bound into the interleaved volume) enclosing a further last-minute note to *Ivanhoe*—expanding a note already added for the Magnum edition—which he hopes comes in time to be inserted. He also takes the opportunity to make a statement of reassurance to his publisher: 'I am determined to finish the whole Magnum before beginning any thing else. It will be a great job off hand.'

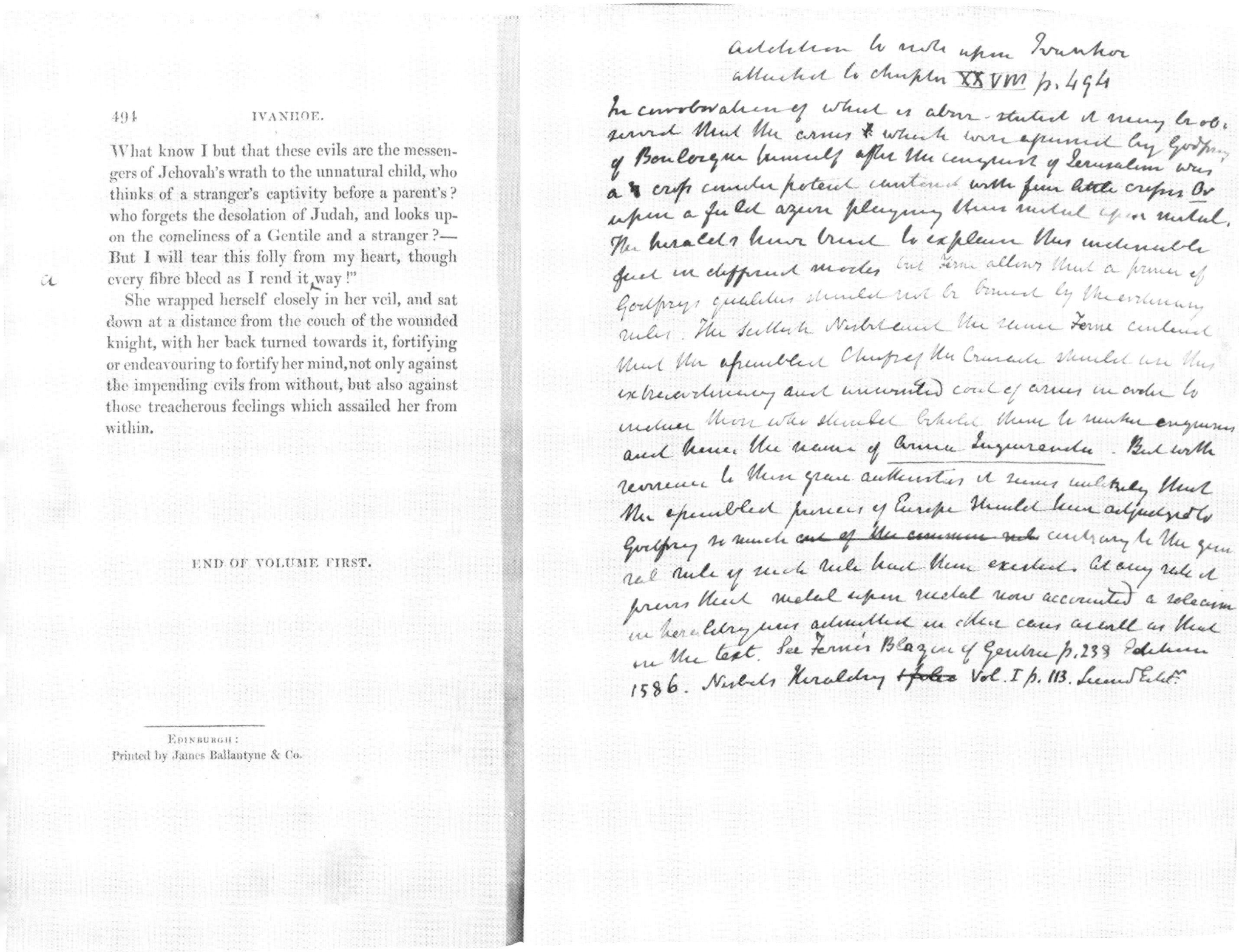
494 IVANHOE.

What know I but that these evils are the messengers of Jehovah's wrath to the unnatural child, who thinks of a stranger's captivity before a parent's? who forgets the desolation of Judah, and looks upon the comeliness of a Gentile and a stranger?— But I will tear this folly from my heart, though every fibre bleed as I rend it a way!"

She wrapped herself closely in her veil, and sat down at a distance from the couch of the wounded knight, with her back turned towards it, fortifying or endeavouring to fortify her mind, not only against the impending evils from without, but also against those treacherous feelings which assailed her from within.

END OF VOLUME FIRST.

EDINBURGH:
Printed by James Ballantyne & Co.

Addition to note upon Ivanhoe
attached to chapter XXVIII p. 494

In corroboration of what is above-stated it may be observed that the arms * which were assumed by Godfrey of Boulogne himself after the conquest of Jerusalem was a * cross counter potent cantoned with four little crosses Or upon a field azure playing thus metal upon metal. The heralds have tried to explain this undeniable fact in different modes but Ferne allows that a prince of Godfrey's qualities should not be bound by the ordinary rules. The Scottish Nisbet and the same Ferne contend that the assembled Chiefs of the Crusade should use this extraordinary and unwonted coat of arms in order to induce those who should behold them to make enquiries and hence the name of Arma Inquirenda. But with reverence to these grave authorities it seems unlikely that the assembled princes of Europe should have adjudged to Godfrey so much ~~out of the common rule~~ contrary to the general rule if such rule had then existed. At any rate it proves that metal upon metal now accounted a solecism in heraldry was admitted in other cases as well as that in the text. See Ferne's Blazon of Gentrie p. 238 Edition 1586. Nisbets Heraldry ~~folio~~ Vol. I p. 113. Second Edit.

PLATE 44 Vol. XIII *IVANHOE*
The last-minute note to the novel (see Plate 43), which expands and corroborates a note on a point of heraldry already added some pages before, during revision for the new edition. (17. 111)

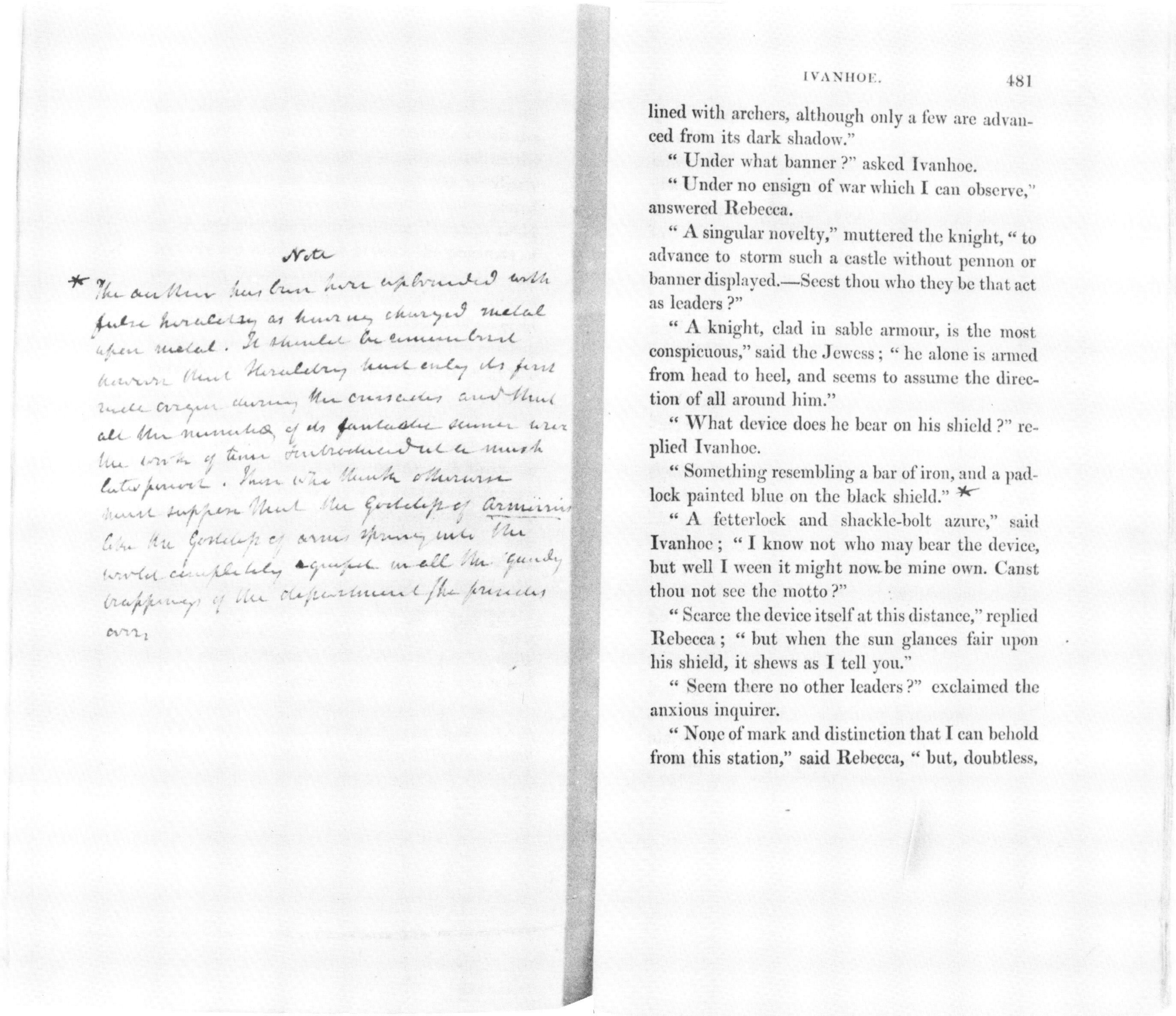

Note

* The author has been here upbraided with false heraldry as having charged metal upon metal. It should be remembered however that Heraldry had only its first rude origin during the crusades and that all the minutiae of its fantastic science were the work of time introduced at a much later period. Those who think otherwise must suppose that the Goddess of Armoiries like the Goddess of arms sprung into the world completely equipped in all the gaudy trappings of the department she presides over.

lined with archers, although only a few are advanced from its dark shadow."

"Under what banner?" asked Ivanhoe.

"Under no ensign of war which I can observe," answered Rebecca.

"A singular novelty," muttered the knight, "to advance to storm such a castle without pennon or banner displayed.—Seest thou who they be that act as leaders?"

"A knight, clad in sable armour, is the most conspicuous," said the Jewess; "he alone is armed from head to heel, and seems to assume the direction of all around him."

"What device does he bear on his shield?" replied Ivanhoe.

"Something resembling a bar of iron, and a padlock painted blue on the black shield." *

"A fetterlock and shackle-bolt azure," said Ivanhoe; "I know not who may bear the device, but well I ween it might now be mine own. Canst thou not see the motto?"

"Scarce the device itself at this distance," replied Rebecca; "but when the sun glances fair upon his shield, it shews as I tell you."

"Seem there no other leaders?" exclaimed the anxious inquirer.

"None of mark and distinction that I can behold from this station," said Rebecca, "but, doubtless,

PLATE 45 Vol. XIII *IVANHOE*

The note referred to above (see Plates 43–44) in which Scott attempts to defend his heraldic mistake in describing the charges and tinctures of a knight's shield by arguing that the laws of armory had taken time to evolve, and that the precise science of heraldry as it was known in his own time had not always been so minutely controlled. This statement caused Scott to append yet a further note late in the day. (17. 99–100)

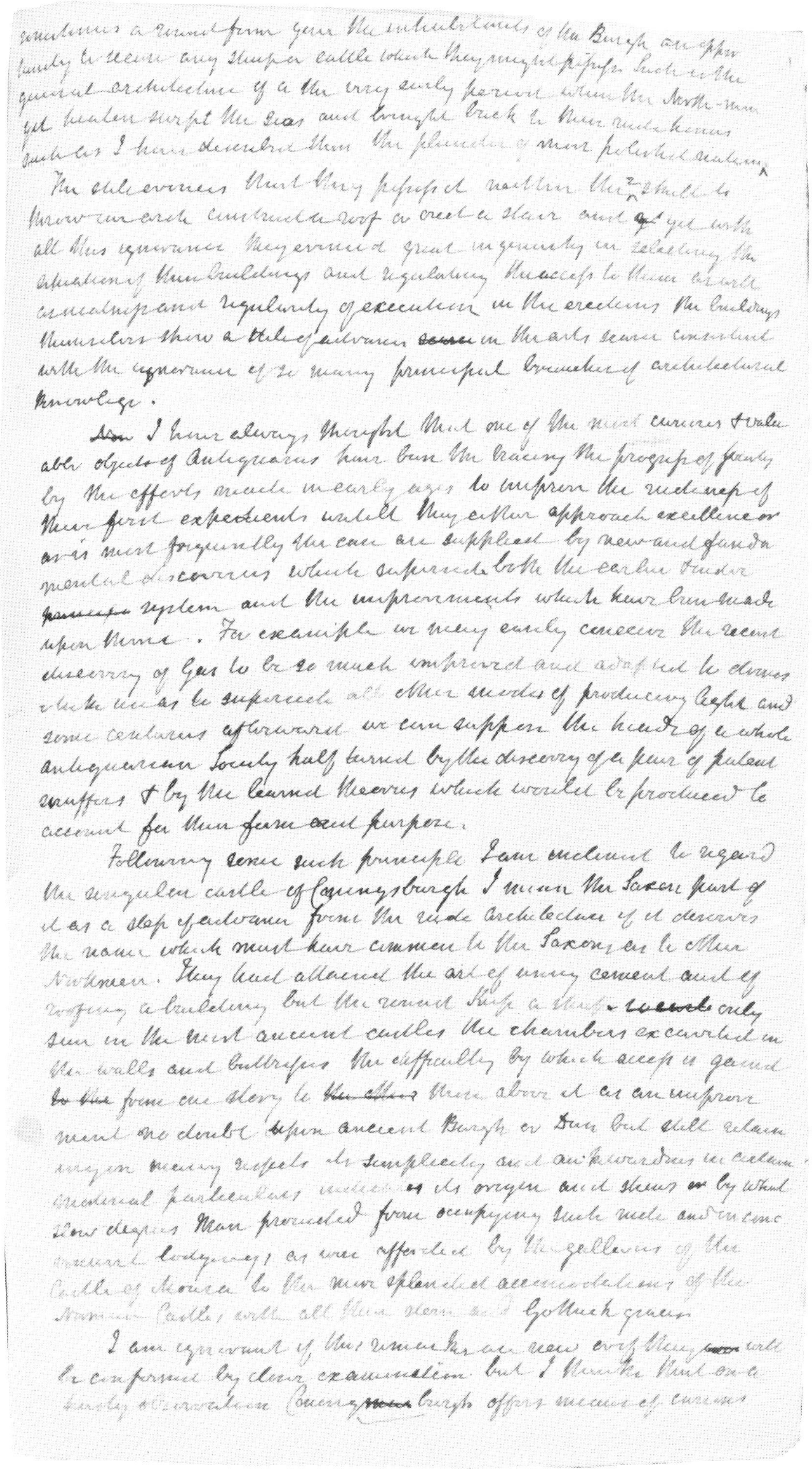

sometimes a wound from year the inhabitants of the Burgh an opportunity to secure any stranger cattle which they might possess. Such is the
general architecture of a the very early period when the North-men
yet beaten swept the seas and brought back to their rude homes
such as I have described them the plunder of more polished nations.
The [illegible] that they possessed neither the skill to
throw an arch construct a roof or erect a stair and yet with
all this ignorance they evinced great ingenuity in selecting the
situation of their buildings and regulating the access to them as well
as neatness and regularity of execution in the erections the buildings
themselves show a state of advance in the arts scarce consistent
with the ignorance of so many principal branches of architectural
knowledge.

I have always thought that one of the most curious & valuable objects of Antiquarians have been the tracing the progress of society
by the efforts made in early ages to improve the rudeness of
their first expedients until they either approach excellence or
as is most frequently the case are supplied by new and funda-
mental discoveries which supersede both the earlier & ruder
system and the improvements which have been made
upon them. For example we may easily conceive the recent
discovery of Gas to be so much improved and adapted to domestic uses as to supersede all other modes of producing light and
some centuries afterward we can suppose the heads of a whole
antiquarian Society half turned by the discovery of a pair of patent
snuffers & by the learned theories which would be produced to
account for their form and purpose.

Following some such principle I am inclined to regard
the singular castle of Coningsburgh I mean the Saxon part of
it as a step of advance from the rude architecture of it deserves
the name which must have common to the Saxons as to other
Northmen. They had attained the art of using cement and of
roofing a building but the round shape a shape only
seen in the most ancient castles the chambers excavated in
the walls and buttresses the difficulty by which access is gained
from one story to those above it as an improve-
ment no doubt upon ancient Burgh or Dun but still retaining in many respects its simplicity and awkwardness in certain
[illegible] particulars which [illegible] its origin and shews by what
slow degrees Man proceeded from occupying such rude and inconve-
nient lodgings as were afforded by the galleries of the
Castle of Mousa to the more splendid accommodations of the
Norman Castles, with all their stern and Gothick graces.

I am ignorant if these remarks are new or if they will
be confirmed by closer examination but I think that on a
hasty observation Coningsburgh offers means of curious

PLATE 46 Vol. XIV *IVANHOE*

Part of a very long discursive note added to a chapter of *Ivanhoe* (and subsequently bound into the interleaved volume) which includes some general thoughts on the progress of society occasioned by consideration of the architecture of brochs in the Northern Isles. The whole note on the Castle of Coningsburgh occupies five pages in the Magnum edition. As an example of progress and technological change he cites the application of gas to domestic lighting, and wonders what a society of antiquaries would make, some hundreds of years in the future, of the discovery of a pair of patent candle-snuffers. It should be remembered that Scott had been chairman of the Edinburgh Oil Gas Light Company since 1823, and that he was much involved in such matters of advancing technology at the time he was writing his later historical novels; and that Abbotsford, the *locus classicus* of the early nineteenth-century Romantic antiquarian interior, was also one of the first houses in Scotland to be lit by gas. (17. 336–37)

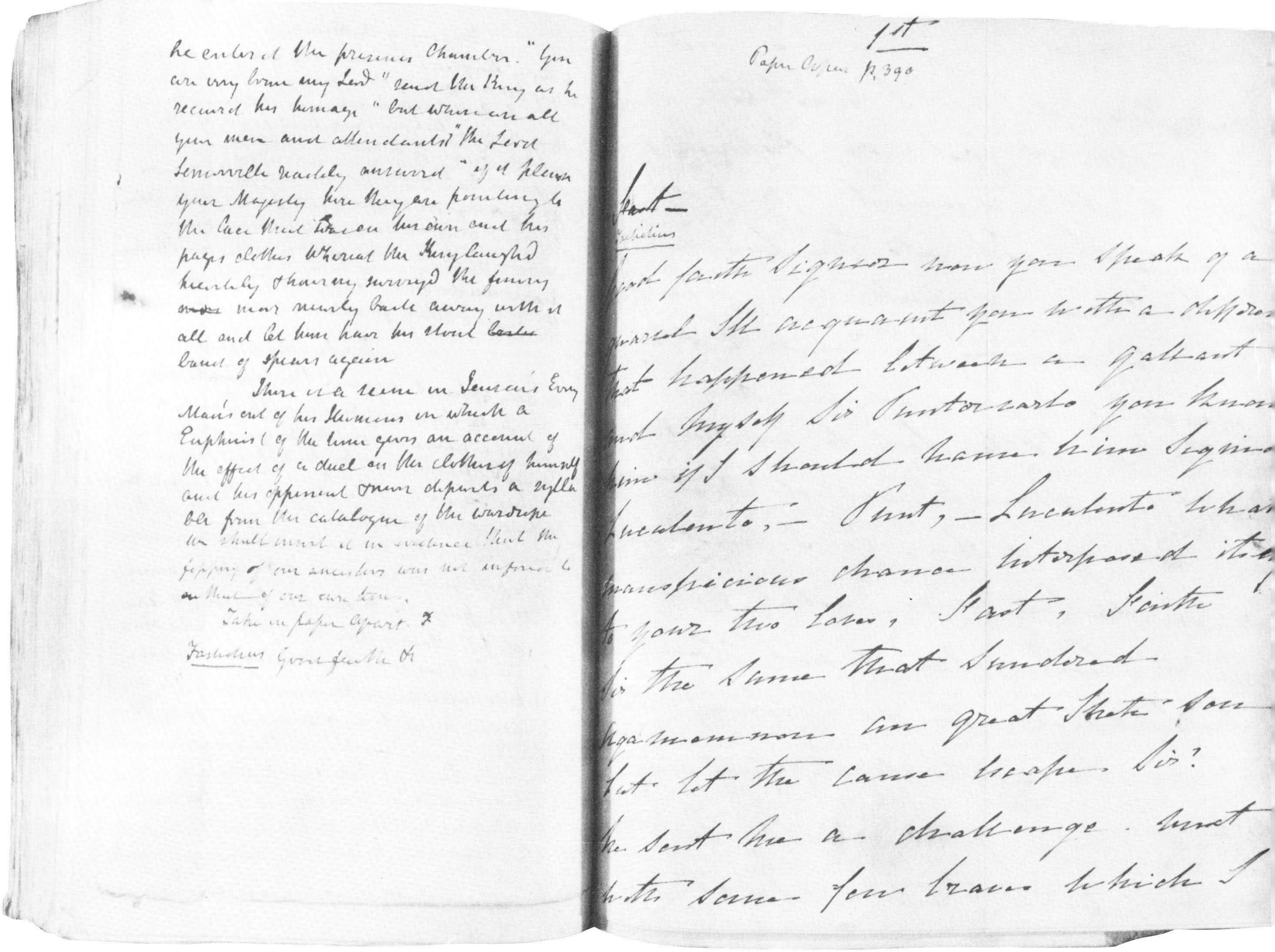

PLATE 47 Vol. XV *THE MONASTERY*

For a long note on 'Foppery of the Sixteenth Century' to be added to the novel, Scott has filled both sides of an interleaf with the historical and critical part of the note, and then makes reference to a paper apart which should be taken in; and that paper, containing long quotations from Jonson's *Every Man out of his Humour* in the hand of Anne Scott, is bound in opposite. (19. 162–63)

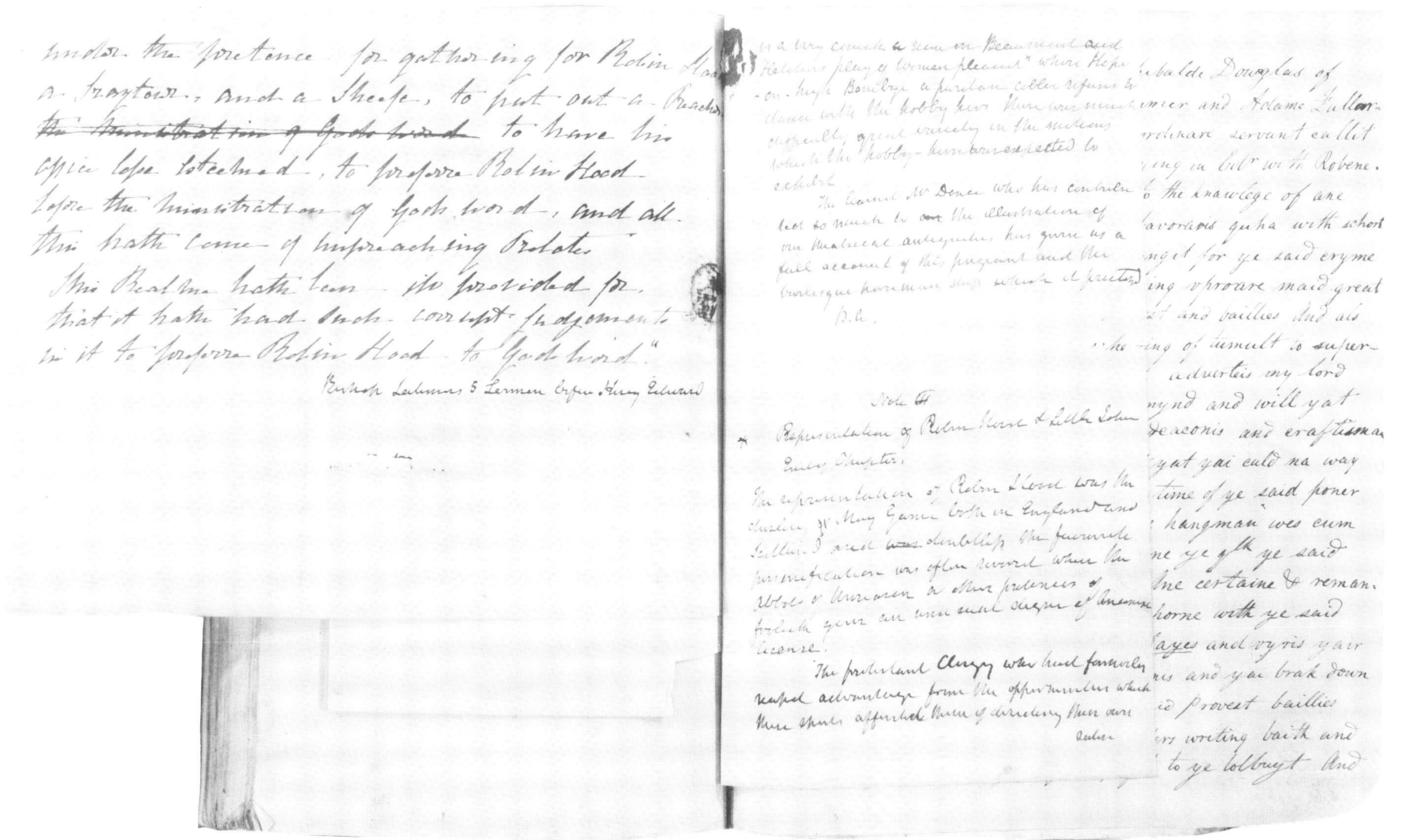
under the pretence for gathering for Robin Hood
a traytour, and a Theefe, to put out a Preacher
~~the ministration of Gods word~~ to have his
office lesse esteemed, to preferre Robin Hood
before the ministration of Gods word, and all
this hath come of unpreaching Prelates.
This Realme hath been ill provided for,
that it hath had such corrupt judgments
in it to preferre Robin Hood to Gods word."
Bishop Latimers 5 Sermon before King Edward

is a very comick scene in Beaumont and Fletchers play of Women pleased" where Hope-on-high Bomby a puritan cobler refuses to dance with the hobby horse. There was much cheerfully great variety in the motions which the hobby-horse was expected to exhibit.
The learned Mr Douce who has contributed so much to the illustration of our theatrical antiquities, has given us a full account of this pageant and the burlesque horseman ...
D.L.

Note III
Representation of Robin Hood & Little John
Every Chapter.
The representation of Robin Hood was the darling ... May Games both in England and Scotland and was doubtless the favourite personification was often revived when the Abbot of Unreason or other pretences of frolick gave an unusual degree of licence.
The protestant Clergy who had formerly reaped advantage from the opportunities which these sports afforded them of directing their ... arrows

...balde Douglas of
...mer and Adame Gullan
...rdinare servant callit
...ing in Edr with Robene.
... the knawlege of ane
...avorovis quha with schort
...ngit for ye said cryme
...ing vproare maid great
...st and baillies and als
...ing of tumult to super-
... adverteis my lord
...nynd and will yat
...deaconis and craftismen
...yat yai culd na way
...time of ye said poner
... hangman wes cum
...ne ye qlk ye said
...the certaine & reman.
...horne with ye said
...ayes and vyris yair
...ris and yai brak doun
...id Provest baillies
...rs writing baith and
... to ye tolbuyt And

PLATE 48 Vol. XVI *THE ABBOT*

Miscellaneous material gathered by Scott the antiquary (on interleaf), or transcribed for him by amanuenses including his daughter Anne (on the papers apart), and used in the composition of three Magnum notes on the general subject of late-medieval masquerades and festivities.
(20. 209–11: notes ii ('The Hobby-Horse') and iii ('Representation of Robin Hood and Little John')

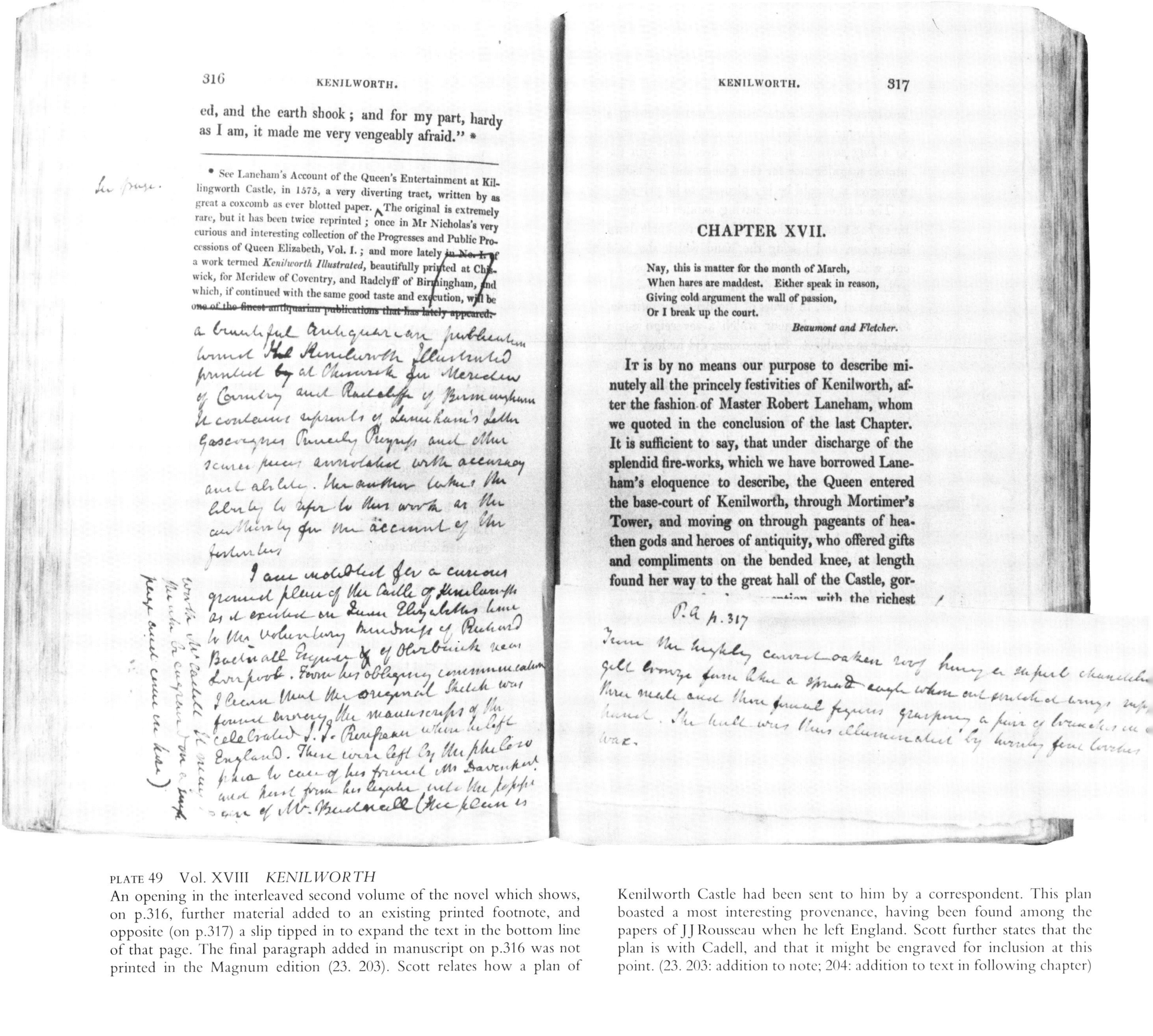

316 KENILWORTH.

ed, and the earth shook; and for my part, hardy as I am, it made me very vengeably afraid." *

* See Laneham's Account of the Queen's Entertainment at Killingworth Castle, in 1575, a very diverting tract, written by as great a coxcomb as ever blotted paper. The original is extremely rare, but it has been twice reprinted; once in Mr Nichols's very curious and interesting collection of the Progresses and Public Processions of Queen Elizabeth, Vol. I.; and more lately in No. I. of a work termed *Kenilworth Illustrated*, beautifully printed at Chiswick, for Meridew of Coventry, and Radclyff of Birmingham, and which, if continued with the same good taste and execution, will be ~~one of the finest antiquarian publications that has lately appeared.~~

KENILWORTH. 317

CHAPTER XVII.

Nay, this is matter for the month of March,
When hares are maddest. Either speak in reason,
Giving cold argument the wall of passion,
Or I break up the court.

Beaumont and Fletcher.

It is by no means our purpose to describe minutely all the princely festivities of Kenilworth, after the fashion of Master Robert Laneham, whom we quoted in the conclusion of the last Chapter. It is sufficient to say, that under discharge of the splendid fire-works, which we have borrowed Laneham's eloquence to describe, the Queen entered the base-court of Kenilworth, through Mortimer's Tower, and moving on through pageants of heathen gods and heroes of antiquity, who offered gifts and compliments on the bended knee, at length found her way to the great hall of the Castle, gor- ... with the richest

PLATE 49 Vol. XVIII *KENILWORTH*

An opening in the interleaved second volume of the novel which shows, on p.316, further material added to an existing printed footnote, and opposite (on p.317) a slip tipped in to expand the text in the bottom line of that page. The final paragraph added in manuscript on p.316 was not printed in the Magnum edition (23. 203). Scott relates how a plan of Kenilworth Castle had been sent to him by a correspondent. This plan boasted a most interesting provenance, having been found among the papers of J J Rousseau when he left England. Scott further states that the plan is with Cadell, and that it might be engraved for inclusion at this point. (23. 203: addition to note; 204: addition to text in following chapter)

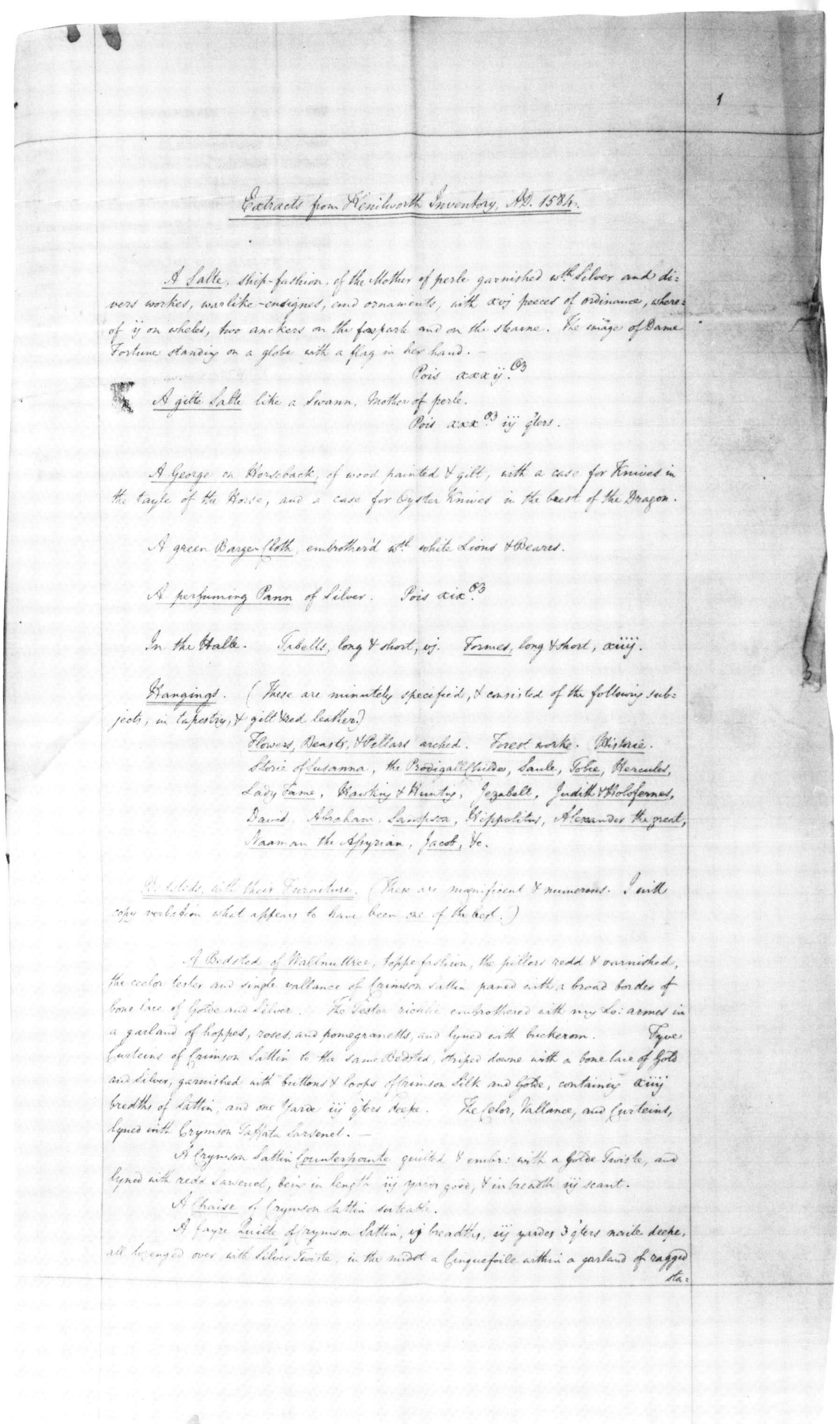

1

Extracts from Kenilworth Inventory, Aº. 1584.

A Salte, ship-fashion, of the Mother of perle garnished wth. Silver and divers workes, warlike-ensignes, and ornaments, with xvj peeces of ordinance, whereof ij on wheles, two anckers on the foreparte and on the sterne. The image of Dame Fortune standing on a globe with a flag in her hand. –

Pois xxxij. oz

A gilte Salte like a Swann, Mother of perle.

Pois xxx oz iij qters.

A George on Horseback, of wood painted & gilt, with a case for Knives in the tayle of the Horse, and a case for Oyster Knives in the brest of the Dragon.

A green Barge-Cloth, embrother'd wth. white Lions & Beares.

A perfuming Pann of Silver. Pois xix. oz

In the Halle. Tabells, long & short, vj. Formes, long & short, xiiij.

Hangings. (These are minutely specified, & consisted of the following subjects, in tapestry, & gilt Red leather.)

Flowers, Beasts, & Pillars arched. Forest worke. Historie.
Storie of Susanna, the Prodigall Childe, Saule, Tobie, Hercules,
Lady Fame, Hawking & Hunting, Jezabell, Judith & Holofernes,
David, Abraham, Sampson, Hippolitus, Alexander the great,
Naaman the Assyrian, Jacob, &c.

Bedsteds, with their Furniture. (These are magnificent & numerous. I will copy verbatim what appears to have been one of the best.)

A Bedsted of Wallnuttree, toppe fashion, the pillers redd & varnished, the ceelor tester and single vallance of Crimson Sattin paned with a broad border of bone lace of Golde and Silver. The Tester richlie embrothered with my Lo: armes in a garland of hoppes, roses, and pomegranetts, and lyned with buckeram. Fyve Curteins of Crimson Sattin to the same Bedsted, striped downe with a bone lace of Golde and Silver, garnished with buttons & loops of Crimson Silk and Golde, containing xiiij bredths of Sattin, and one Yarde iij qters deepe. The Celor, Vallance, and Curteins, lyned with Crymson Taffata Sarsenet. –

A Crymson Sattin Counterpointe quilted & embr: with a Golde Twiste, and lyned with redd Sarsenet, being in length iij yards good, & in breadth iij scant.

A Chaise of Crymson Sattin suteable.

A fayre Quilte of Crymson Sattin, vj breadths, iij yardes 3 qters naile deepe, all lozenged over with Silver Twiste, in the midst a Cinquefoile within a garland of ragged sta-

PLATE 50 Vol. XVIII *KENILWORTH*
Part of a letter of William Hamper to Scott, 2 June 1829, containing extracts from inventories of plenishings of Kenilworth Castle, many of which quotations were used to supplement Scott's description of 'the princely pleasures of Kenilworth'. Material extracted from Hamper's letter (which was subsequently bound into the interleaved volume) forms the notes on Magnum 23. 237–41.

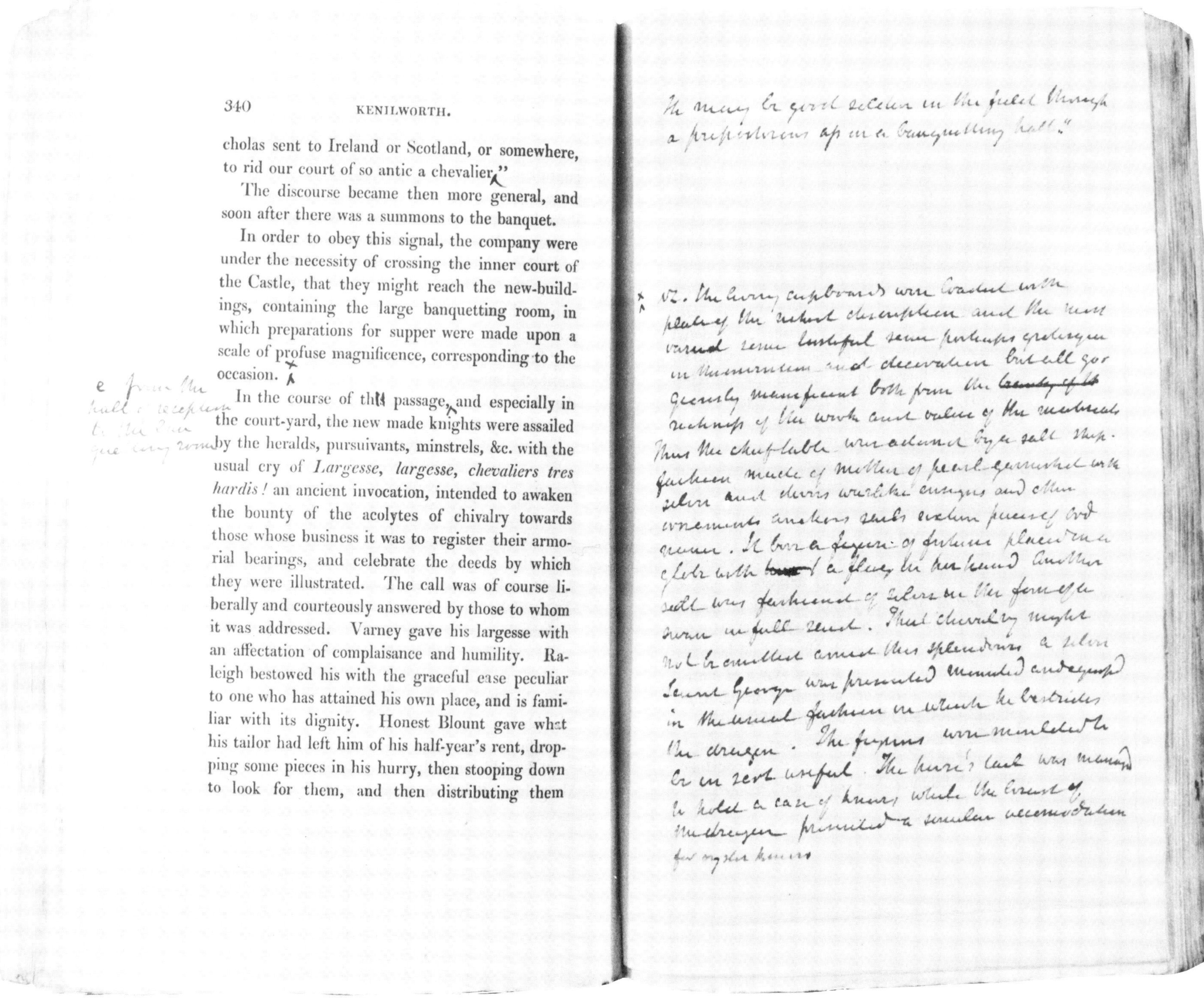

cholas sent to Ireland or Scotland, or somewhere, to rid our court of so antic a chevalier."

The discourse became then more general, and soon after there was a summons to the banquet.

In order to obey this signal, the company were under the necessity of crossing the inner court of the Castle, that they might reach the new-buildings, containing the large banquetting room, in which preparations for supper were made upon a scale of profuse magnificence, corresponding to the occasion.

In the course of this passage, and especially in the court-yard, the new made knights were assailed by the heralds, pursuivants, minstrels, &c. with the usual cry of *Largesse, largesse, chevaliers tres hardis!* an ancient invocation, intended to awaken the bounty of the acolytes of chivalry towards those whose business it was to register their armorial bearings, and celebrate the deeds by which they were illustrated. The call was of course liberally and courteously answered by those to whom it was addressed. Varney gave his largesse with an affectation of complaisance and humility. Raleigh bestowed his with the graceful ease peculiar to one who has attained his own place, and is familiar with its dignity. Honest Blount gave what his tailor had left him of his half-year's rent, dropping some pieces in his hurry, then stooping down to look for them, and then distributing them

PLATE 51 Vol. XVIII *KENILWORTH*
A digest of some of William Hamper's information about Kenilworth also appears in this lengthy and detailed descriptive passage added as an extra paragraph to the text itself. (23. 226)

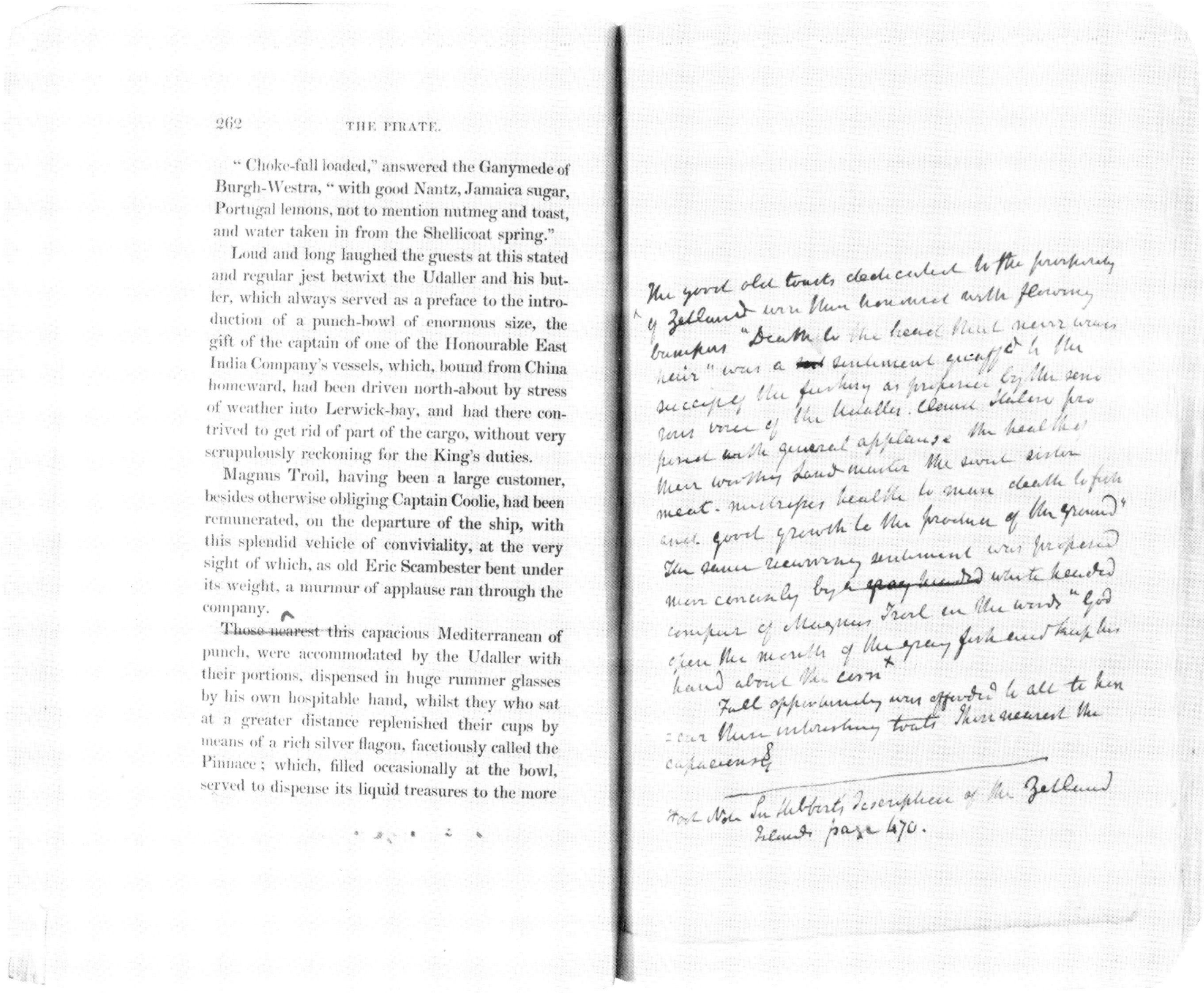

262 THE PIRATE.

"Choke-full loaded," answered the Ganymede of Burgh-Westra, "with good Nantz, Jamaica sugar, Portugal lemons, not to mention nutmeg and toast, and water taken in from the Shellicoat spring."

Loud and long laughed the guests at this stated and regular jest betwixt the Udaller and his butler, which always served as a preface to the introduction of a punch-bowl of enormous size, the gift of the captain of one of the Honourable East India Company's vessels, which, bound from China homeward, had been driven north-about by stress of weather into Lerwick-bay, and had there contrived to get rid of part of the cargo, without very scrupulously reckoning for the King's duties.

Magnus Troil, having been a large customer, besides otherwise obliging Captain Coolie, had been remunerated, on the departure of the ship, with this splendid vehicle of conviviality, at the very sight of which, as old Eric Scambester bent under its weight, a murmur of applause ran through the company.

~~Those nearest~~ this capacious Mediterranean of punch, were accommodated by the Udaller with their portions, dispensed in huge rummer glasses by his own hospitable hand, whilst they who sat at a greater distance replenished their cups by means of a rich silver flagon, facetiously called the Pinnace; which, filled occasionally at the bowl, served to dispense its liquid treasures to the more

The good old toasts dedicated to the prosperity of Zetland were then honoured with flowing bumpers "Death to the head that never wears hair" was a ~~[illegible]~~ sentiment quaffed to the success of the fishery as proposed by the sonorous voice of the Udaller. Claud Halcro proposed with general applause the health of their worthy Land-master the sweet sister meat. mistress health to man death to fish and good growth to the produce of the ground" The same recurring sentiment was proposed more concisely by ~~a grey headed~~ white headed companion of Magnus Troil in the words "God open the mouth of the grey fish and keep his hand about the corn[x]"

Full opportunity was afforded to all to [illegible] these interesting toasts. Those nearest the capacious &c

---

Foot Note See Hibberts Description of the Zetland Islands page 470.

PLATE 52 Vol. XIX *THE PIRATE*

Background material on Zetland toasts, which might well have been the stuff of a note in the novel, is here incorporated in the text itself, the bare reference being relegated to a footnote. (24. 235)

Paper apart ~~cut to~~ page 421 in the preceding chapter

The author has ~~has~~ supposed that a very ancient northern custom used by those who were accounted sooth saying women might have survived though in a more ~~latter~~ altered form among the Zetlanders their descendants. The following original account of such a scene will shew the ancient importance of such a character as was assumed by Norna.

"There lived in the the same territory (Greenland) a woman named Thorbiorga who was a prophetess and call the little Vola (or fatal sister) the ~~sister~~ only one of nine sisters who survived. Thorbiorga during the winter ~~season~~ used to frequent the festivities of the season invited by those who were desirous of knowing their own ~~fu~~ fortune and the future events which impended. Torquil being a man of consequence in the country it fell to his lot to enquire how long the dearth was to endure with which the country was then afflicted. He therefore invited the prophetess to his house having made liberal preparation ~~for~~ as was the custom ~~for~~ ~~sitting~~ receiving a guest of such ~~cong~~ consequence. The seat of the soothsayer was placed in an eminent situation and covered with pillows filled with the softest eider down. In the evening she herself arrived together with a person who had been sent to meet her and shew her the way to Torquils habitation. She was attired as follows She had a sky-blue tunic having the front ornamented with gems from the top to the bottom x and wore around her throat a necklace of glass-beads x Her headgear was of ~~fu~~ black lambs skin the lining being the fur of a ~~wild~~ white wild cat. She leant on a staff having a ~~globe~~ or ball at the top x2 The staff was ornamented with brass and the ball or globe with gems or pebbles ~~&c~~ ~~and~~ x.a. She wore gloves of the wild cats skin with the fur inmost. As this venerable person entered the hall all saluted her with due respect but she only returned the compliments of such as were agreeable to her. Torquil conducted her with reverence to the seat prepared for her and requested she would purify the apartment and company assembled by casting her eyes over them. She was by no means sparing of her ... The table being at length covered such viands were placed before Thorbiorga ... was a preparation ~~on~~ of goats milk ... animals. The prophetess used ... handle of which was composed of a whales ... The table, being removed Torquil ad... ...room and guests at the same time ... company were desirous to consult ... for her to answer their enquiries ... unable

x.a. She wore a Hunland girdle to which were attached a large pouch in which she kept her magical implements. Her shoes were of seals skin dressed with the hair outside and secured by long and thick straps fastened by brazen clasps. She wore gloves &

x' we may suppose the beads to have been of ... potent adder stone to which so many virtues were ascribed

Like those anciently borne by porters at the gates of distinguished persons as a badge of office

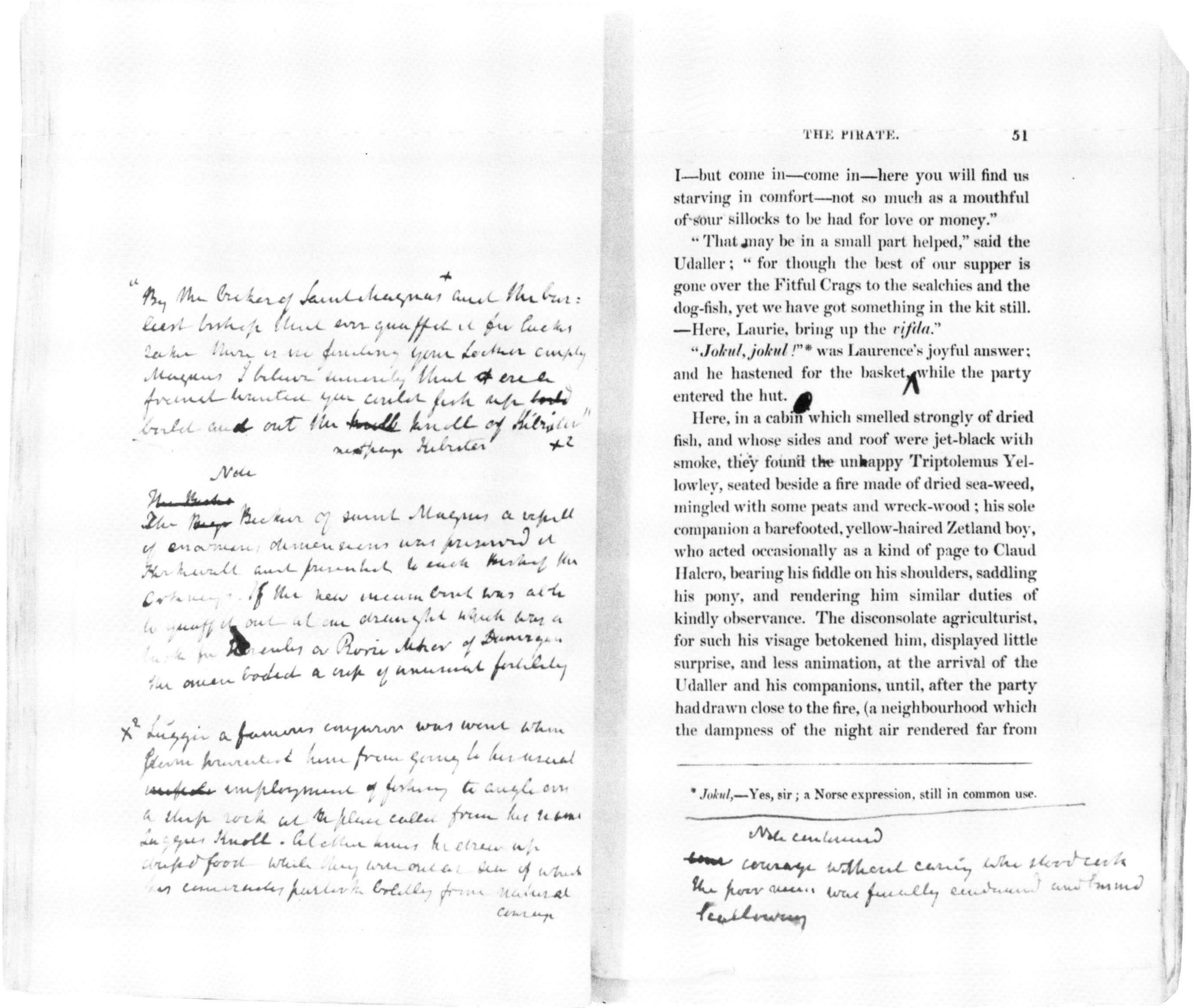
"By the Becker of Saint Magnus and the bar:
best bishop that ever quaffed it for luck's
sake there is no finding your locker empty
Magnus I believe sincerely that ere a
friend wanted you could fish up
boiled and out the Knoll of Kibrister"
next page Kebister x2
Note
The Becker of Saint Magnus a vessel
of enormous dimensions was preserved at
Kirkwall and presented to each Bishop of the
Orkneys. If the new incumbent was able
to quaff it out at one draught which was a
task for Hercules or Rorie More of Dunvegan
the omen boded a crop of unusual fertility
x2 Luggie a famous conjuror was wont when
storms prevented him from going to his usual
employment of fishing to angle over
a steep rock at the place called from his name
Luggies Knoll. At other times he drew up
dressed food while they were out at sea of which
his comrades partook boldly from natural
courage
THE PIRATE. 51
I—but come in—come in—here you will find us starving in comfort—not so much as a mouthful of sour sillocks to be had for love or money."
"That may be in a small part helped," said the Udaller; "for though the best of our supper is gone over the Fitful Crags to the sealchies and the dog-fish, yet we have got something in the kit still. —Here, Laurie, bring up the rifila."
"Jokul, jokul!"* was Laurence's joyful answer; and he hastened for the basket, while the party entered the hut.
Here, in a cabin which smelled strongly of dried fish, and whose sides and roof were jet-black with smoke, they found the unhappy Triptolemus Yellowley, seated beside a fire made of dried sea-weed, mingled with some peats and wreck-wood; his sole companion a barefooted, yellow-haired Zetland boy, who acted occasionally as a kind of page to Claud Halcro, bearing his fiddle on his shoulders, saddling his pony, and rendering him similar duties of kindly observance. The disconsolate agriculturist, for such his visage betokened him, displayed little surprise, and less animation, at the arrival of the Udaller and his companions, until, after the party had drawn close to the fire, (a neighbourhood which the dampness of the night air rendered far from
* Jokul,—Yes, sir; a Norse expression, still in common use.
Note continued
courage without caring who stood cook
the poor man was finally condemned and burned

facing page

PLATE 53 Vol. XIX *THE PIRATE*
A long note (on soothsaying women in Greenland) written on a paper apart is further expanded by the addition of two sentences inscribed on a small slip of paper. The place where the contents of this second paper apart are to be taken into the first is marked rather over half-way down the sheet with the abbreviation 'p.a.'. (25. 21–22)

above

PLATE 54 Vol. XX *THE PIRATE*
An additional paragraph of speech containing certain obscure allusions is inserted as a 'peg' on which Scott can then hang two new notes relating to traditions of the Northern Isles. This is an excellent example of Scott's compulsive desire to annotate. If the opportunity for him to do so was not already present he would, as here, create the circumstances necessary for editorial enjoyment. (25. 157)

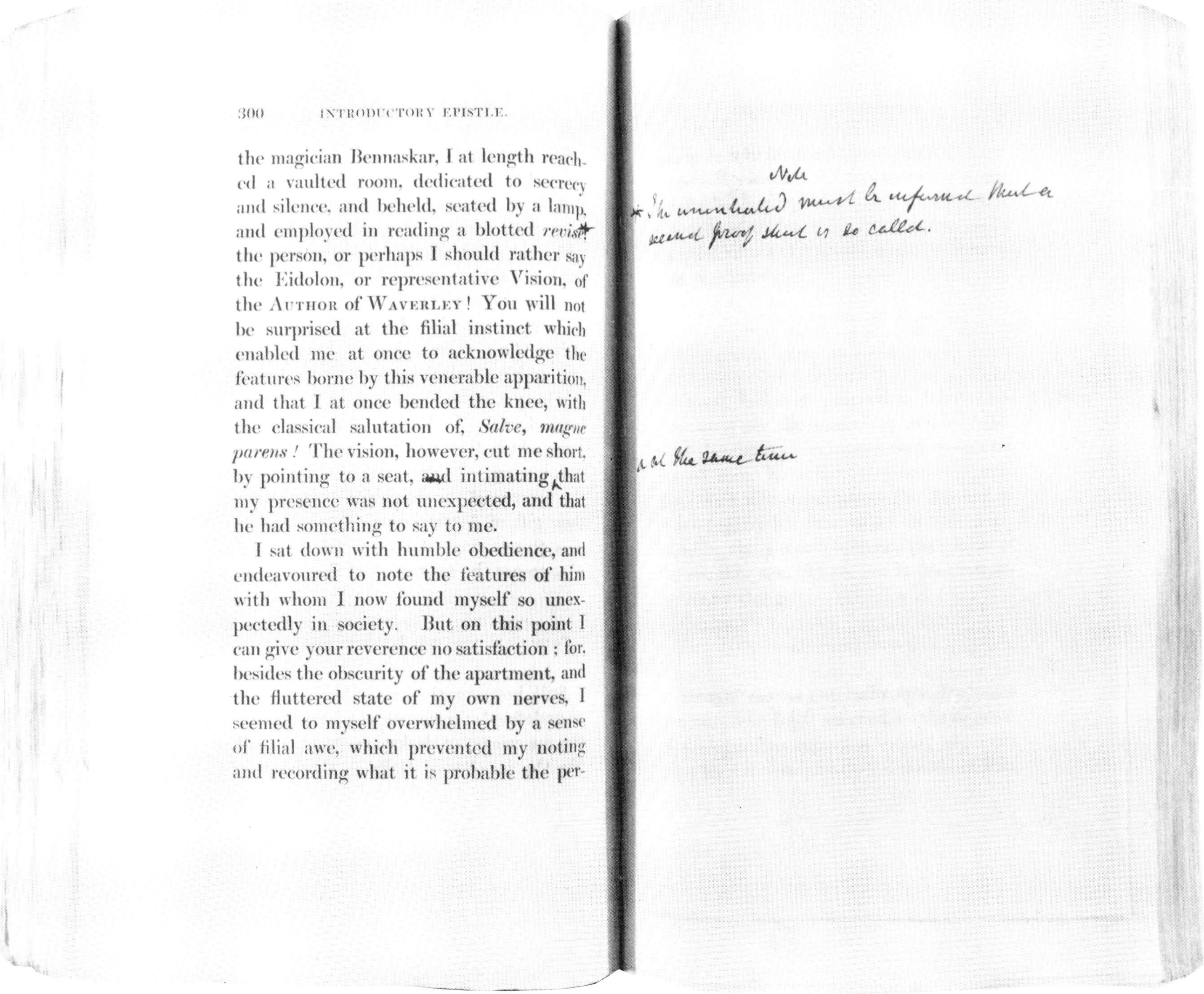

the magician Bennaskar, I at length reached a vaulted room, dedicated to secrecy and silence, and beheld, seated by a lamp, and employed in reading a blotted *revise*,* the person, or perhaps I should rather say the Eidolon, or representative Vision, of the AUTHOR of WAVERLEY! You will not be surprised at the filial instinct which enabled me at once to acknowledge the features borne by this venerable apparition, and that I at once bended the knee, with the classical salutation of, *Salve, magne parens!* The vision, however, cut me short, by pointing to a seat, and intimating that my presence was not unexpected, and that he had something to say to me.

I sat down with humble obedience, and endeavoured to note the features of him with whom I now found myself so unexpectedly in society. But on this point I can give your reverence no satisfaction; for, besides the obscurity of the apartment, and the fluttered state of my own nerves, I seemed to myself overwhelmed by a sense of filial awe, which prevented my noting and recording what it is probable the per-

Note
* The uninitiated must be informed that a second proof sheet is so called.

at the same time

PLATE 55 Vol. XX *THE FORTUNES OF NIGEL*
Evidence for the belief that in the Magnum edition Scott was writing for a different, perhaps rather less well-educated class of readership, which he felt needed greater instruction than had his earlier followers, is furnished by the appearance of this pedantic note to Captain Clutterbuck's letter to the Rev Dr Dryasdust which forms the introductory epistle to the novel. Here the 'uninitiated' are told that a 'revise' is a second proof. (26. xxv)

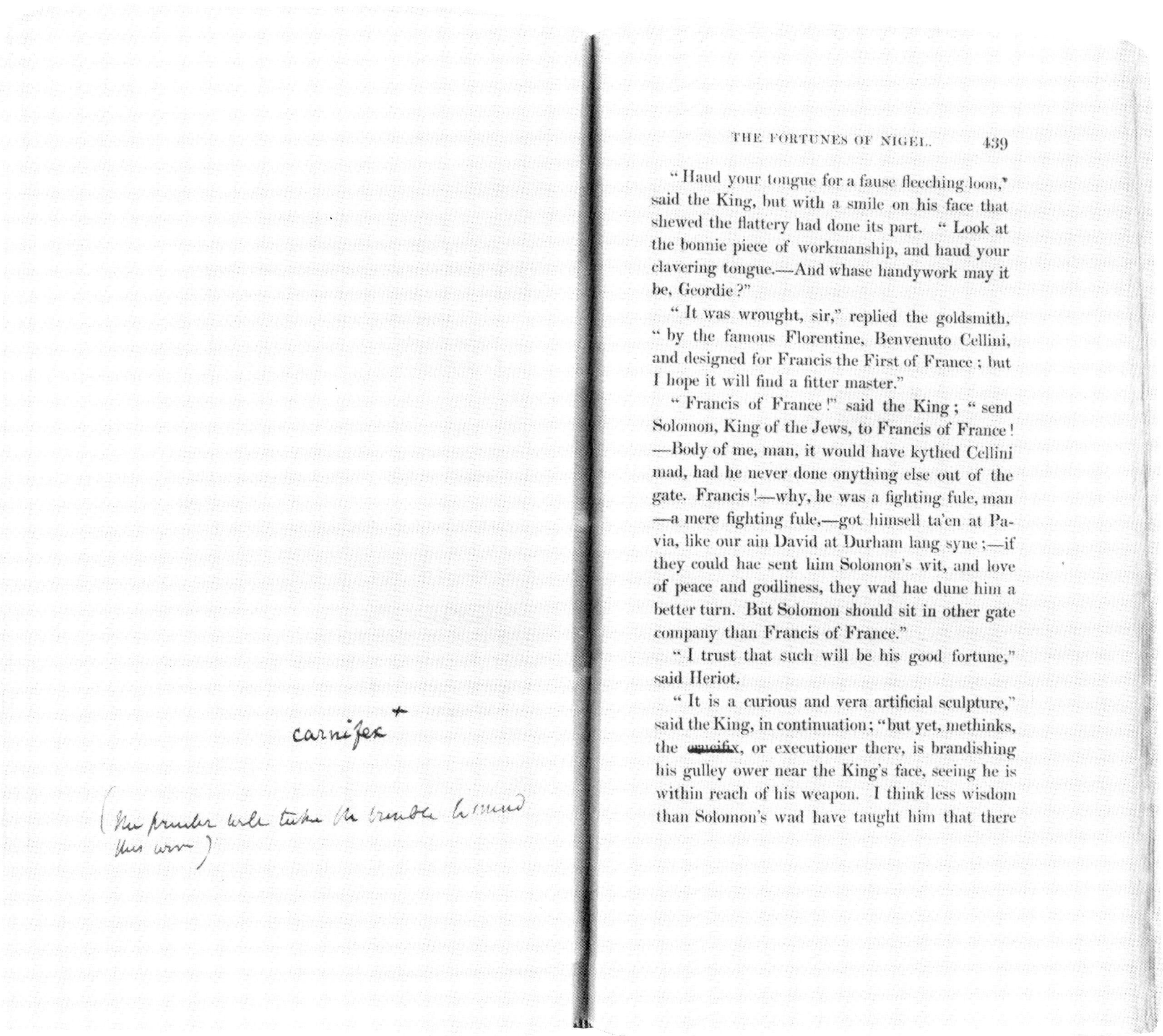
THE FORTUNES OF NIGEL. 439

"Haud your tongue for a fause fleeching loon," said the King, but with a smile on his face that shewed the flattery had done its part. "Look at the bonnie piece of workmanship, and haud your clavering tongue.—And whase handywork may it be, Geordie?"

"It was wrought, sir," replied the goldsmith, "by the famous Florentine, Benvenuto Cellini, and designed for Francis the First of France; but I hope it will find a fitter master."

"Francis of France!" said the King; "send Solomon, King of the Jews, to Francis of France! —Body of me, man, it would have kythed Cellini mad, had he never done onything else out of the gate. Francis!—why, he was a fighting fule, man —a mere fighting fule,—got himsell ta'en at Pavia, like our ain David at Durham lang syne;—if they could hae sent him Solomon's wit, and love of peace and godliness, they wad hae dune him a better turn. But Solomon should sit in other gate company than Francis of France."

"I trust that such will be his good fortune," said Heriot.

"It is a curious and vera artificial sculpture," said the King, in continuation; "but yet, methinks, the ~~crucifix~~, or executioner there, is brandishing his gulley ower near the King's face, seeing he is within reach of his weapon. I think less wisdom than Solomon's wad have taught him that there

carnifex +

(the printer will take the trouble to mind this word)

PLATE 56 Vol. XX *THE FORTUNES OF NIGEL*

An uncommon word had caused problems for the printer. Scott here wrote out the word 'carnifex' in a clear, bold hand; deleted the word 'crucifix' in the text (for thus had the compositor read the intended antiquated synonym for 'executioner'); and added a plea for the printer to take care in setting the word correctly. (26. 100)

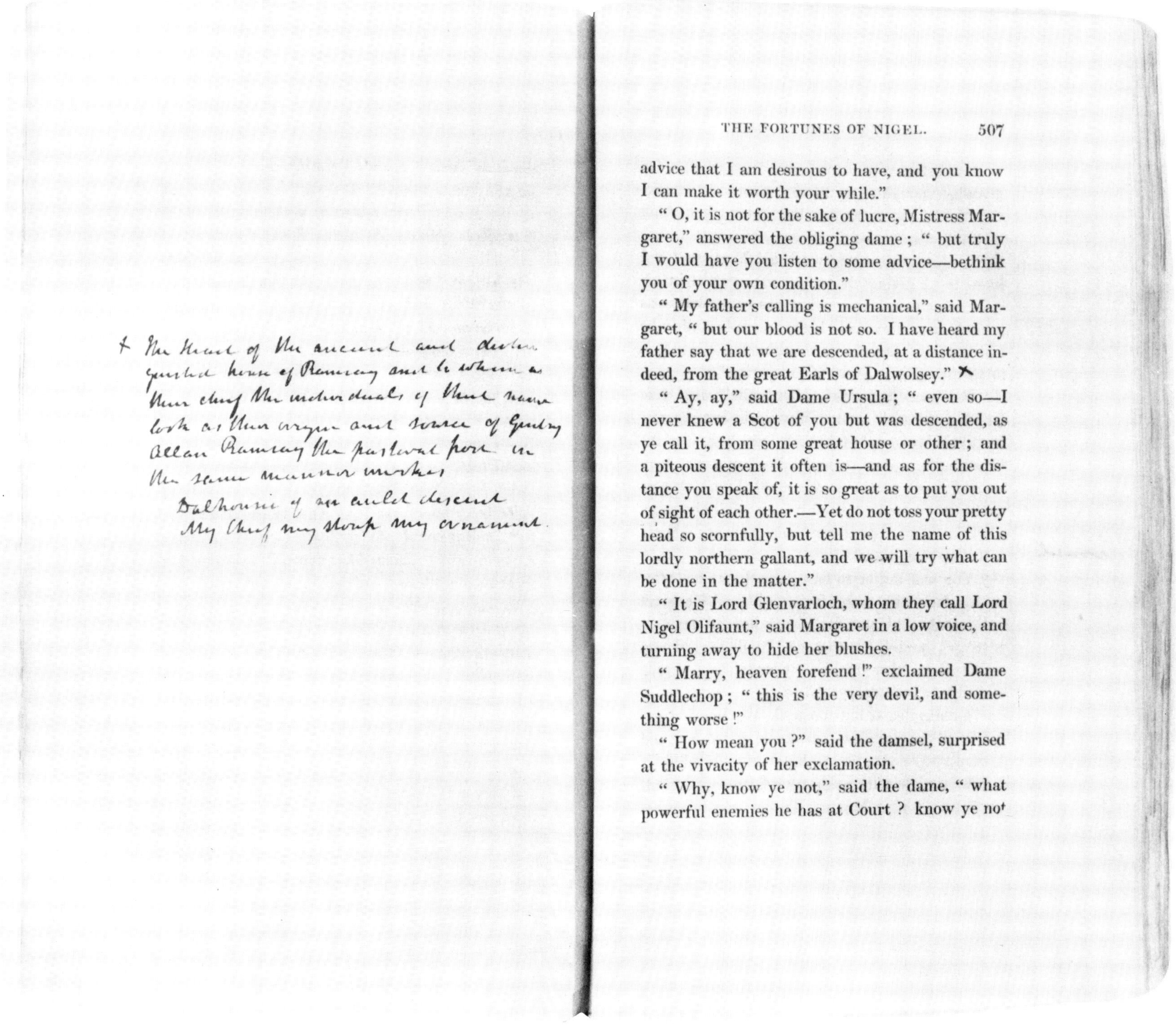

+ the Head of the ancient and distinguished house of Ramsay and to whom as their chief the individuals of that name look as their origin and source of gentry Allan Ramsay the pastoral poet in the same manner makes
Dalhousie of an auld descent
My chief my stoup my ornament.

advice that I am desirous to have, and you know I can make it worth your while."

"O, it is not for the sake of lucre, Mistress Margaret," answered the obliging dame; "but truly I would have you listen to some advice—bethink you of your own condition."

"My father's calling is mechanical," said Margaret, "but our blood is not so. I have heard my father say that we are descended, at a distance indeed, from the great Earls of Dalwolsey." +

"Ay, ay," said Dame Ursula; "even so—I never knew a Scot of you but was descended, as ye call it, from some great house or other; and a piteous descent it often is—and as for the distance you speak of, it is so great as to put you out of sight of each other.—Yet do not toss your pretty head so scornfully, but tell me the name of this lordly northern gallant, and we will try what can be done in the matter."

"It is Lord Glenvarloch, whom they call Lord Nigel Olifaunt," said Margaret in a low voice, and turning away to hide her blushes.

"Marry, heaven forefend!" exclaimed Dame Suddlechop; "this is the very devil, and something worse!"

"How mean you?" said the damsel, surprised at the vivacity of her exclamation.

"Why, know ye not," said the dame, "what powerful enemies he has at Court? know ye not

PLATE 57 Vol. XX *THE FORTUNES OF NIGEL*
Scott had made a character in the novel, Margaret Ramsay, claim descent from the Ramsays, Earls of Dalhousie. In revising his text he now adds substance to the claim by reminding his readers that Allan Ramsay, too, had thought of that noble house as his kinsfolk, and the 'origin and source of gentry'. Fact was adduced in support of fiction. (26. 162)

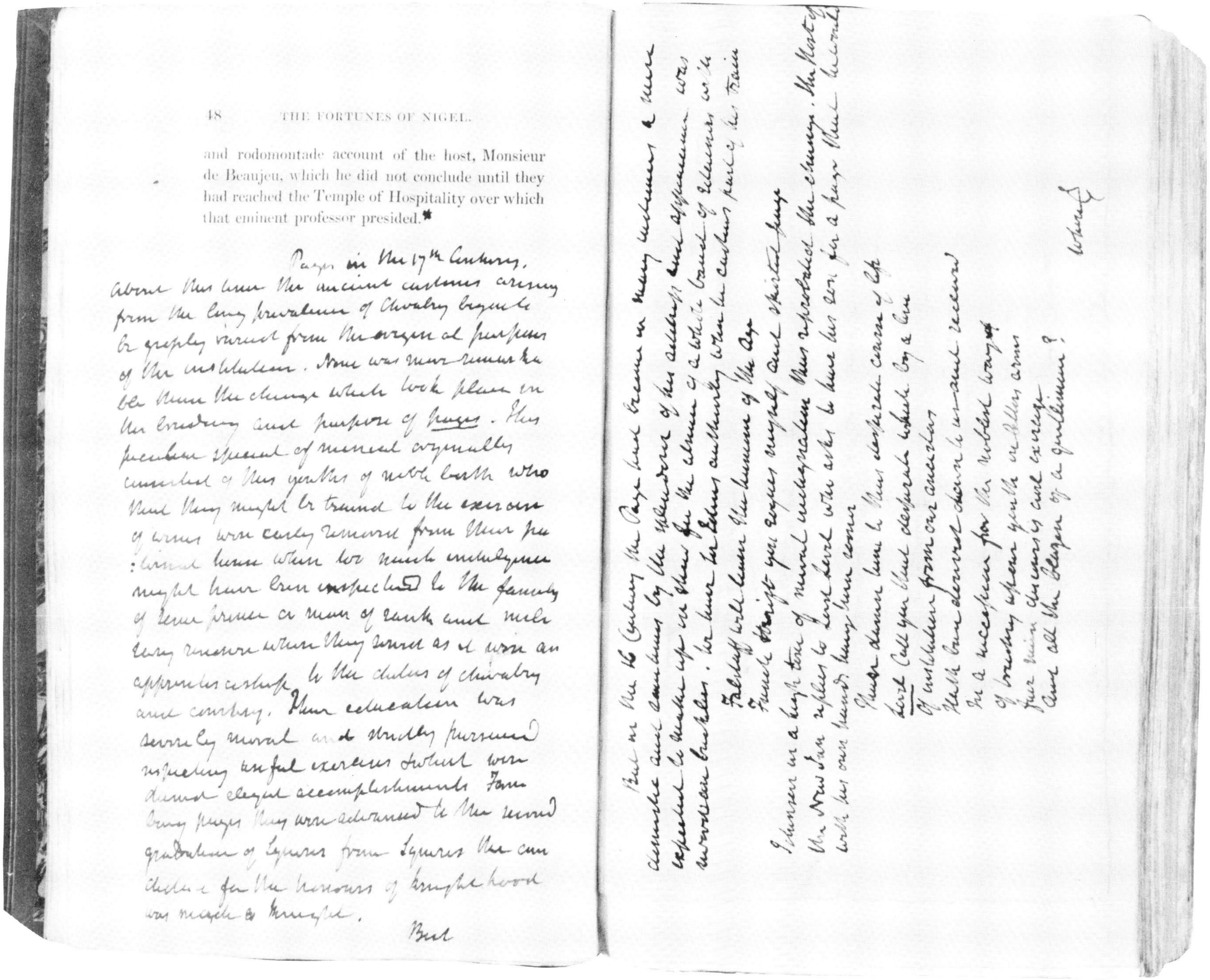
48 THE FORTUNES OF NIGEL.

and rodomontade account of the host, Monsieur de Beaujeu, which he did not conclude until they had reached the Temple of Hospitality over which that eminent professor presided.*

PLATE 58 Vol. XXI *THE FORTUNES OF NIGEL*

Annotation at its heaviest and most tiresome. Scott allows himself an extensive digression on the rôle of pages in the seventeenth century, which is illustrated by an excessively long quotation from Ben Jonson's *The New Inn*. The quotation extends over both sides of two interleaves. There are also several long quotations in the notes to the succeeding chapter. (26. 237–38)

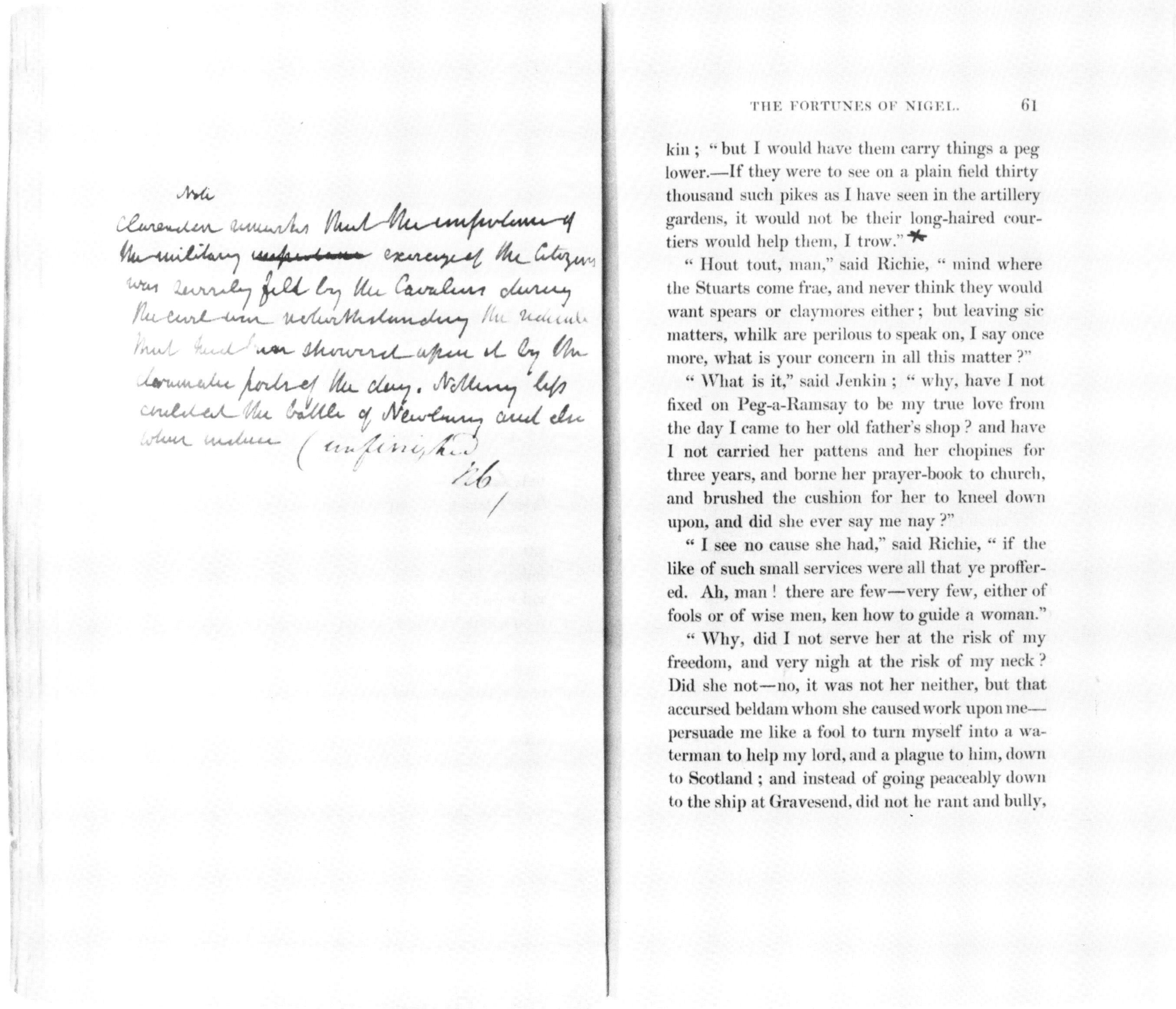

Note

Clarendon remarks that the importance of the military ~~importance~~ exercise of the Citizens was severely felt by the Cavaliers during the civil war notwithstanding the ridicule that had been showered upon it by the dramatic poets of the day. Nothing less could at the battle of Newbury and the other instances (unfinished)

JC

THE FORTUNES OF NIGEL. 61

kin; "but I would have them carry things a peg lower.—If they were to see on a plain field thirty thousand such pikes as I have seen in the artillery gardens, it would not be their long-haired courtiers would help them, I trow." *

"Hout tout, man," said Richie, "mind where the Stuarts come frae, and never think they would want spears or claymores either; but leaving sic matters, whilk are perilous to speak on, I say once more, what is your concern in all this matter?"

"What is it," said Jenkin; "why, have I not fixed on Peg-a-Ramsay to be my true love from the day I came to her old father's shop? and have I not carried her pattens and her chopines for three years, and borne her prayer-book to church, and brushed the cushion for her to kneel down upon, and did she ever say me nay?"

"I see no cause she had," said Richie, "if the like of such small services were all that ye proffered. Ah, man! there are few—very few, either of fools or of wise men, ken how to guide a woman."

"Why, did I not serve her at the risk of my freedom, and very nigh at the risk of my neck? Did she not—no, it was not her neither, but that accursed beldam whom she caused work upon me—persuade me like a fool to turn myself into a waterman to help my lord, and a plague to him, down to Scotland; and instead of going peaceably down to the ship at Gravesend, did not he rant and bully,

PLATE 59 Vol. XXII *THE FORTUNES OF NIGEL*
A note on the military training of the citizenry which made up the Parliamentary army in the Civil War has been left unfinished, and is so marked by Cadell. It was presumably modified and concluded at proof stage (or just conceivably in a later paper apart which is now lost). (27. 347–48)

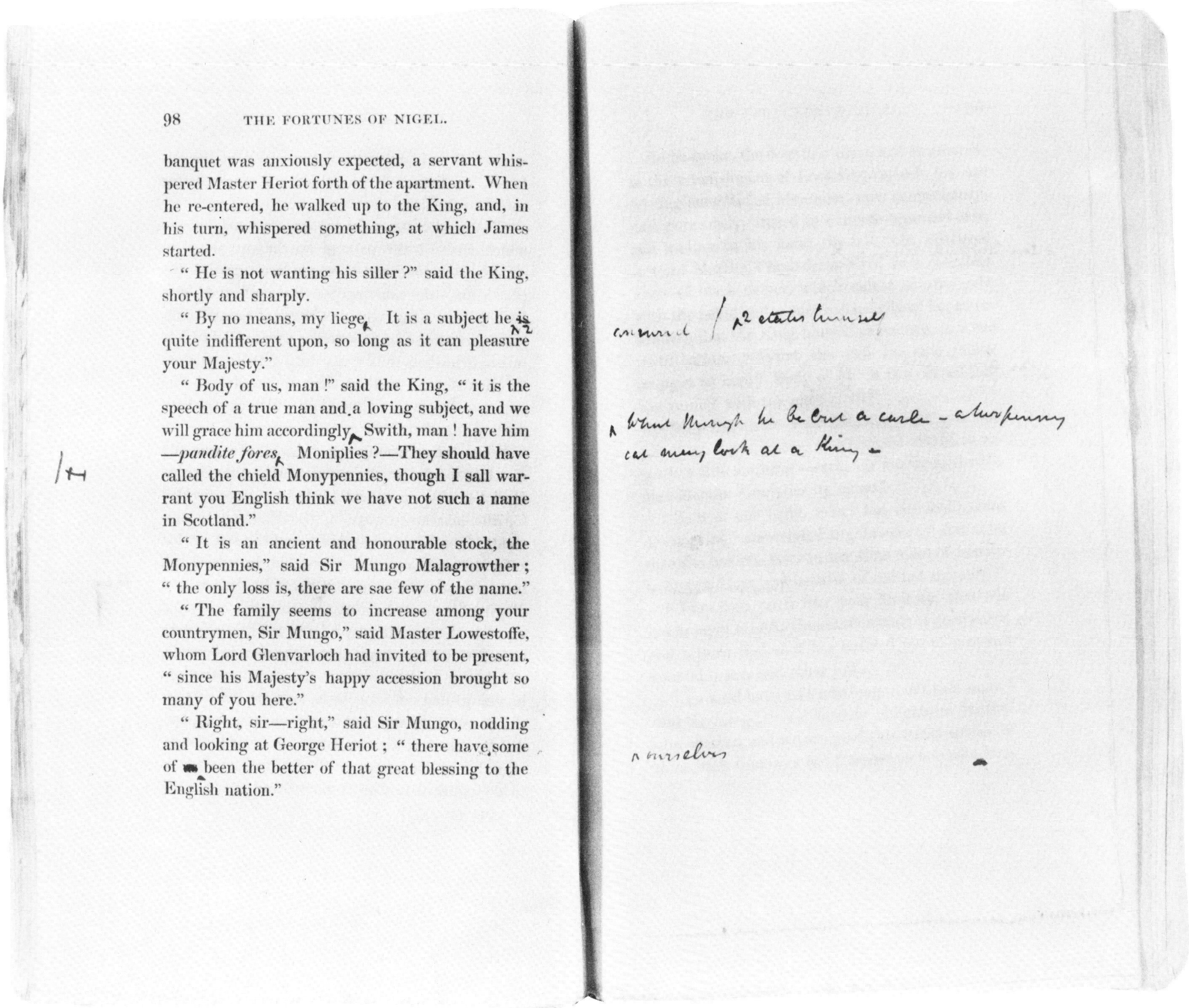
98 THE FORTUNES OF NIGEL.

banquet was anxiously expected, a servant whispered Master Heriot forth of the apartment. When he re-entered, he walked up to the King, and, in his turn, whispered something, at which James started.

"He is not wanting his siller?" said the King, shortly and sharply.

"By no means, my liege. It is a subject he is quite indifferent upon, so long as it can pleasure your Majesty."

"Body of us, man!" said the King, "it is the speech of a true man and a loving subject, and we will grace him accordingly. Swith, man! have him —*pandite fores*. Moniplies?—They should have called the chield Monypennies, though I sall warrant you English think we have not such a name in Scotland."

"It is an ancient and honourable stock, the Monypennies," said Sir Mungo Malagrowther; "the only loss is, there are sae few of the name."

"The family seems to increase among your countrymen, Sir Mungo," said Master Lowestoffe, whom Lord Glenvarloch had invited to be present, "since his Majesty's happy accession brought so many of you here."

"Right, sir—right," said Sir Mungo, nodding and looking at George Heriot; "there have some of been the better of that great blessing to the English nation."

PLATE 60 Vol. XXII *THE FORTUNES OF NIGEL*
By inserting two lines into a speech—'what though he be but a carle—a twopenny cat may look at a king'—Scott adds humanity and tolerance to the character of James VI and I. (27. 382)